TALES FROM
HARROW
◆ DEATH'S CHOIR ◆
COUNTY

TALES FROM
HARROW

→ DEATH'S CHOIR ←

COUNTY

Created by
CULLEN BUNN
TYLER CROOK

Script
CULLEN BUNN

Art
NAOMI FRANQUIZ

President and Publisher
MIKE RICHARDSON

Editor
DANIEL CHABON

Assistant Editor
CHUCK HOWITT

Designer
KEITH WOOD

Digital Art Technician
JOSIE CHRISTENSEN

NEIL HANKERSON Executive Vice President · **TOM WEDDLE** Chief Financial Officer

RANDY STRADLEY Vice President of Publishing · **NICK McWHORTER** Chief Business Development Officer

DALE LaFOUNTAIN Chief Information Officer · **MATT PARKINSON** Vice President of Marketing

VANESSA TODD-HOLMES Vice President of Production and Scheduling · **MARK BERNARDI** Vice President of Book Trade and Digital Sales

KEN LIZZI General Counsel · **DAVE MARSHALL** Editor in Chief · **DAVEY ESTRADA** Editorial Director

CHRIS WARNER Senior Books Editor · **CARY GRAZZINI** Director of Specialty Projects · **LIA RIBACCHI** Art Director

MATT DRYER Director of Digital Art and Prepress · **MICHAEL GOMBOS** Senior Director of Licensed Publications

KARI YADRO Director of Custom Programs · **KARI TORSON** Director of International Licensing · **SEAN BRICE** Director of Trade Sales

Published by Dark Horse Books
A division of Dark Horse Comics LLC
10956 SE Main Street
Milwaukie, OR 97222

First edition: July 2020
ISBN: 978-1-50671-681-7

Comic Shop Locator Service: comicshoplocator.com

Tales from Harrow County Volume 1: Death's Choir

This volume collects Tales from Harrow County #1–#4.

10 9 8 7 6 5 4 3 2 1
Printed in China

DarkHorse.com

Library of Congress Cataloging-in-Publication Data

Names: Bunn, Cullen, author. | Franquiz, Naomi, artist. | Crook, Tyler, illustrator.

Title: Death's choir / script, Cullen Bunn ; art, Naomi Franquiz ; lettering, Tyler Crook.

Description: First edition. | Milwaukie, OR : Dark Horse Book, 2020. | Series: Tales from Harrow County ; volume 1 | "This volume collects Tales from Harrow County #1-#4."

Identifiers: LCCN 2020002804 | ISBN 9781506716817 (paperback) | ISBN 9781506716688 (ebook)

Subjects: LCSH: Comic books, strips, etc.

Classification: LCC PN6728.H369 B8576 2020 | DDC 741.5/973--dc23

LC record available at https://lccn.loc.gov/2020002804

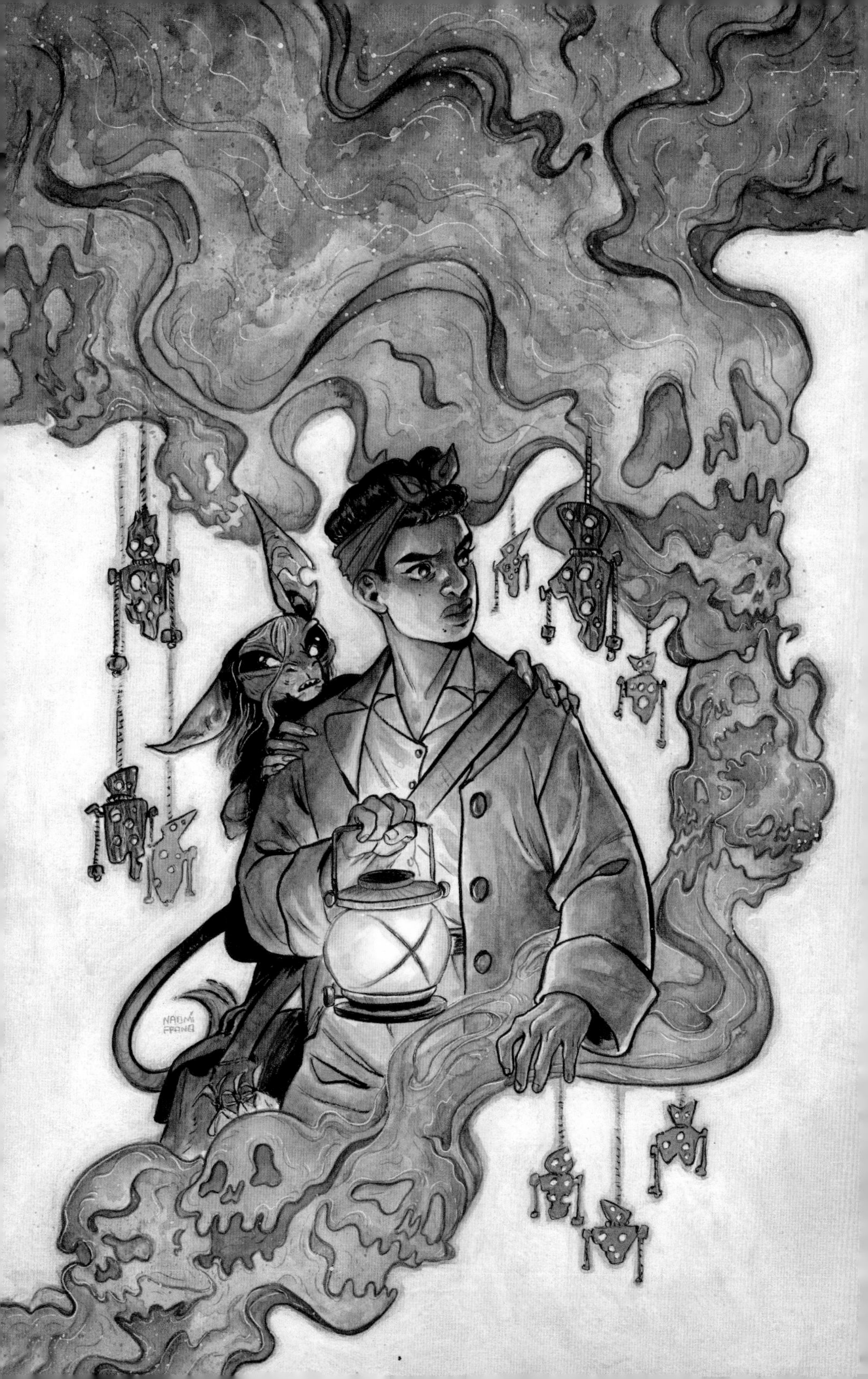
NAOMÍ
FRANQ

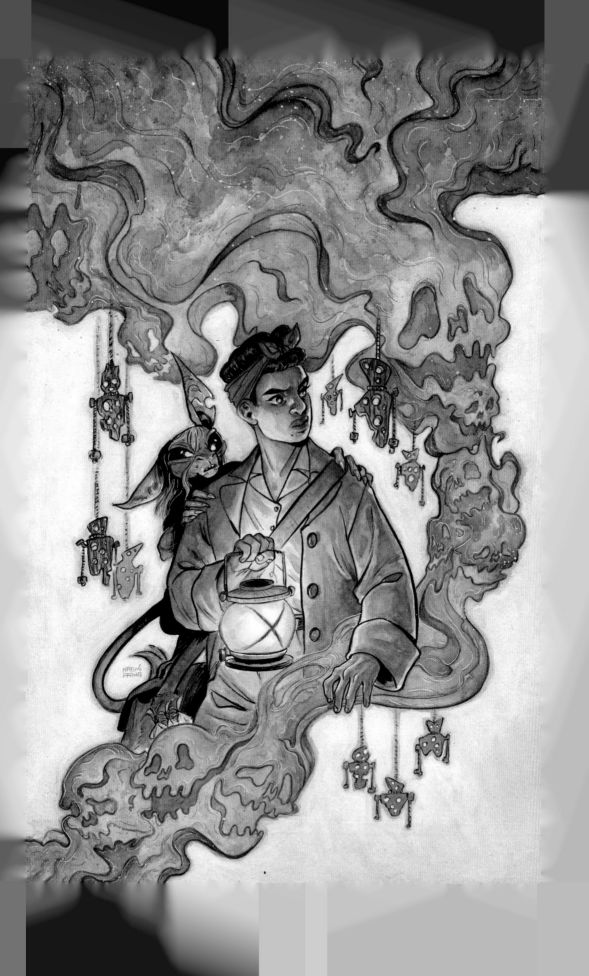

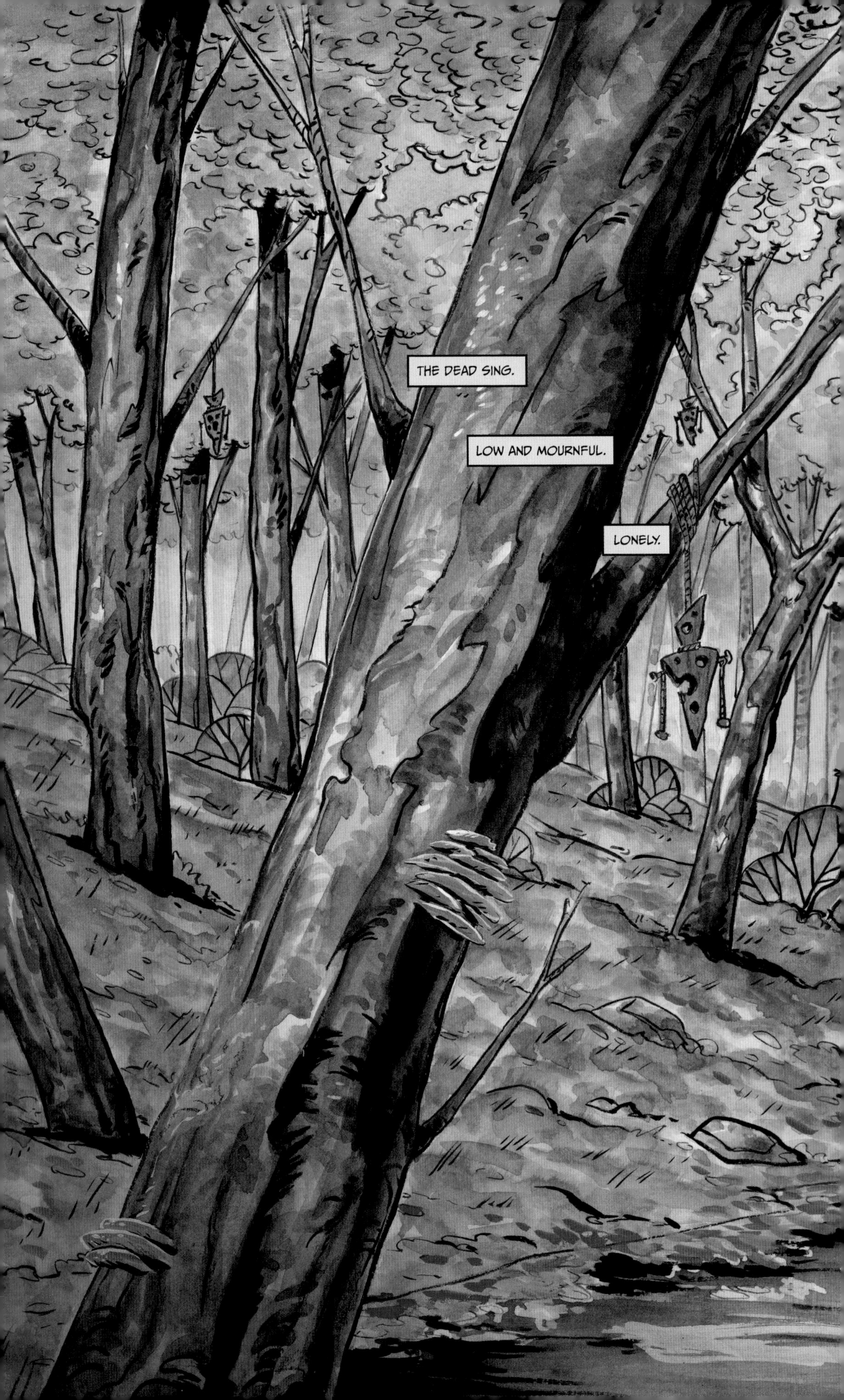
THE DEAD SING.
LOW AND MOURNFUL.
LONELY.

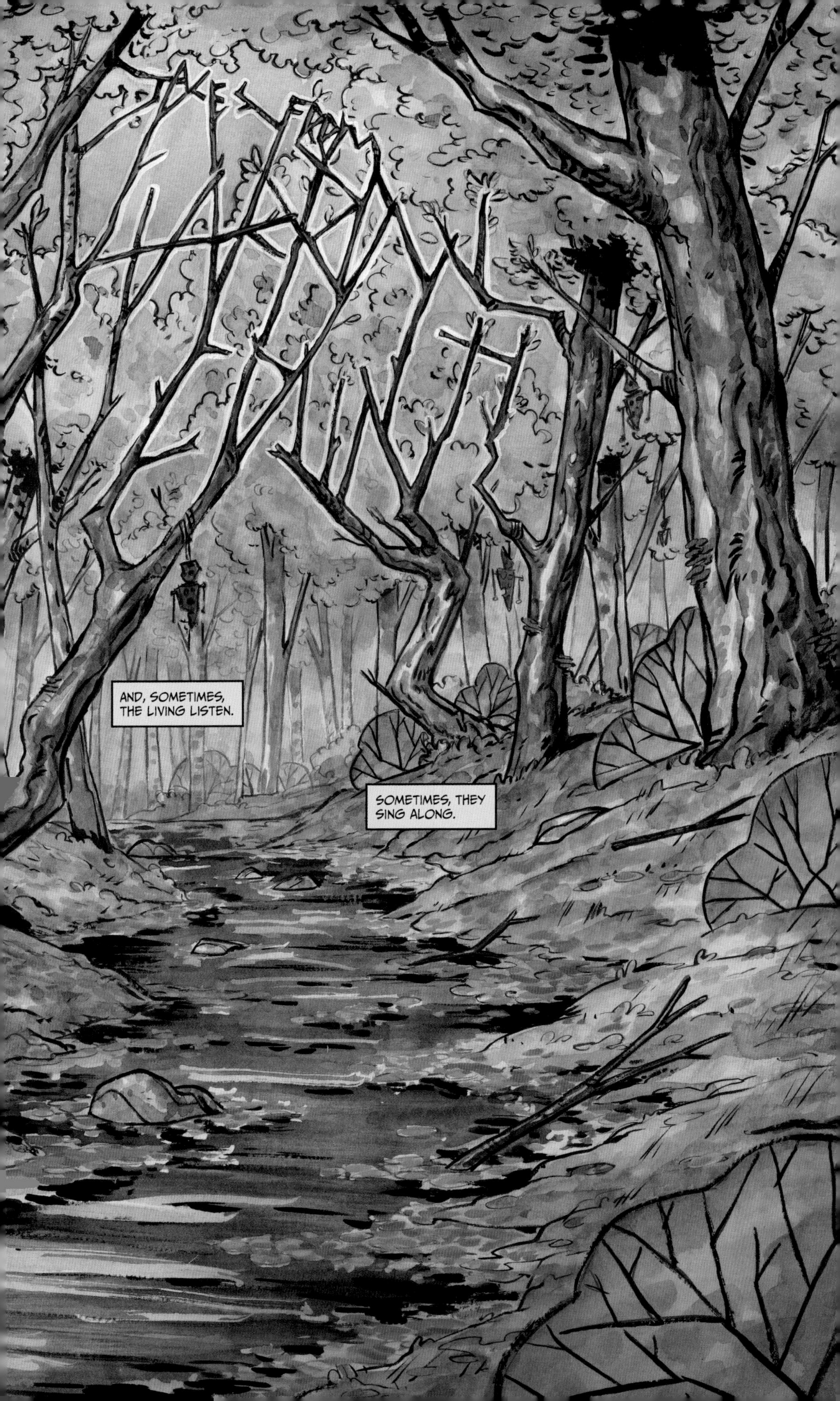
AND, SOMETIMES, THE LIVING LISTEN.
SOMETIMES, THEY SING ALONG.

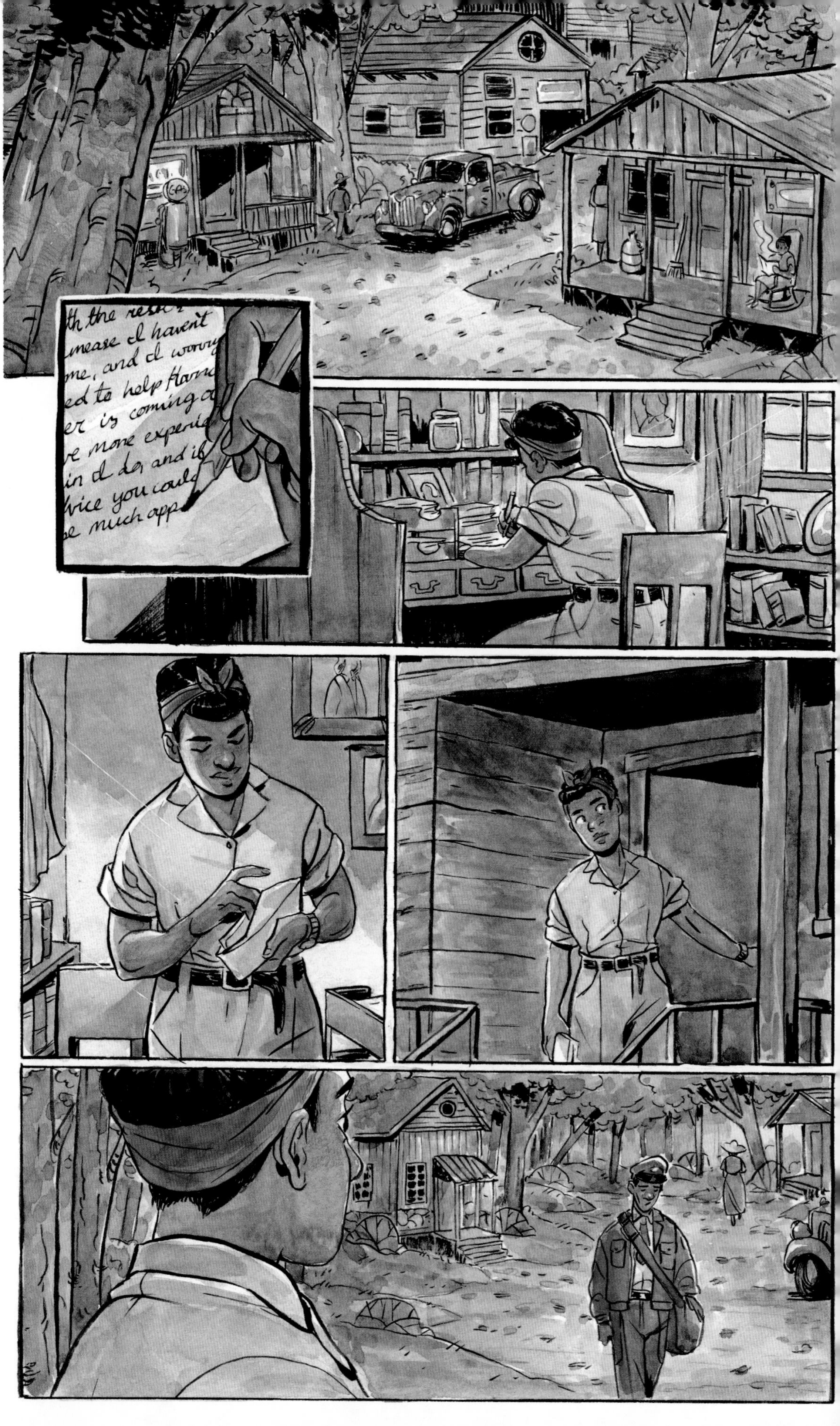

GAS
th the rest
mease I haven't
me, and I worry
ed to help Harri
er is coming o
e more experie
in I do, and if
vice you could
e much app

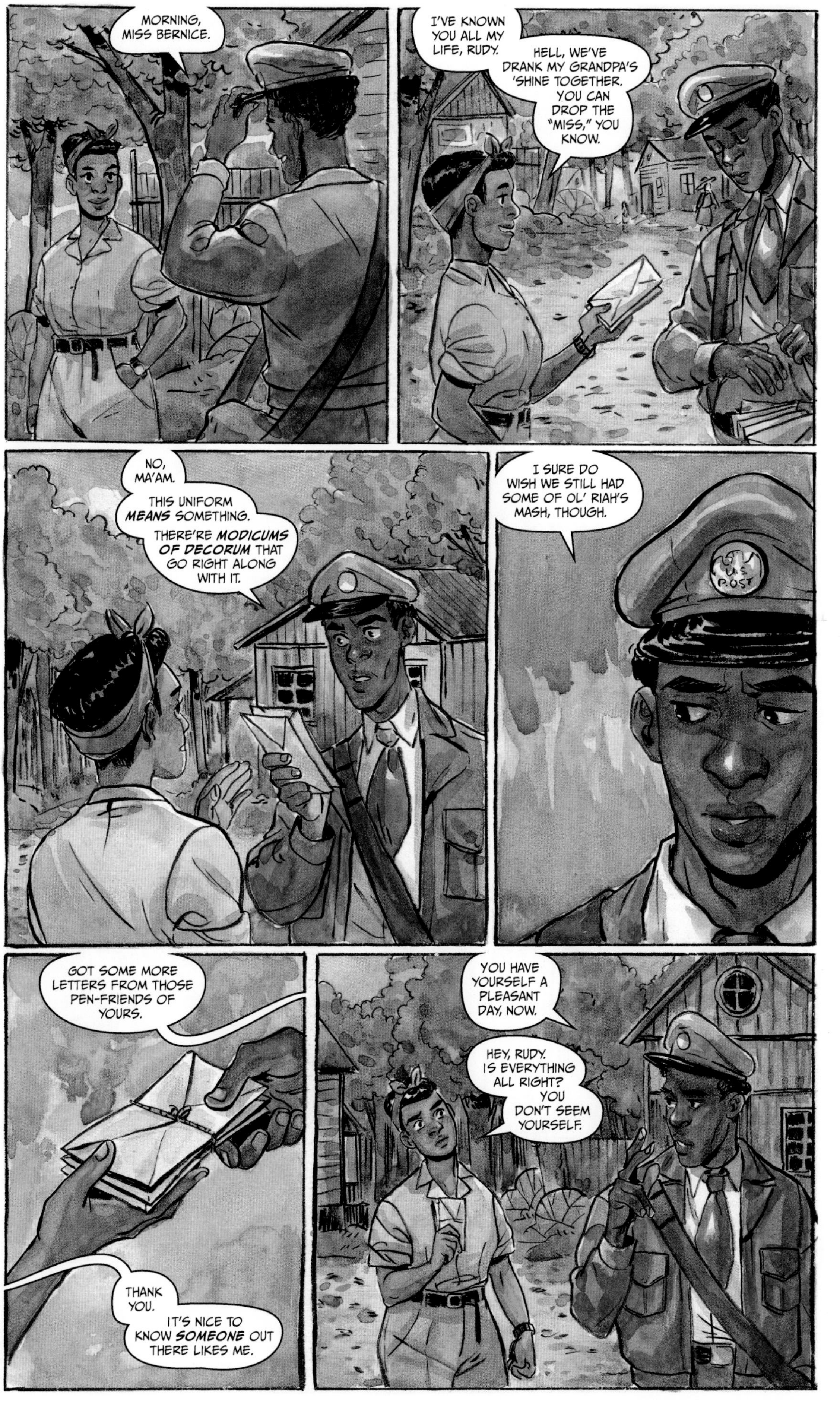
MORNING, MISS BERNICE.
I'VE KNOWN YOU ALL MY LIFE, RUDY.
HELL, WE'VE DRANK MY GRANDPA'S 'SHINE TOGETHER. YOU CAN DROP THE "MISS," YOU KNOW.
NO, MA'AM.
THIS UNIFORM MEANS SOMETHING.
THERE'RE MODICUMS OF DECORUM THAT GO RIGHT ALONG WITH IT.
I SURE DO WISH WE STILL HAD SOME OF OL' RIAH'S MASH, THOUGH.
U.S. POST
GOT SOME MORE LETTERS FROM THOSE PEN-FRIENDS OF YOURS.
THANK YOU.
IT'S NICE TO KNOW SOMEONE OUT THERE LIKES ME.
YOU HAVE YOURSELF A PLEASANT DAY, NOW.
HEY, RUDY. IS EVERYTHING ALL RIGHT?
YOU DON'T SEEM YOURSELF.

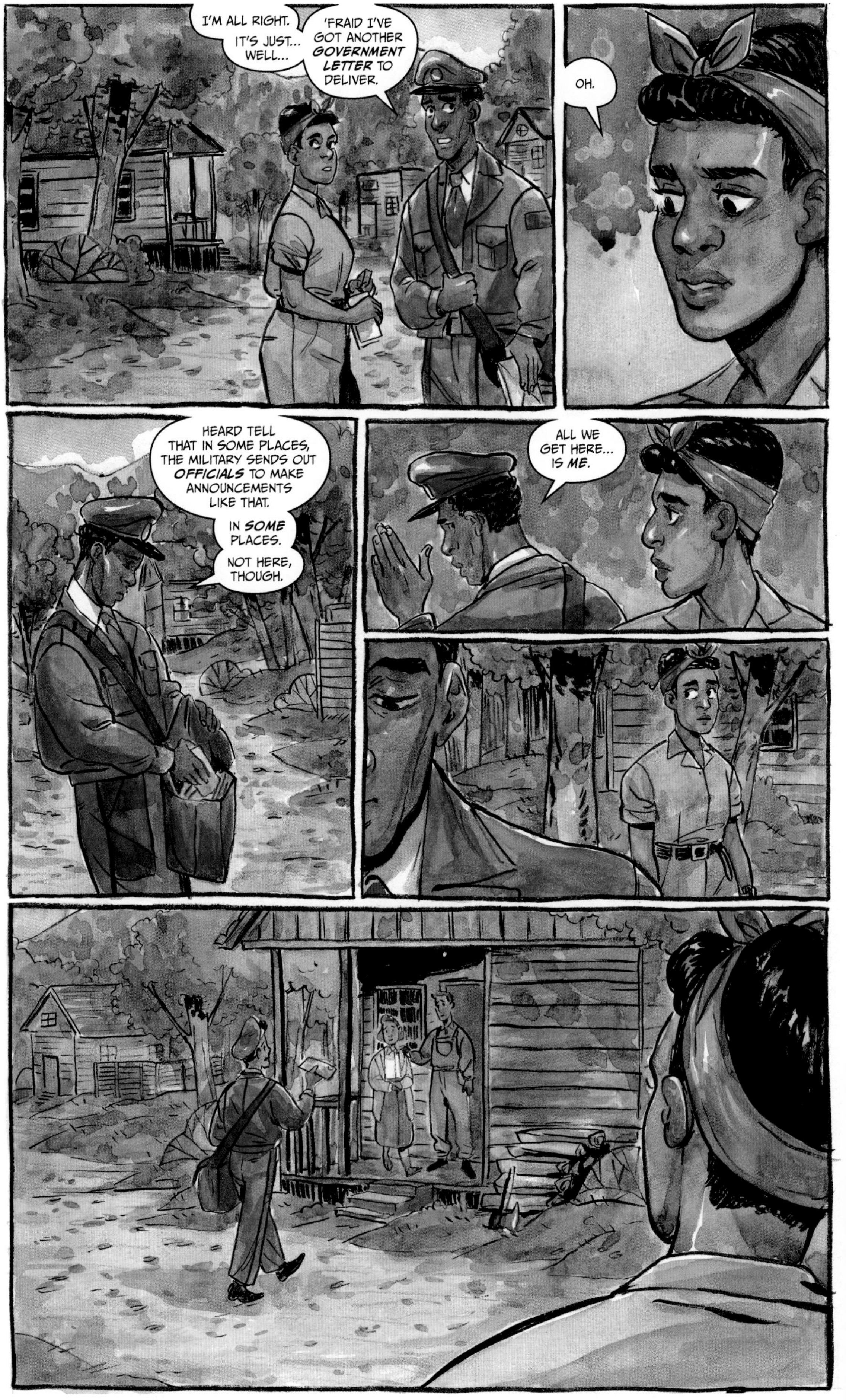
I'M ALL RIGHT.
IT'S JUST... WELL...
'FRAID I'VE GOT ANOTHER GOVERNMENT LETTER TO DELIVER.
OH.
HEARD TELL THAT IN SOME PLACES, THE MILITARY SENDS OUT OFFICIALS TO MAKE ANNOUNCEMENTS LIKE THAT.
IN SOME PLACES.
NOT HERE, THOUGH.
ALL WE GET HERE... IS ME.

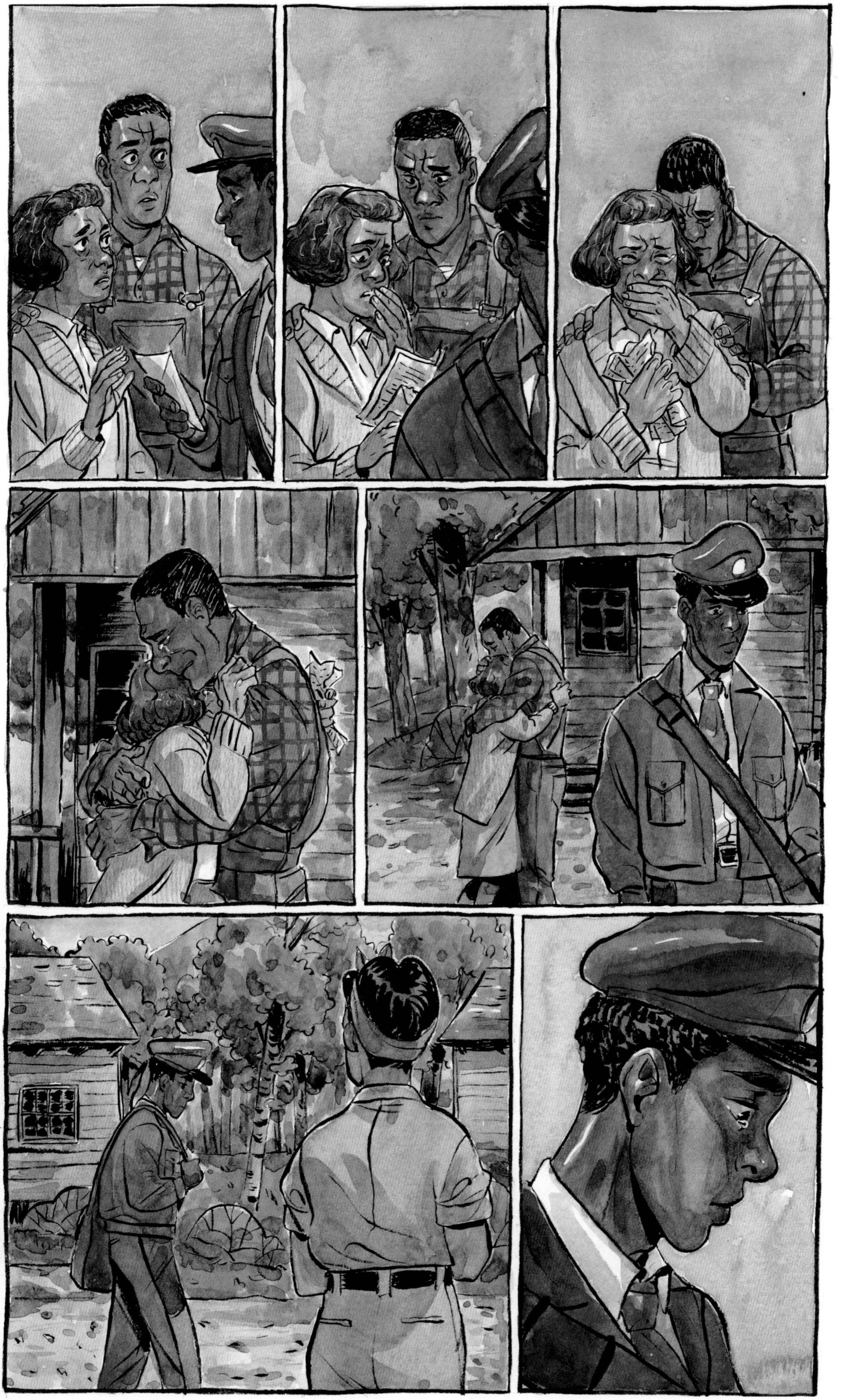

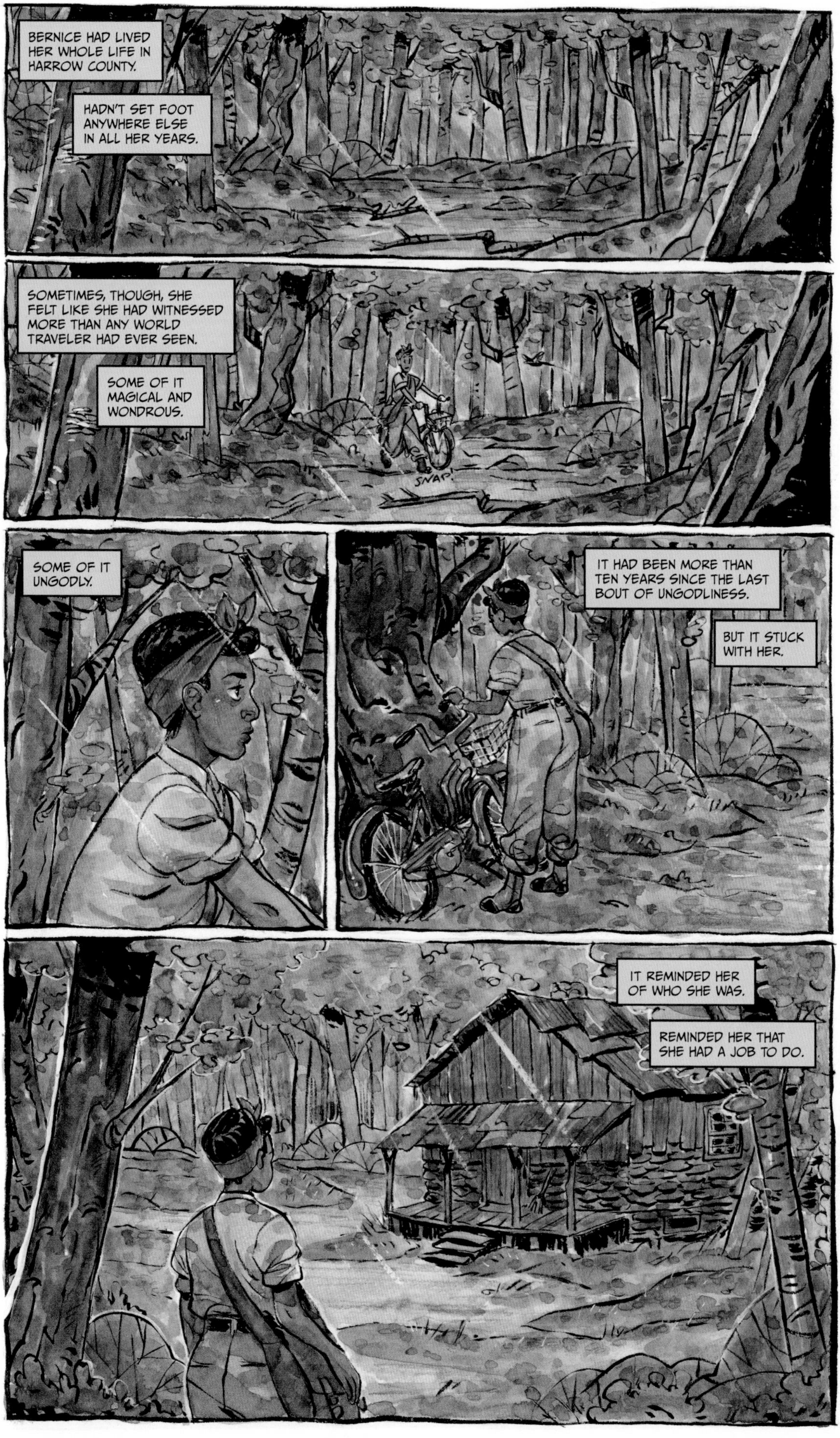
BERNICE HAD LIVED HER WHOLE LIFE IN HARROW COUNTY.
HADN'T SET FOOT ANYWHERE ELSE IN ALL HER YEARS.
SOMETIMES, THOUGH, SHE FELT LIKE SHE HAD WITNESSED MORE THAN ANY WORLD TRAVELER HAD EVER SEEN.
SOME OF IT MAGICAL AND WONDROUS.
SNAP!
SOME OF IT UNGODLY.
IT HAD BEEN MORE THAN TEN YEARS SINCE THE LAST BOUT OF UNGODLINESS.
BUT IT STUCK WITH HER.
IT REMINDED HER OF WHO SHE WAS.
REMINDED HER THAT SHE HAD A JOB TO DO.

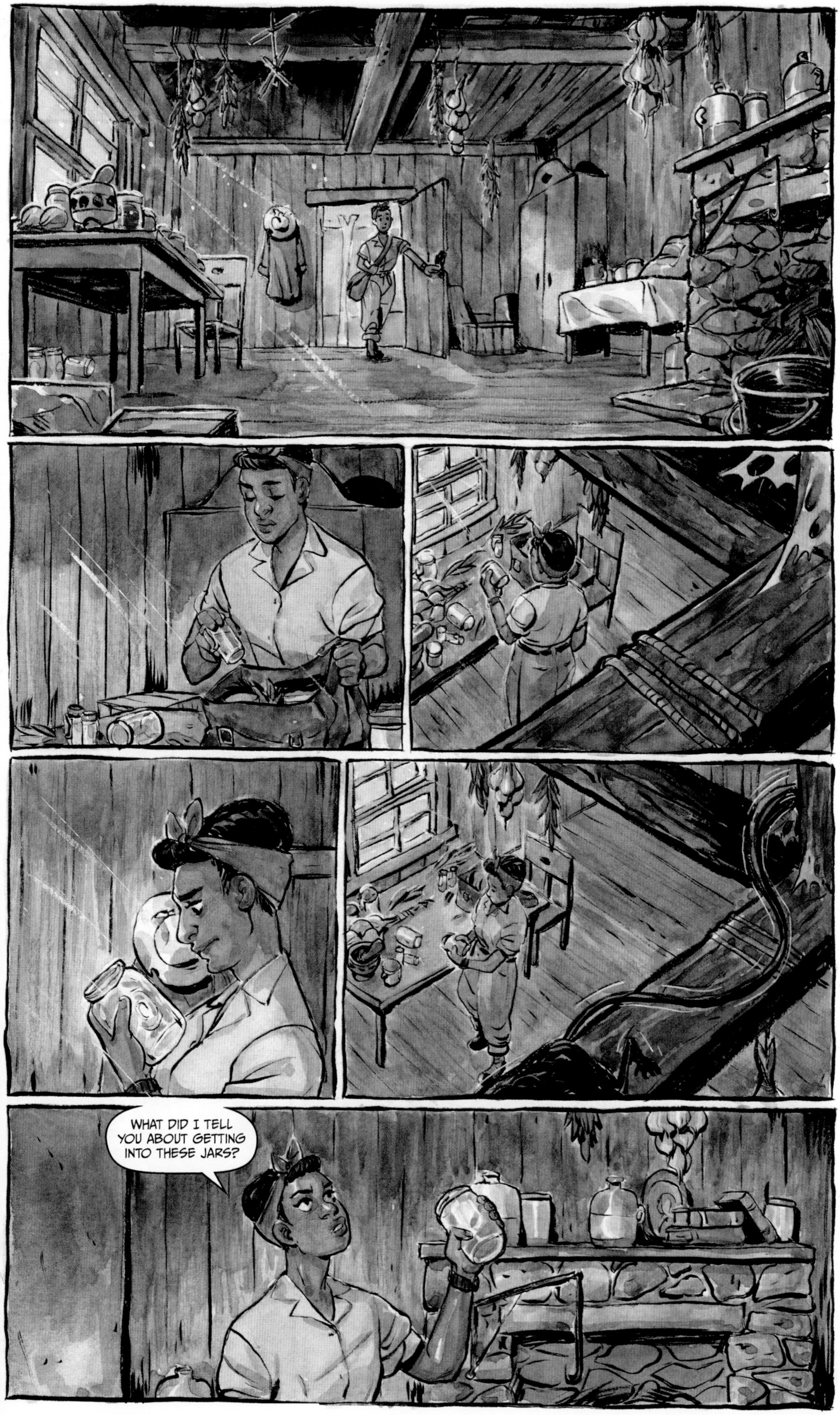
WHAT DID I TELL YOU ABOUT GETTING INTO THESE JARS?

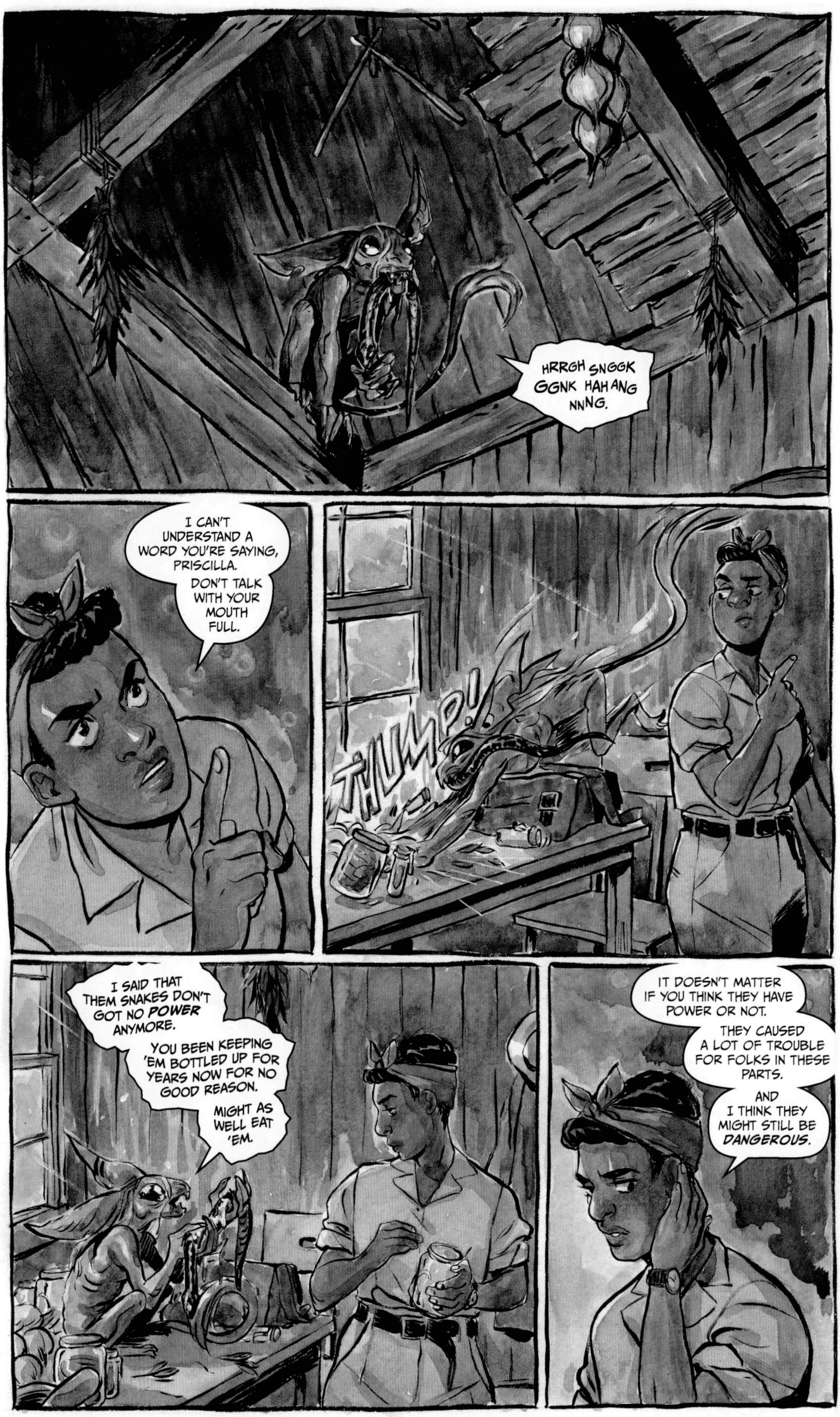
HRRGH SNGGK GGNK HAH ANG NNNG.
I CAN'T UNDERSTAND A WORD YOU'RE SAYING, PRISCILLA.
DON'T TALK WITH YOUR MOUTH FULL.
THUMP!
I SAID THAT THEM SNAKES DON'T GOT NO **POWER** ANYMORE.
YOU BEEN KEEPING 'EM BOTTLED UP FOR YEARS NOW FOR NO GOOD REASON.
MIGHT AS WELL EAT 'EM.
IT DOESN'T MATTER IF YOU THINK THEY HAVE POWER OR NOT.
THEY CAUSED A LOT OF TROUBLE FOR FOLKS IN THESE PARTS.
AND I THINK THEY MIGHT STILL BE ***DANGEROUS***.

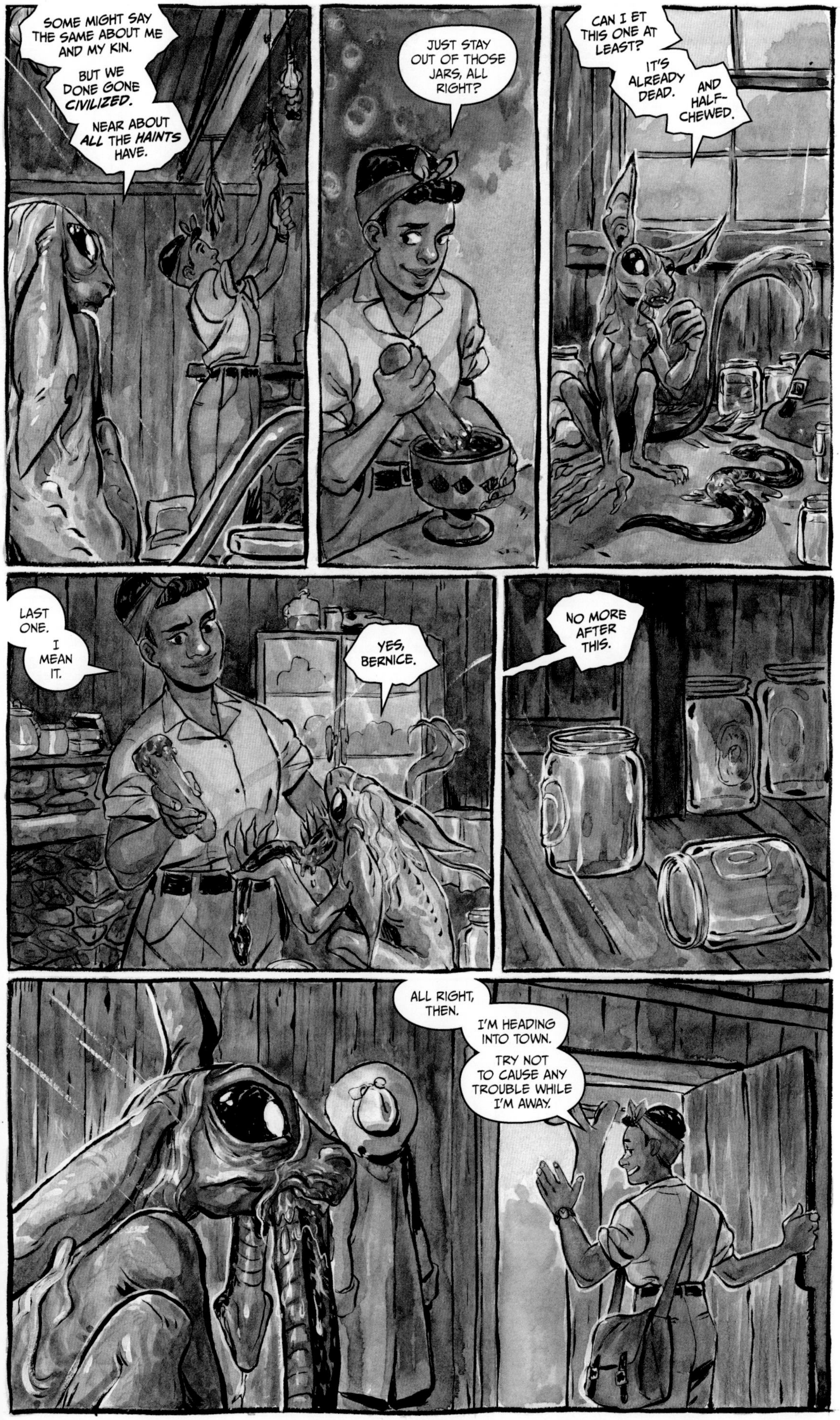
SOME MIGHT SAY THE SAME ABOUT ME AND MY KIN.
BUT WE DONE GONE *CIVILIZED*.
NEAR ABOUT *ALL* THE *HAINTS* HAVE.
JUST STAY OUT OF THOSE JARS, ALL RIGHT?
CAN I ET THIS ONE AT LEAST?
IT'S ALREADY DEAD.
AND HALF-CHEWED.
LAST ONE.
I MEAN IT.
YES, BERNICE.
NO MORE AFTER THIS.
ALL RIGHT, THEN.
I'M HEADING INTO TOWN.
TRY NOT TO CAUSE ANY TROUBLE WHILE I'M AWAY.

BERNICE WOULD BE LYING...

...TO HERSELF AND ANYONE ELSE WHO WAS LISTENING...

...IF SHE SAID SHE NEVER THOUGHT ABOUT LEAVING.

THERE HAD BEEN MORE THAN A FEW DAYS WHEN SHE SET OFF ON THAT PATH.

SET OFF TO FIND...

...SOMETHING ELSE.

BUT SHE ALWAYS TURNED BACK BEFORE SHE MADE IT FAR.

SHE KNEW WHERE SHE BELONGED.

ON THE OTHER HAND...

...SHE DIDN'T HAVE ANY IDEA WHAT WOULD HAPPEN TO HER FRIENDS OR NEIGHBORS IF SHE LEFT.

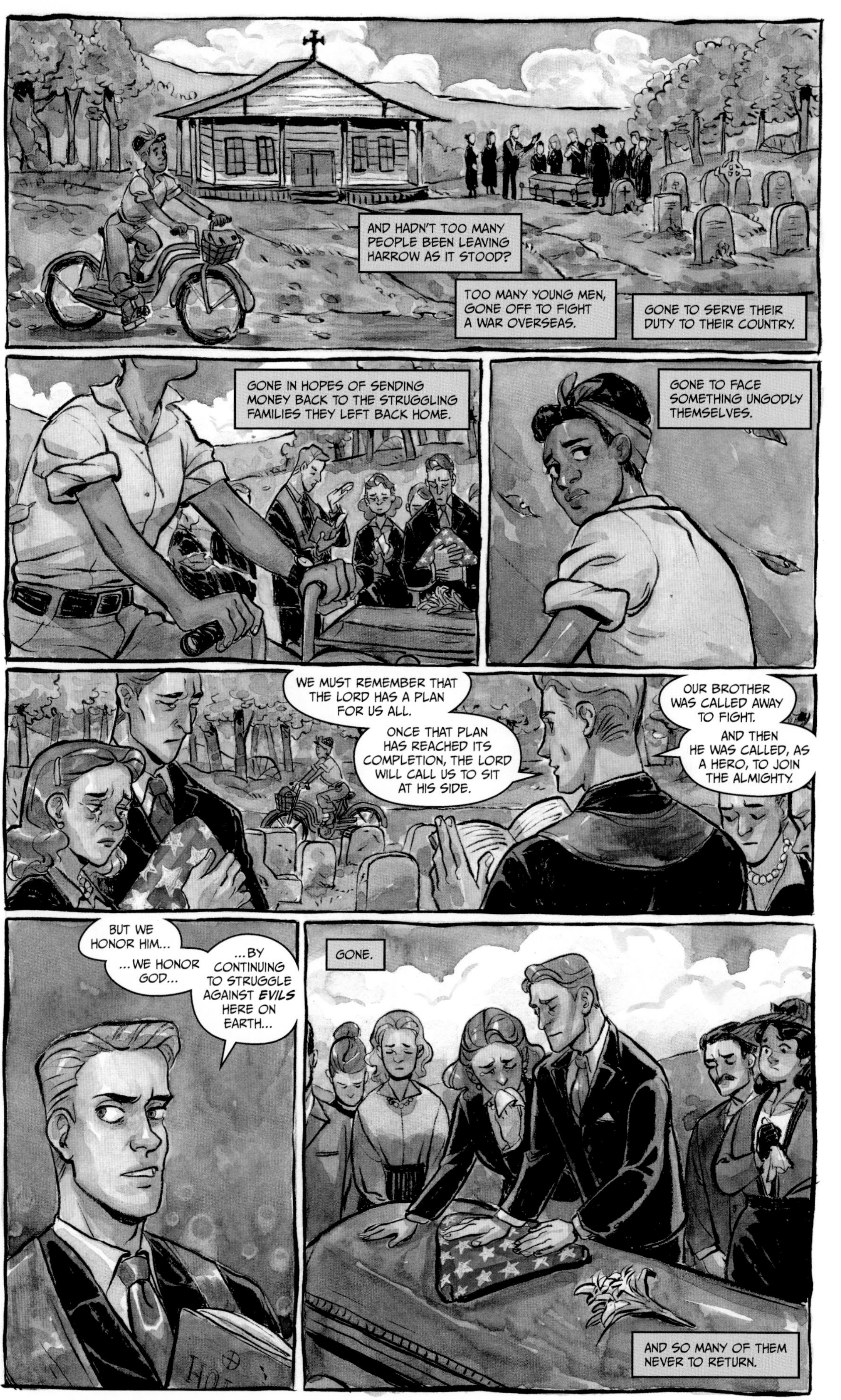
AND HADN'T TOO MANY PEOPLE BEEN LEAVING HARROW AS IT STOOD?
TOO MANY YOUNG MEN, GONE OFF TO FIGHT A WAR OVERSEAS.
GONE TO SERVE THEIR DUTY TO THEIR COUNTRY.
GONE IN HOPES OF SENDING MONEY BACK TO THE STRUGGLING FAMILIES THEY LEFT BACK HOME.
GONE TO FACE SOMETHING UNGODLY THEMSELVES.
WE MUST REMEMBER THAT THE LORD HAS A PLAN FOR US ALL.
ONCE THAT PLAN HAS REACHED ITS COMPLETION, THE LORD WILL CALL US TO SIT AT HIS SIDE.
OUR BROTHER WAS CALLED AWAY TO FIGHT.
AND THEN HE WAS CALLED, AS A HERO, TO JOIN THE ALMIGHTY.
BUT WE HONOR HIM...
...WE HONOR GOD...
...BY CONTINUING TO STRUGGLE AGAINST EVILS HERE ON EARTH...
GONE.
AND SO MANY OF THEM NEVER TO RETURN.

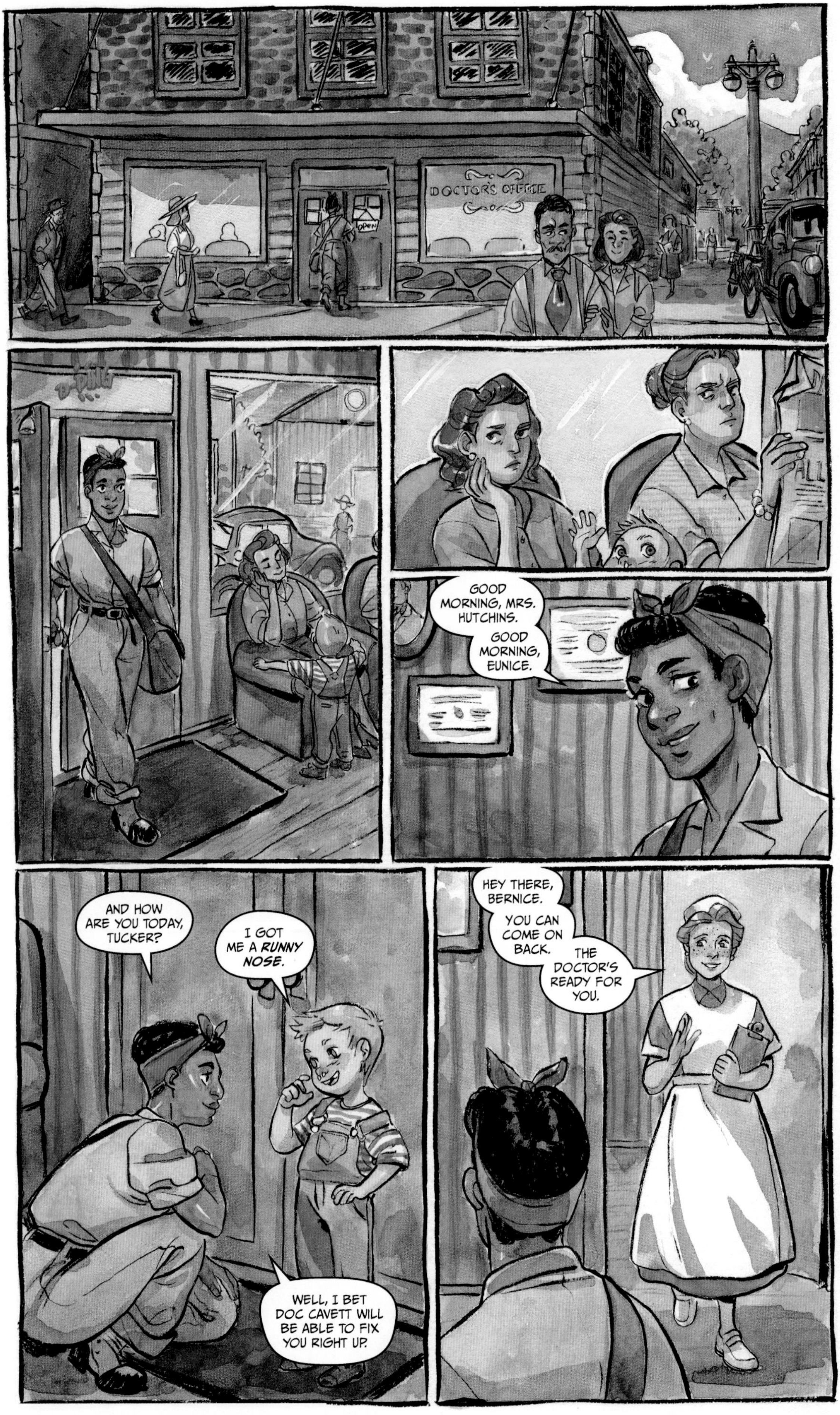
DOCTOR'S OFFICE
OPEN
D-DING
GOOD MORNING, MRS. HUTCHINS.
GOOD MORNING, EUNICE.
AND HOW ARE YOU TODAY, TUCKER?
I GOT ME A ***RUNNY NOSE.***
WELL, I BET DOC CAVETT WILL BE ABLE TO FIX YOU RIGHT UP.
HEY THERE, BERNICE.
YOU CAN COME ON BACK.
THE DOCTOR'S READY FOR YOU.

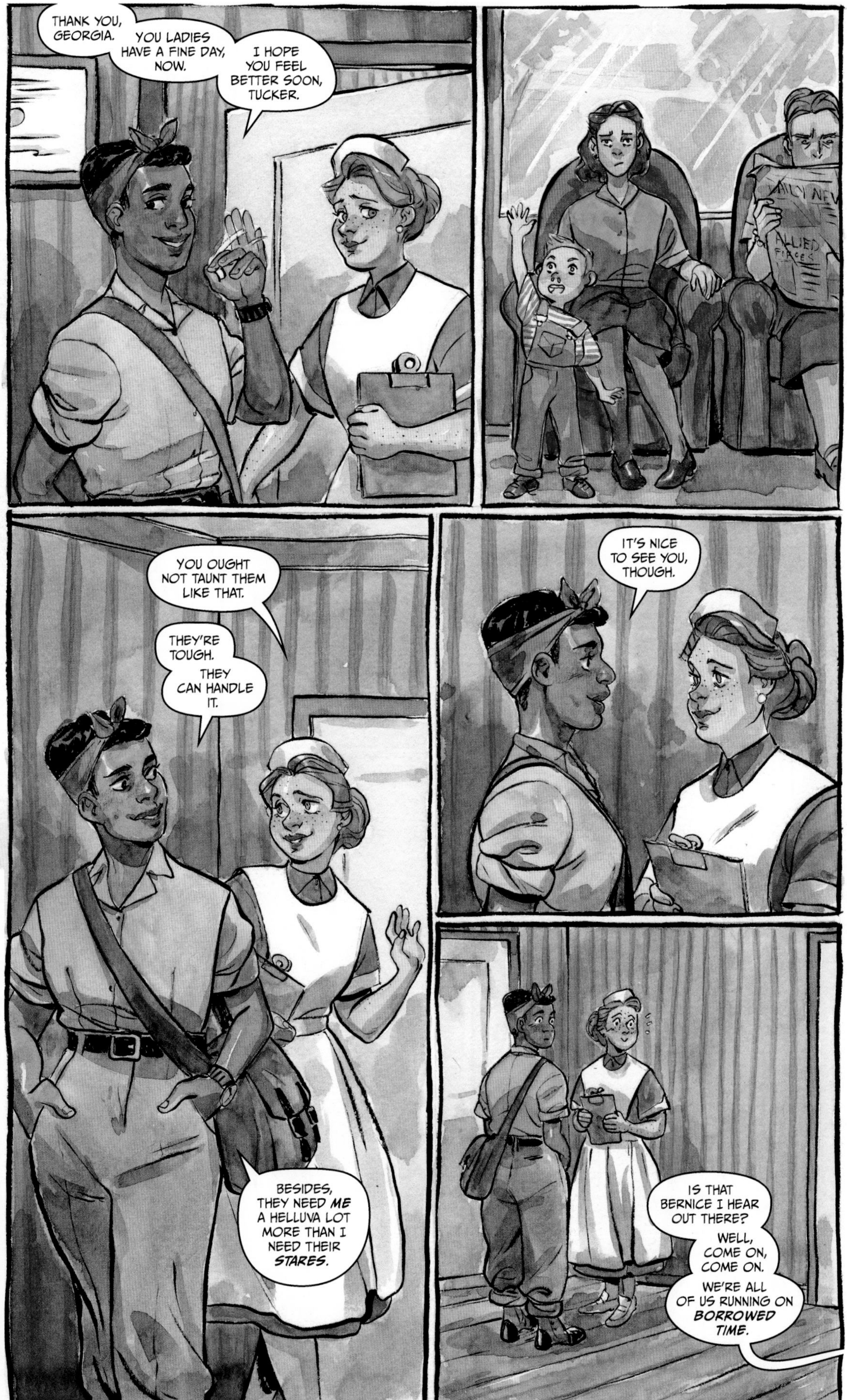
THANK YOU, GEORGIA.
YOU LADIES HAVE A FINE DAY, NOW.
I HOPE YOU FEEL BETTER SOON, TUCKER.
YOU OUGHT NOT TAUNT THEM LIKE THAT.
THEY'RE TOUGH.
THEY CAN HANDLE IT.
BESIDES, THEY NEED ME A HELLUVA LOT MORE THAN I NEED THEIR STARES.
IT'S NICE TO SEE YOU, THOUGH.
IS THAT BERNICE I HEAR OUT THERE?
WELL, COME ON, COME ON.
WE'RE ALL OF US RUNNING ON BORROWED TIME.

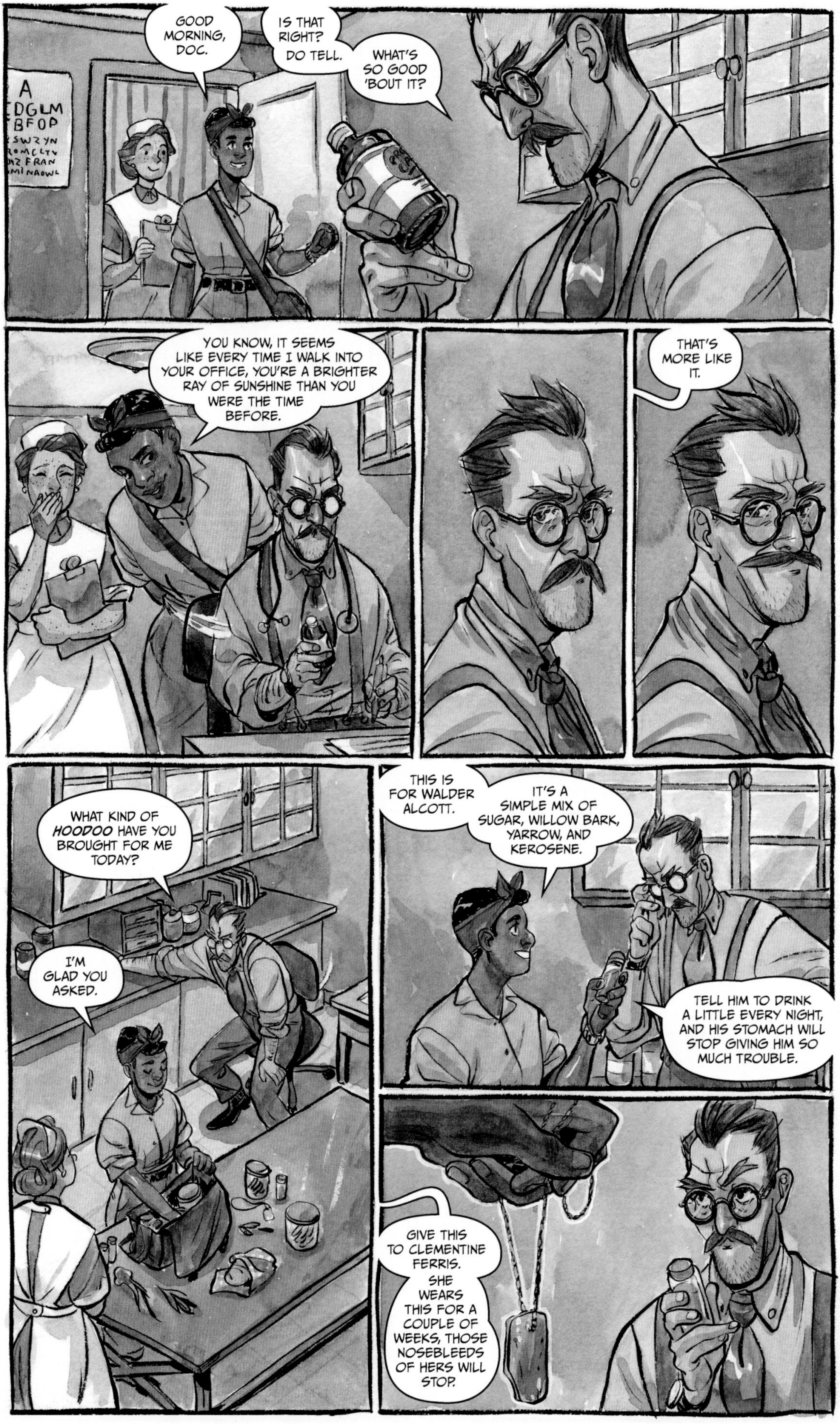
GOOD MORNING, DOC.
IS THAT RIGHT?
DO TELL.
WHAT'S SO GOOD 'BOUT IT?
YOU KNOW, IT SEEMS LIKE EVERY TIME I WALK INTO YOUR OFFICE, YOU'RE A BRIGHTER RAY OF SUNSHINE THAN YOU WERE THE TIME BEFORE.
THAT'S MORE LIKE IT.
WHAT KIND OF *HOODOO* HAVE YOU BROUGHT FOR ME TODAY?
I'M GLAD YOU ASKED.
THIS IS FOR WALDER ALCOTT.
IT'S A SIMPLE MIX OF SUGAR, WILLOW BARK, YARROW, AND KEROSENE.
TELL HIM TO DRINK A LITTLE EVERY NIGHT, AND HIS STOMACH WILL STOP GIVING HIM SO MUCH TROUBLE.
GIVE THIS TO CLEMENTINE FERRIS.
SHE WEARS THIS FOR A COUPLE OF WEEKS, THOSE NOSEBLEEDS OF HERS WILL STOP.

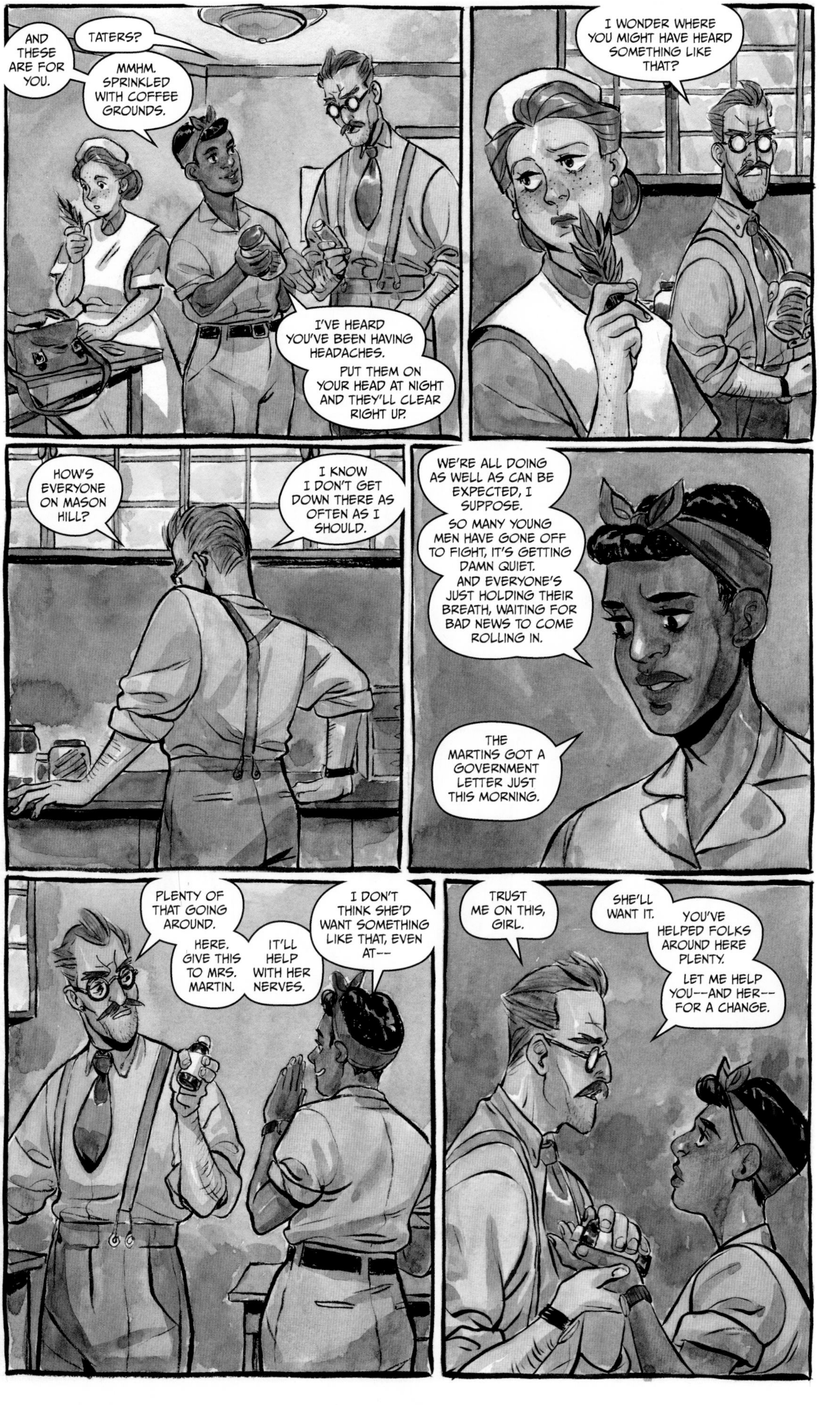
AND THESE ARE FOR YOU.
TATERS?
MMHM. SPRINKLED WITH COFFEE GROUNDS.
I'VE HEARD YOU'VE BEEN HAVING HEADACHES.
PUT THEM ON YOUR HEAD AT NIGHT AND THEY'LL CLEAR RIGHT UP.
I WONDER WHERE YOU MIGHT HAVE HEARD SOMETHING LIKE THAT?
HOW'S EVERYONE ON MASON HILL?
I KNOW I DON'T GET DOWN THERE AS OFTEN AS I SHOULD.
WE'RE ALL DOING AS WELL AS CAN BE EXPECTED, I SUPPOSE.
SO MANY YOUNG MEN HAVE GONE OFF TO FIGHT, IT'S GETTING DAMN QUIET.
AND EVERYONE'S JUST HOLDING THEIR BREATH, WAITING FOR BAD NEWS TO COME ROLLING IN.
THE MARTINS GOT A GOVERNMENT LETTER JUST THIS MORNING.
PLENTY OF THAT GOING AROUND.
HERE. GIVE THIS TO MRS. MARTIN.
IT'LL HELP WITH HER NERVES.
I DON'T THINK SHE'D WANT SOMETHING LIKE THAT, EVEN AT--
TRUST ME ON THIS, GIRL.
SHE'LL WANT IT.
YOU'VE HELPED FOLKS AROUND HERE PLENTY.
LET ME HELP YOU--AND HER--FOR A CHANGE.

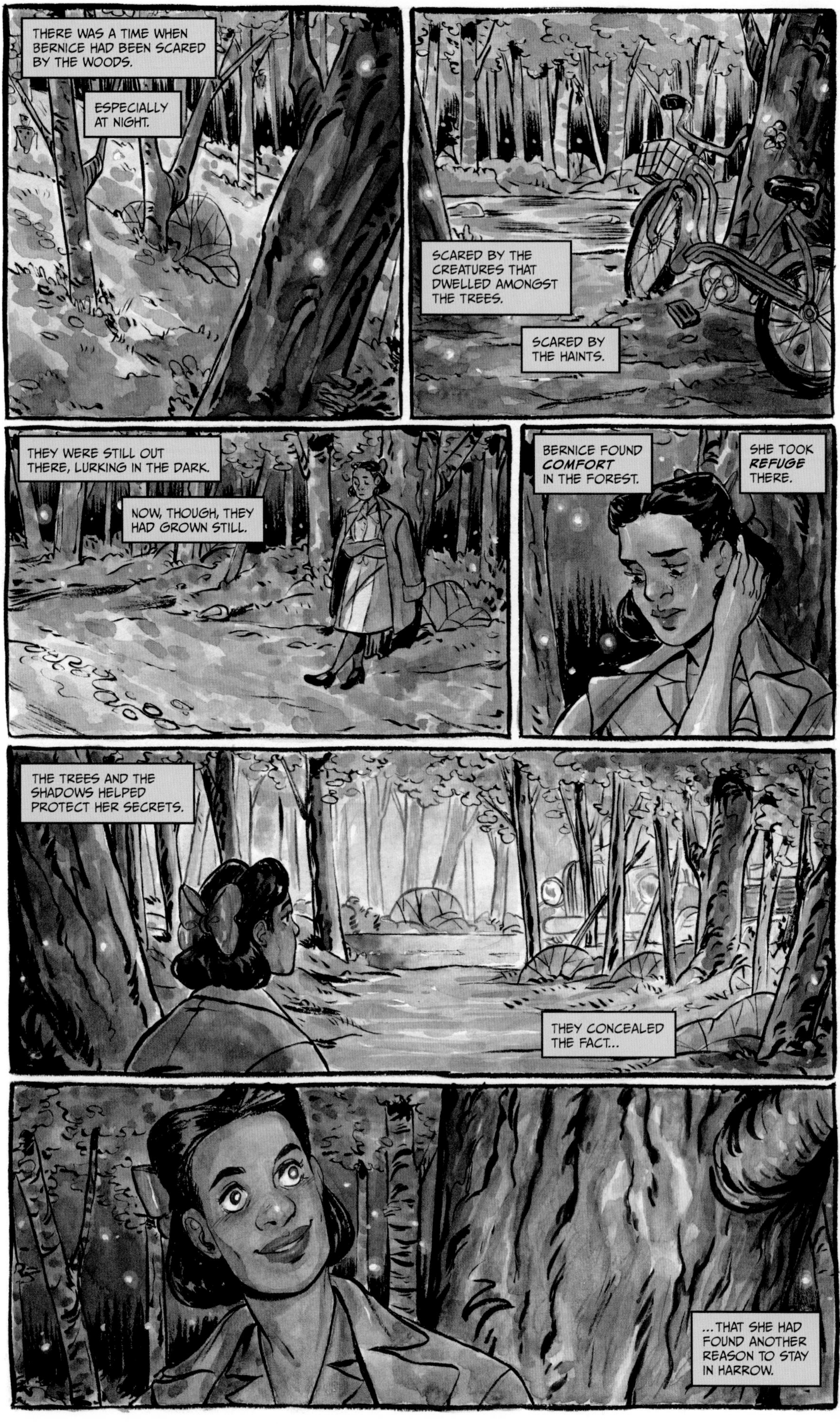
THERE WAS A TIME WHEN BERNICE HAD BEEN SCARED BY THE WOODS.
ESPECIALLY AT NIGHT.
SCARED BY THE CREATURES THAT DWELLED AMONGST THE TREES.
SCARED BY THE HAINTS.
THEY WERE STILL OUT THERE, LURKING IN THE DARK.
NOW, THOUGH, THEY HAD GROWN STILL.
BERNICE FOUND **COMFORT** IN THE FOREST.
SHE TOOK **REFUGE** THERE.
THE TREES AND THE SHADOWS HELPED PROTECT HER SECRETS.
THEY CONCEALED THE FACT...
...THAT SHE HAD FOUND ANOTHER REASON TO STAY IN HARROW.

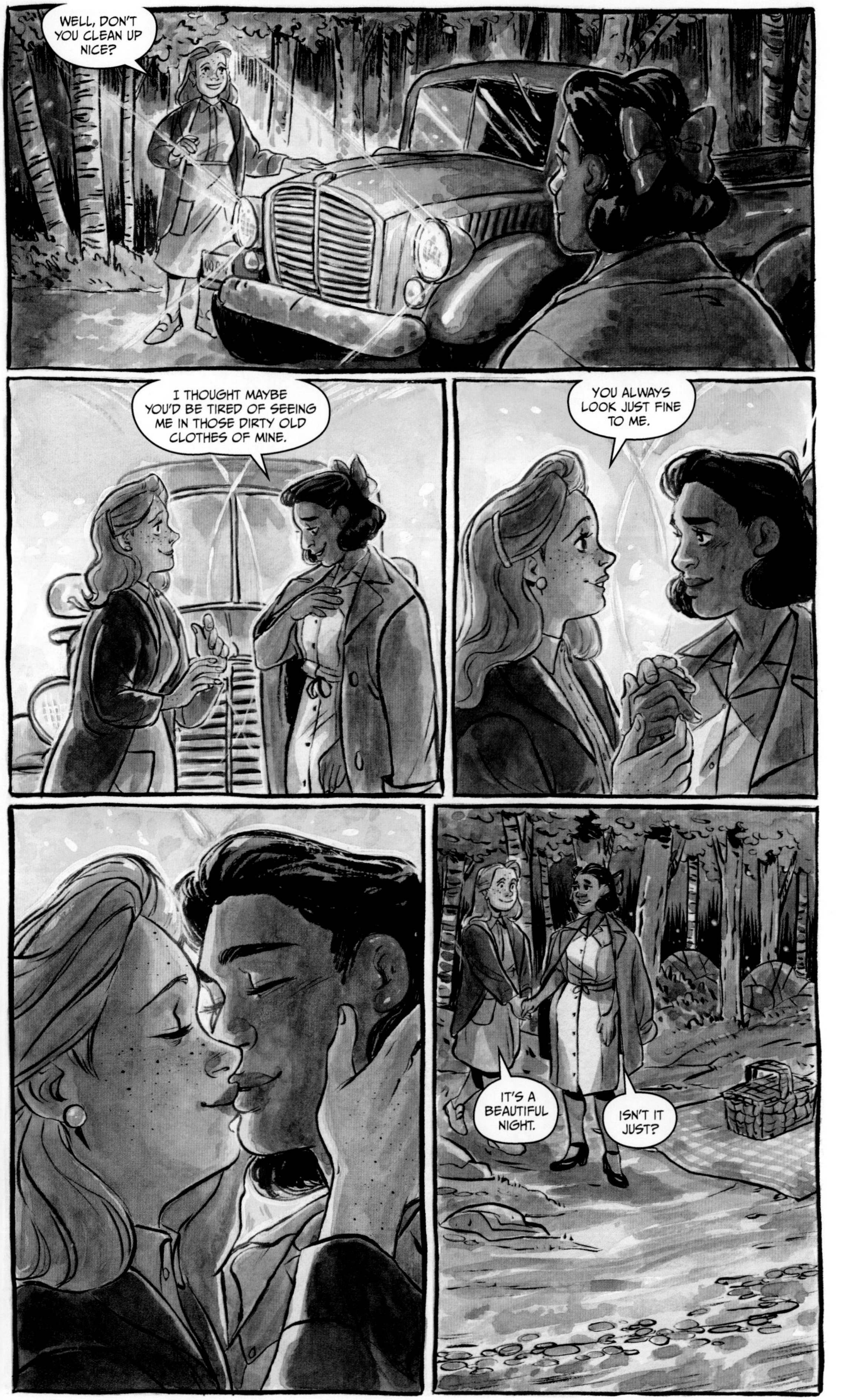
WELL, DON'T YOU CLEAN UP NICE?
I THOUGHT MAYBE YOU'D BE TIRED OF SEEING ME IN THOSE DIRTY OLD CLOTHES OF MINE.
YOU ALWAYS LOOK JUST FINE TO ME.
IT'S A BEAUTIFUL NIGHT.
ISN'T IT JUST?

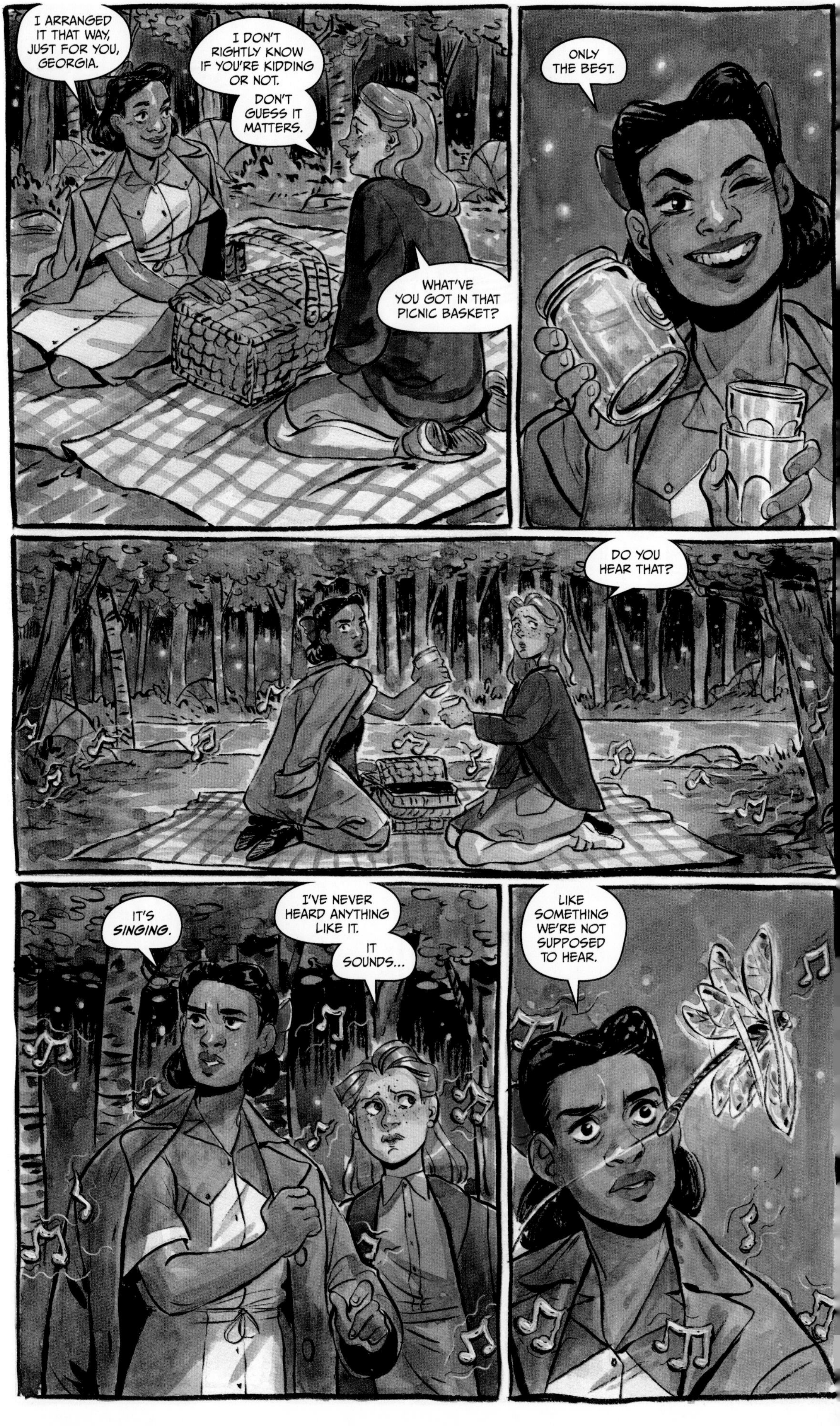
I ARRANGED IT THAT WAY, JUST FOR YOU, GEORGIA.
I DON'T RIGHTLY KNOW IF YOU'RE KIDDING OR NOT.
DON'T GUESS IT MATTERS.
WHAT'VE YOU GOT IN THAT PICNIC BASKET?
ONLY THE BEST.
DO YOU HEAR THAT?
IT'S *SINGING*.
I'VE NEVER HEARD ANYTHING LIKE IT.
IT SOUNDS...
LIKE SOMETHING WE'RE NOT SUPPOSED TO HEAR.

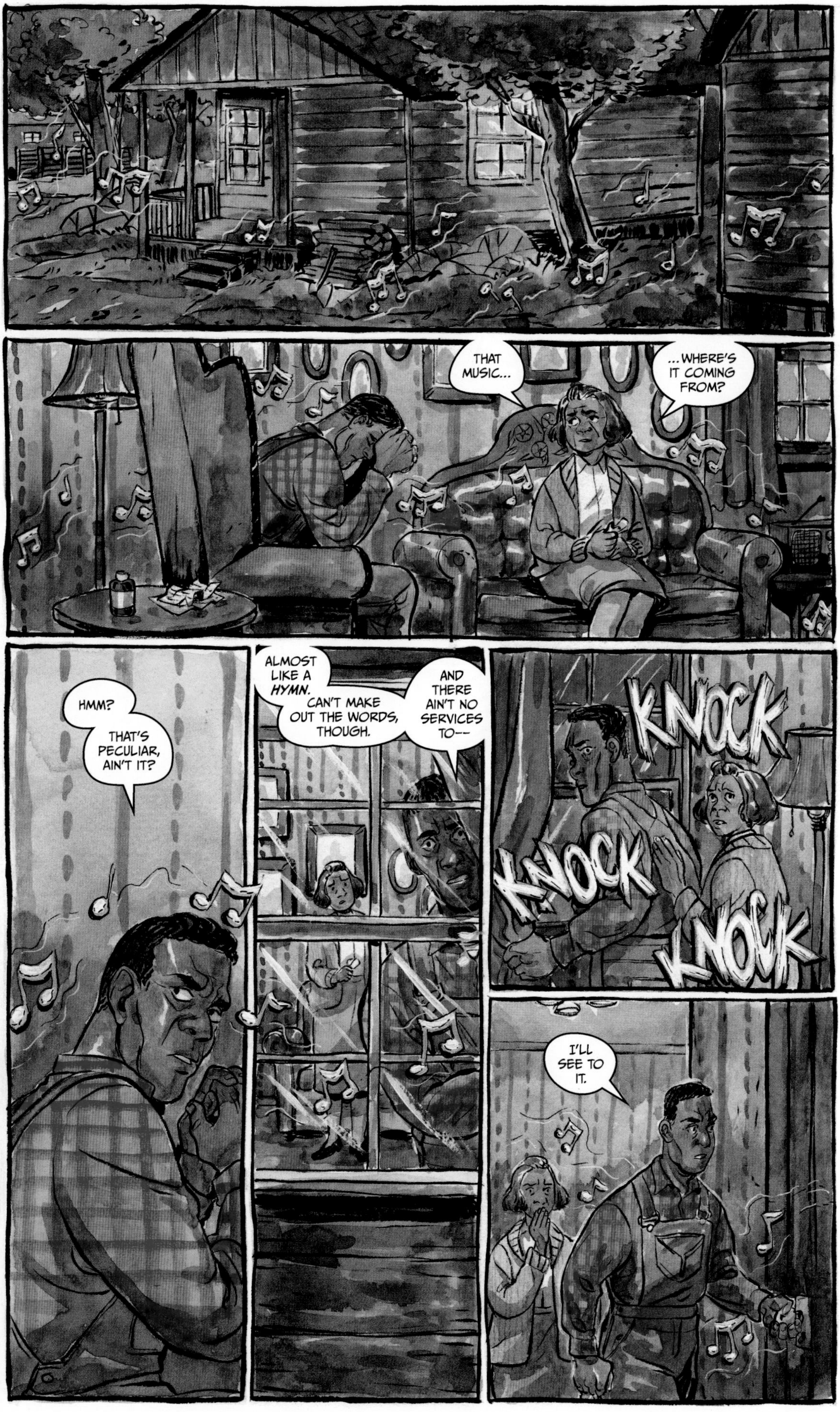
THAT MUSIC...
...WHERE'S IT COMING FROM?
HMM?
THAT'S PECULIAR, AIN'T IT?
ALMOST LIKE A *HYMN*.
CAN'T MAKE OUT THE WORDS, THOUGH.
AND THERE AIN'T NO SERVICES TO--
KNOCK
KNOCK
KNOCK
I'LL SEE TO IT.

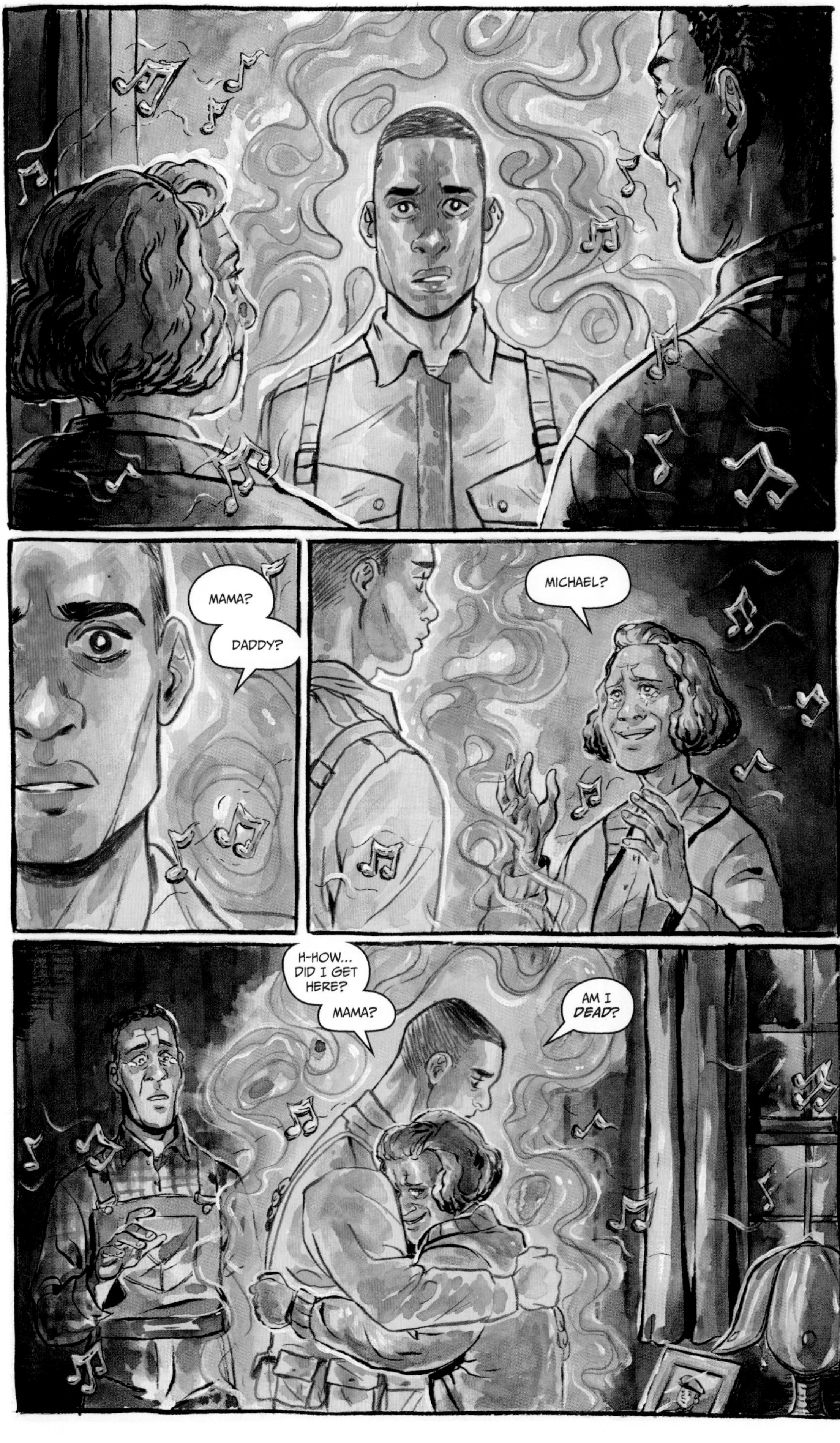
MAMA?
DADDY?
MICHAEL?
H-HOW... DID I GET HERE?
MAMA?
AM I *DEAD*?

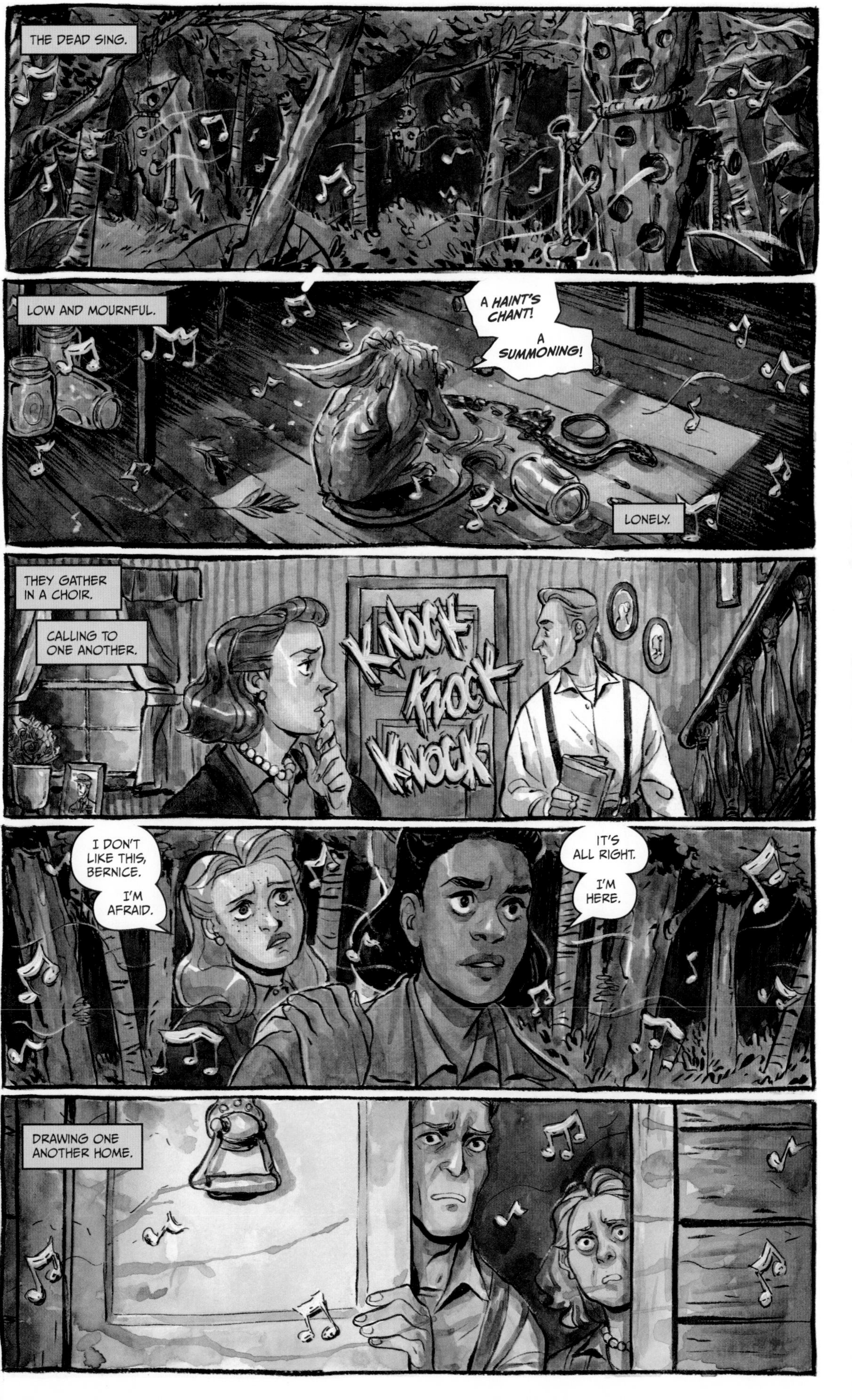
THE DEAD SING.
LOW AND MOURNFUL.
A HAINT'S CHANT!
A SUMMONING!
LONELY.
THEY GATHER IN A CHOIR.
CALLING TO ONE ANOTHER.
KNOCK KNOCK KNOCK
I DON'T LIKE THIS, BERNICE.
I'M AFRAID.
IT'S ALL RIGHT.
I'M HERE.
DRAWING ONE ANOTHER HOME.

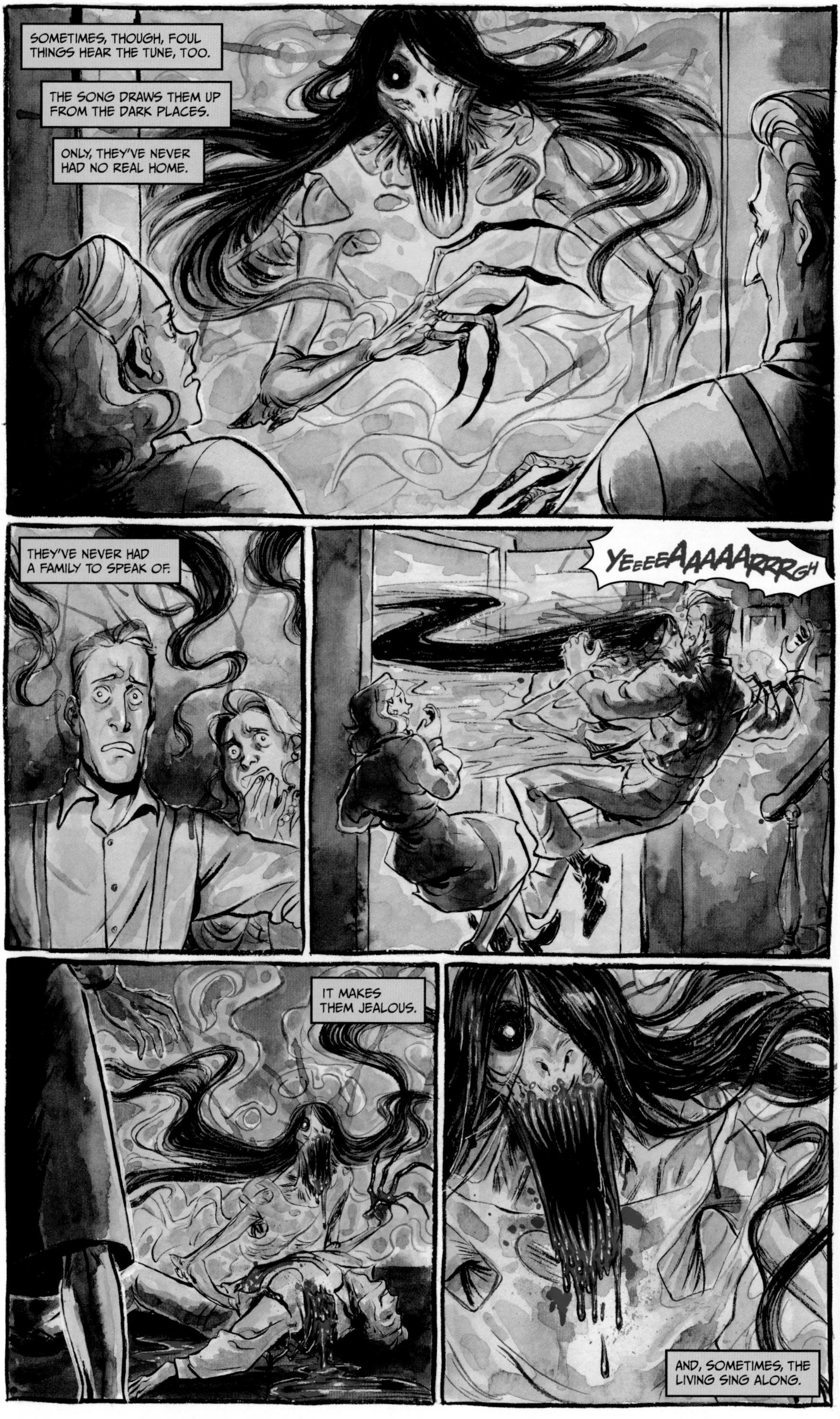
SOMETIMES, THOUGH, FOUL THINGS HEAR THE TUNE, TOO.
THE SONG DRAWS THEM UP FROM THE DARK PLACES.
ONLY, THEY'VE NEVER HAD NO REAL HOME.
THEY'VE NEVER HAD A FAMILY TO SPEAK OF.
YEEEEAAAAARRRGH
IT MAKES THEM JEALOUS.
AND, SOMETIMES, THE LIVING SING ALONG.

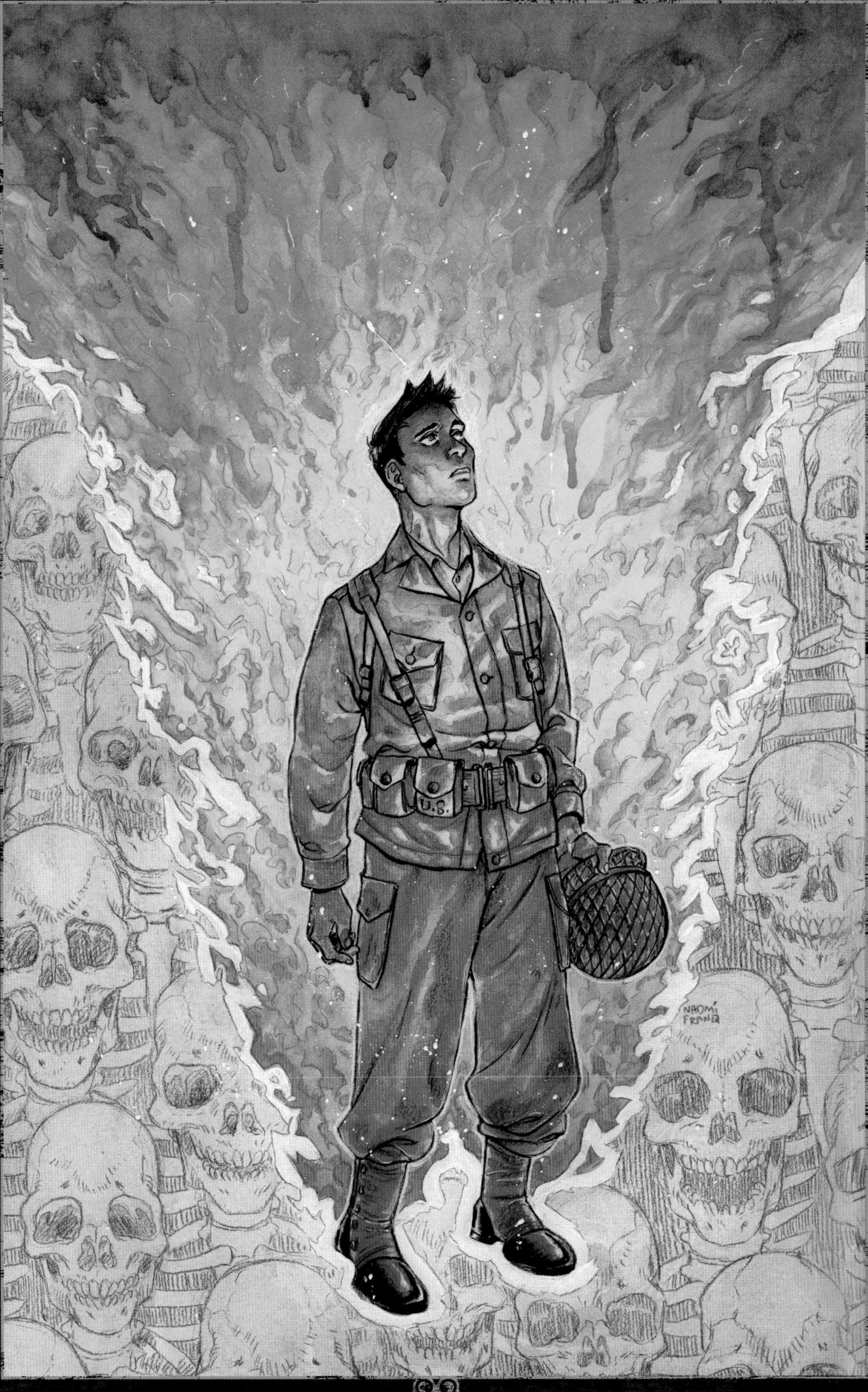
U.S.
NAOMI FRANQ

TWO

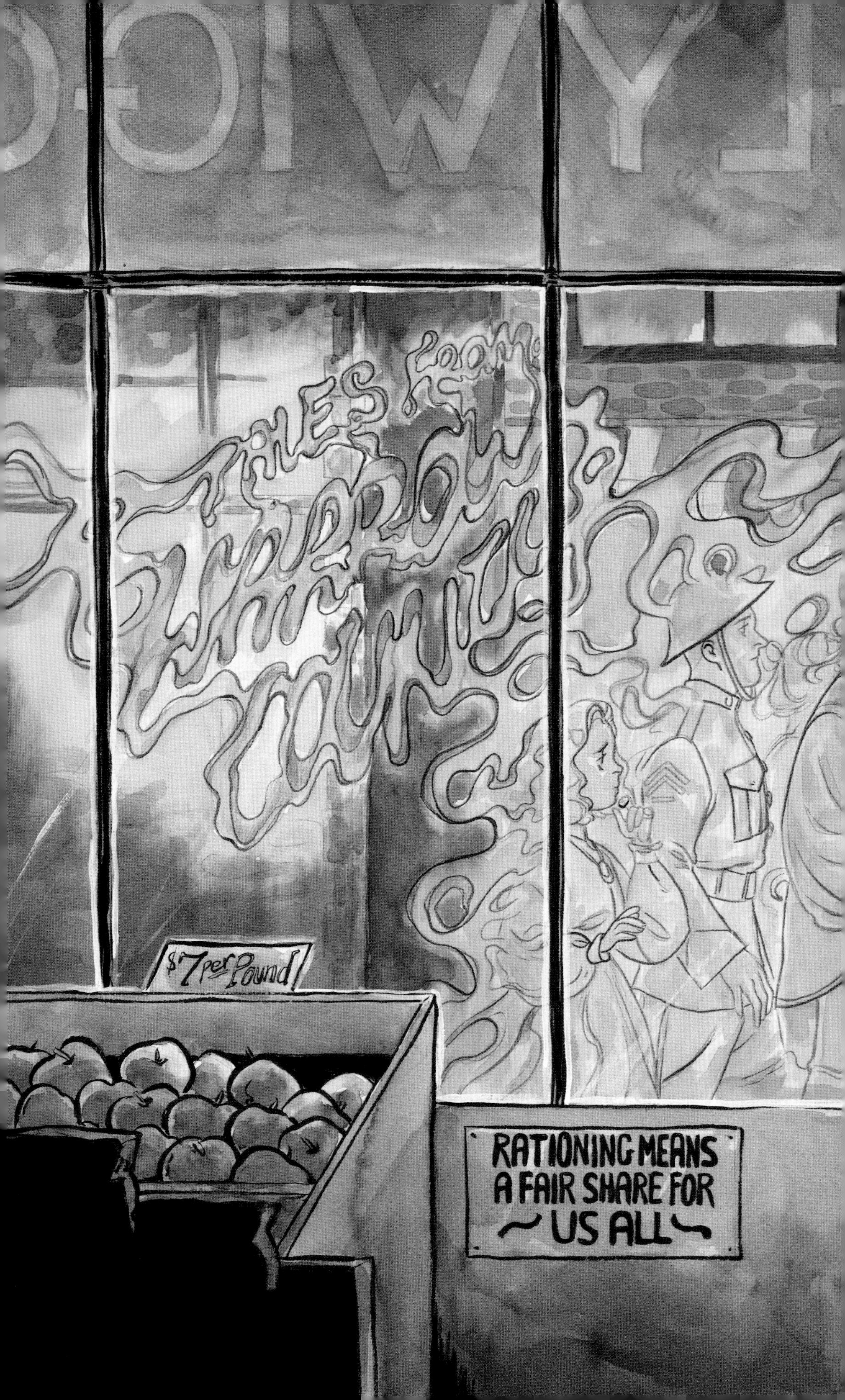
$7 per Pound
RATIONING MEANS A FAIR SHARE FOR ~US ALL~

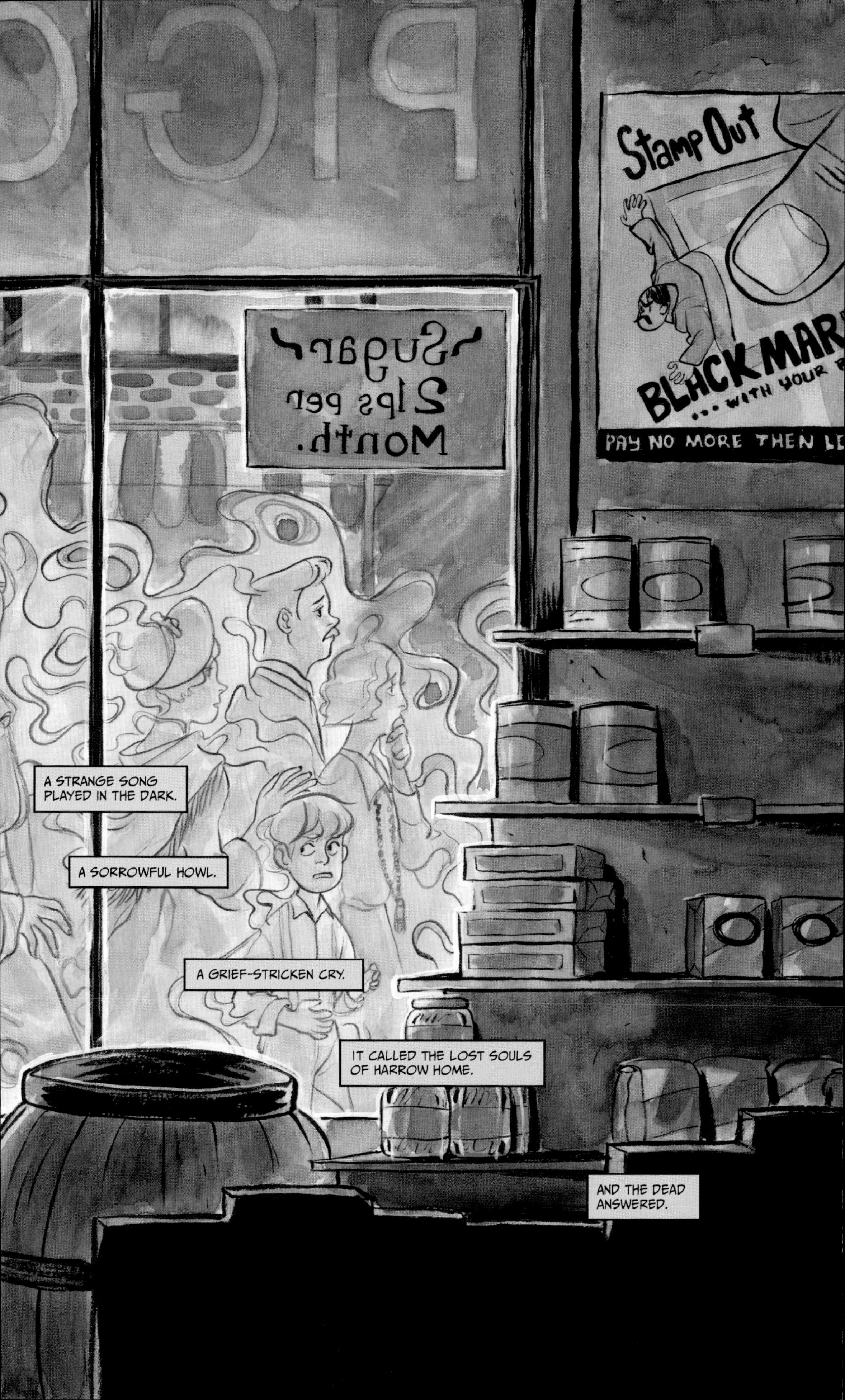
Stamp Out
A STRANGE SONG PLAYED IN THE DARK.
A SORROWFUL HOWL.
A GRIEF-STRICKEN CRY.
IT CALLED THE LOST SOULS OF HARROW HOME.
AND THE DEAD ANSWERED.

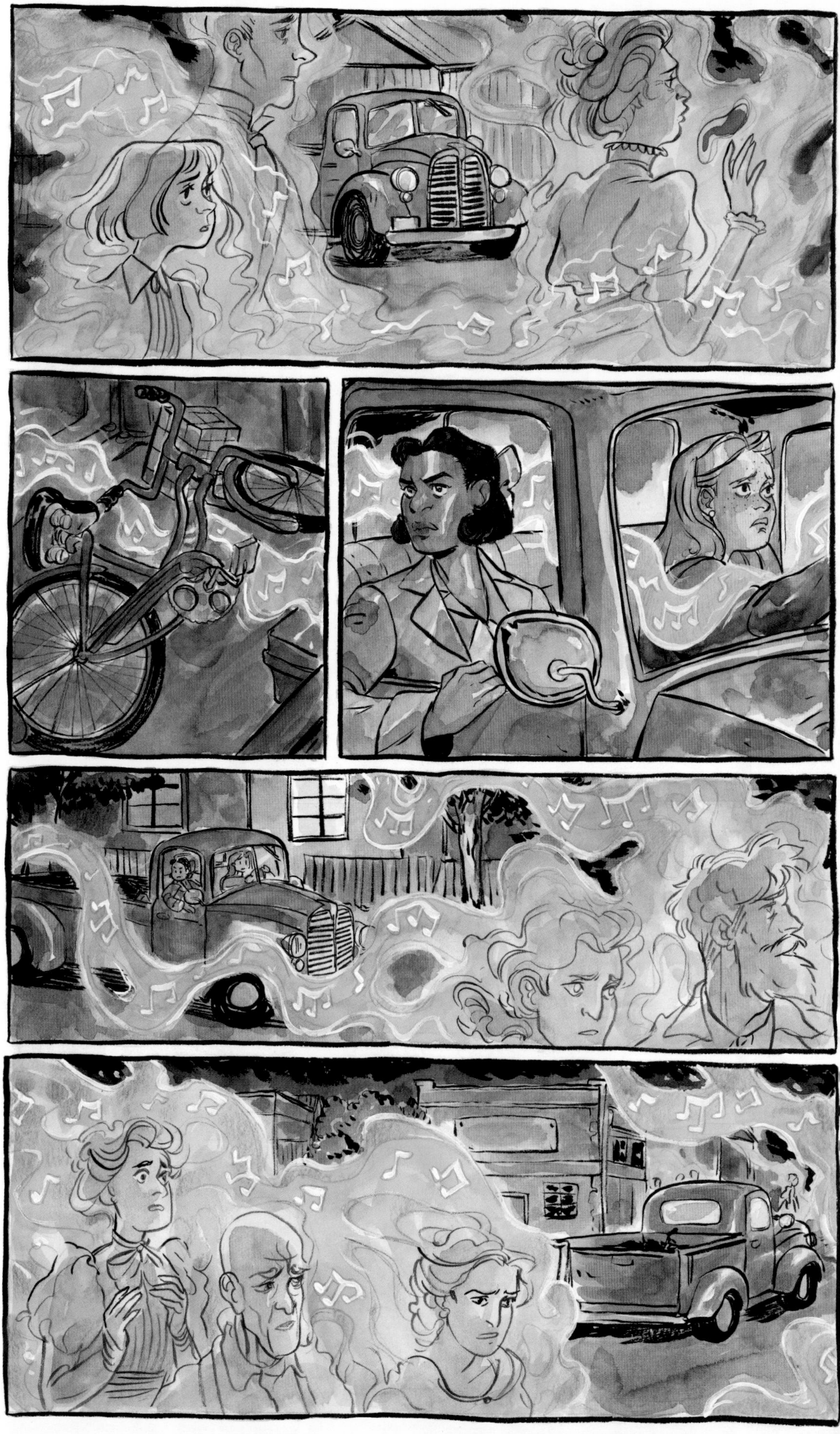

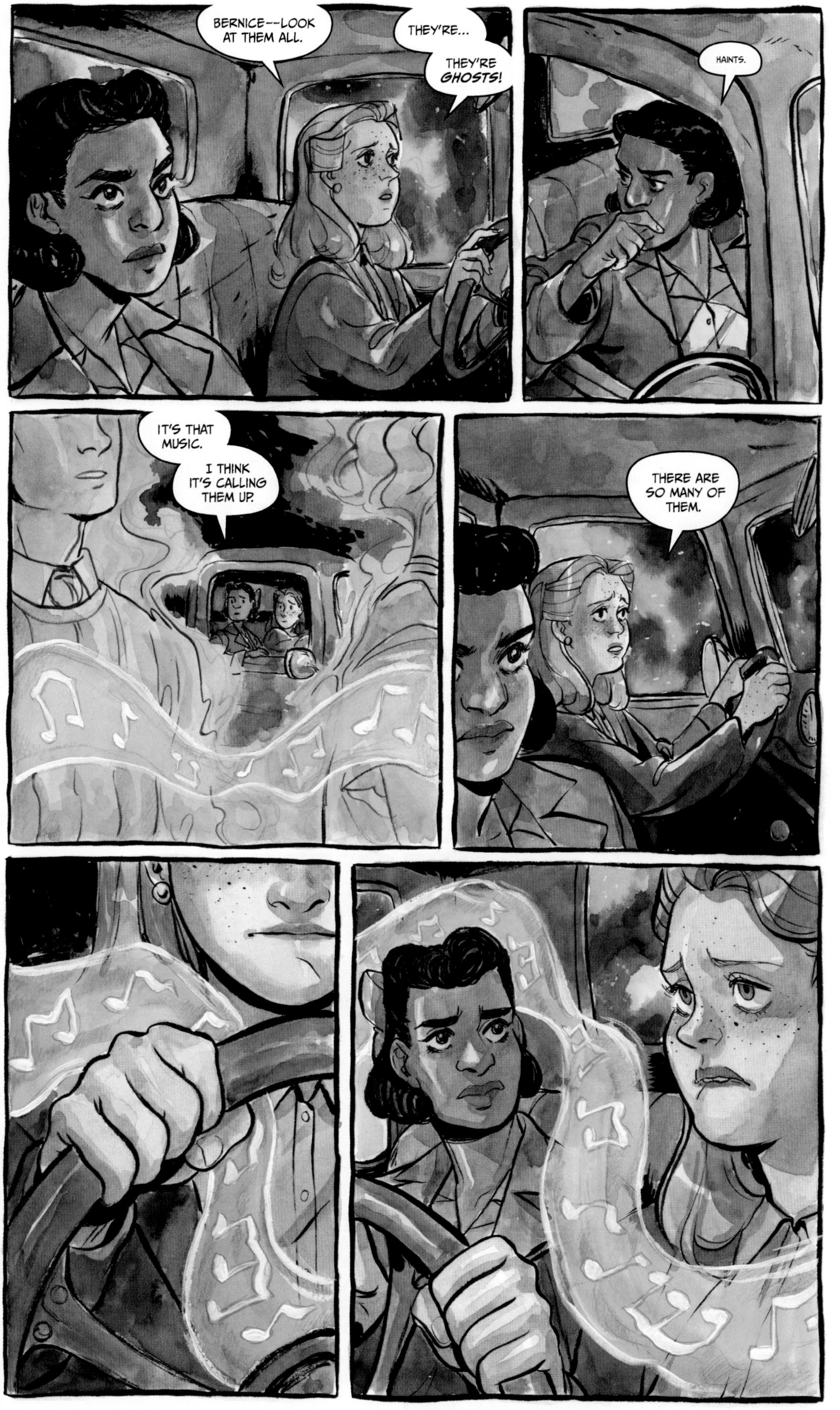

BERNICE--LOOK AT THEM ALL.
THEY'RE...
THEY'RE *GHOSTS!*
HAINTS.
IT'S THAT MUSIC.
I THINK IT'S CALLING THEM UP.
THERE ARE SO MANY OF THEM.

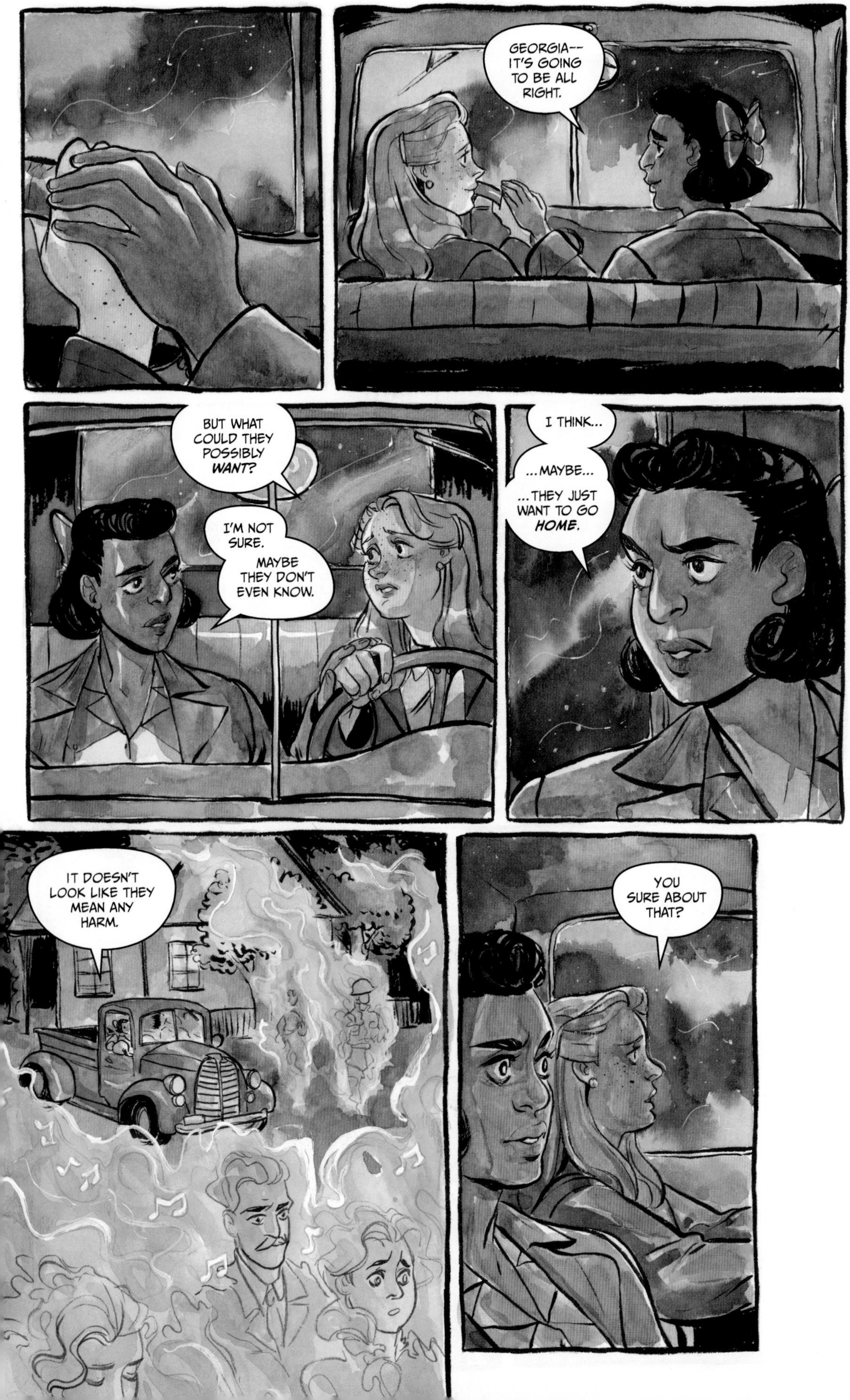
GEORGIA-- IT'S GOING TO BE ALL RIGHT.
BUT WHAT COULD THEY POSSIBLY *WANT*?
I'M NOT SURE.
MAYBE THEY DON'T EVEN KNOW.
I THINK...
...MAYBE...
...THEY JUST WANT TO GO *HOME*.
IT DOESN'T LOOK LIKE THEY MEAN ANY HARM.
YOU SURE ABOUT THAT?

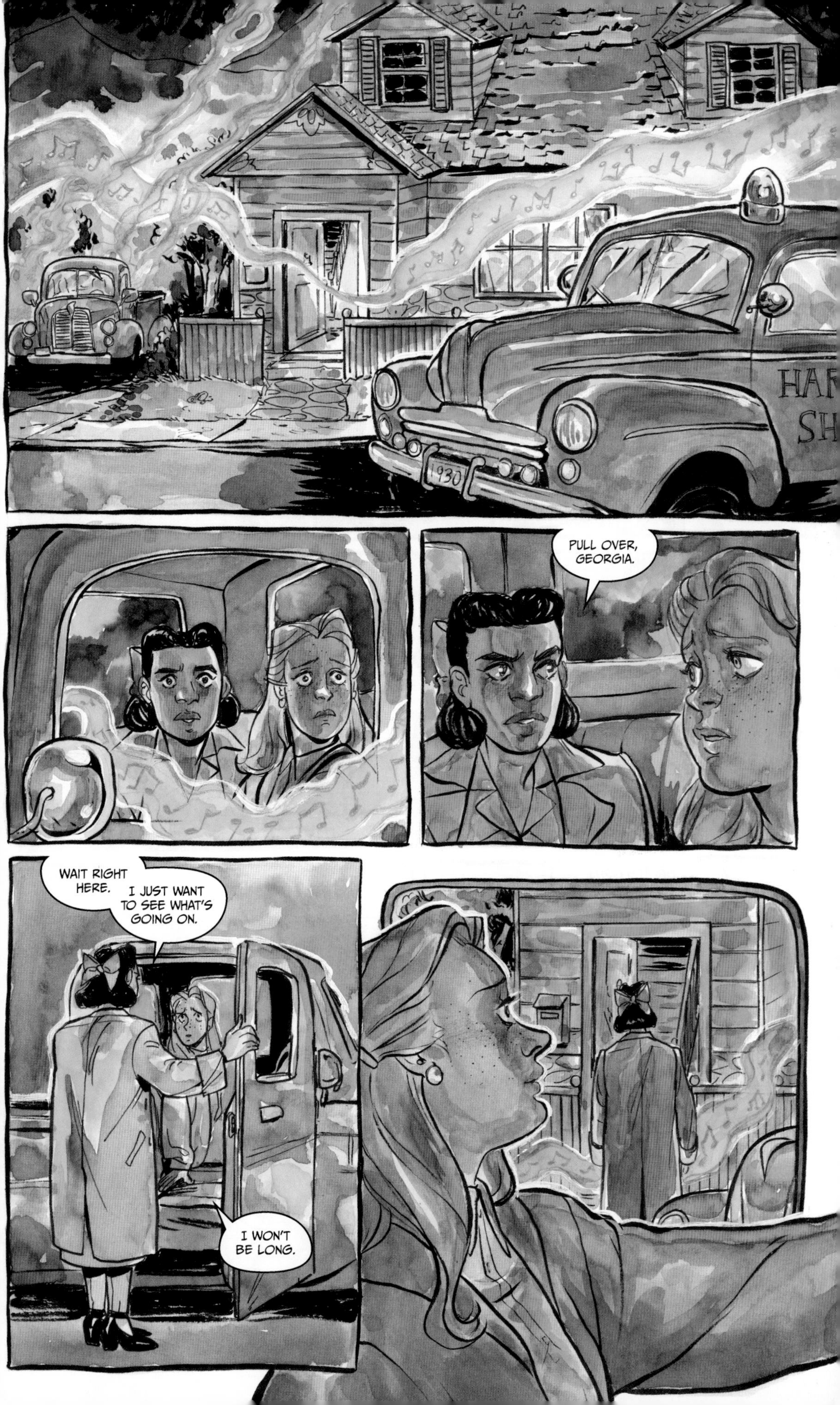
PULL OVER, GEORGIA.
WAIT RIGHT HERE.
I JUST WANT TO SEE WHAT'S GOING ON.
I WON'T BE LONG.

SHERIFF--

COME ON IN, BERNICE. I WAS WONDERING WHEN YOU MIGHT SHOW UP.

I SHOULD WARN YOU, THOUGH, IT AIN'T A PRETTY SIGHT.

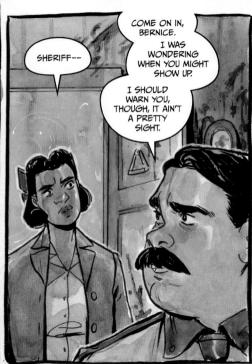

OH, NO.

MR. AND MRS. GRANGER.

WHAT HAPPENED? WHAT DID THIS TO THEM?

I'D SAY IT'S QUITE OBVIOUS WHAT HAPPENED HERE.

THERE'S NOT A THING OBVIOUS ABOUT THIS, REVEREND.

IT'S SATAN'S BUSINESS. HIS DEMONS ROAM THE STREETS.

CAN'T YOU HEAR IT?

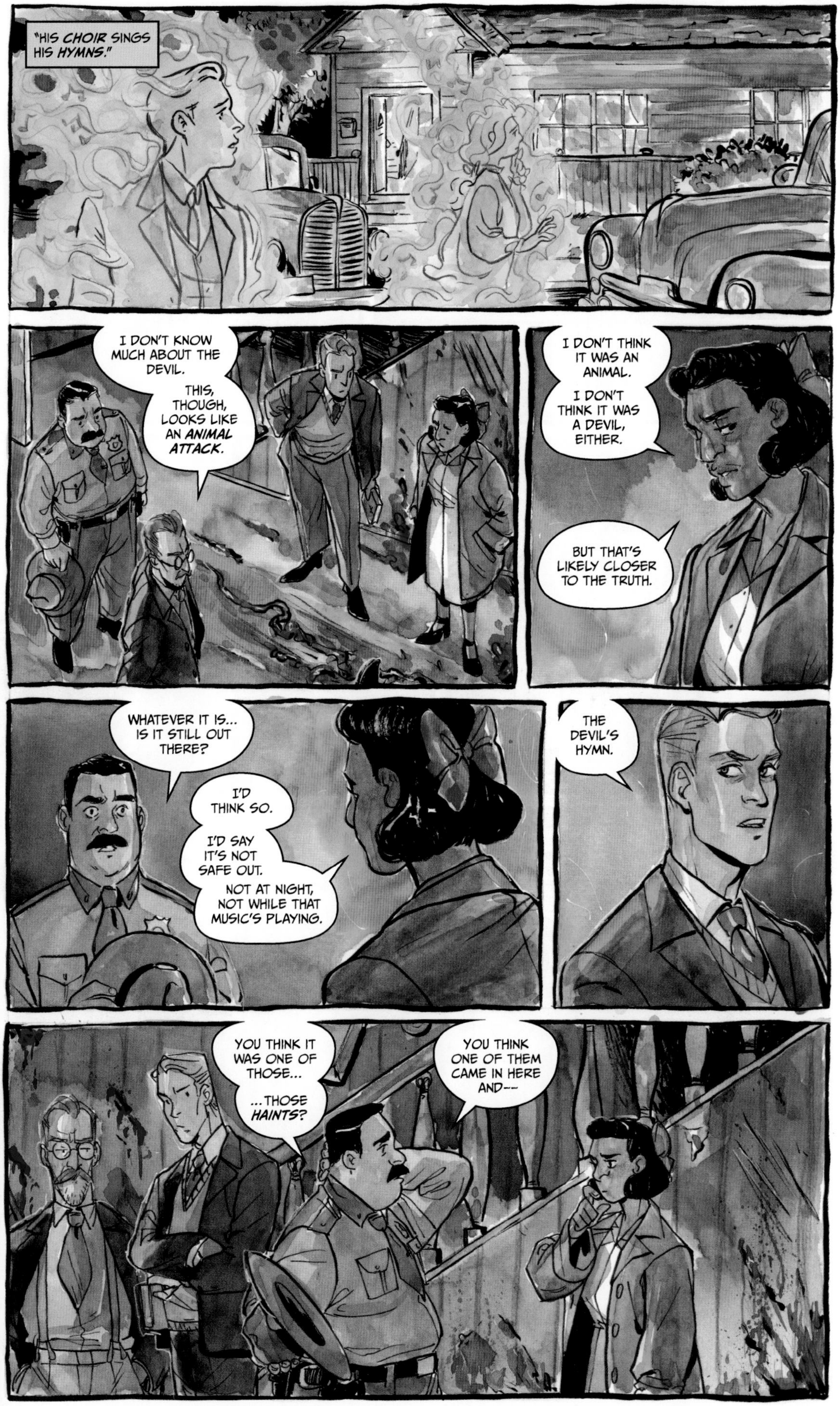
"HIS *CHOIR* SINGS HIS *HYMNS*."
I DON'T KNOW MUCH ABOUT THE DEVIL.
THIS, THOUGH, LOOKS LIKE AN *ANIMAL ATTACK*.
I DON'T THINK IT WAS AN ANIMAL.
I DON'T THINK IT WAS A DEVIL, EITHER.
BUT THAT'S LIKELY CLOSER TO THE TRUTH.
WHATEVER IT IS... IS IT STILL OUT THERE?
I'D THINK SO.
I'D SAY IT'S NOT SAFE OUT.
NOT AT NIGHT, NOT WHILE THAT MUSIC'S PLAYING.
THE DEVIL'S HYMN.
YOU THINK IT WAS ONE OF THOSE...
...THOSE *HAINTS*?
YOU THINK ONE OF THEM CAME IN HERE AND--

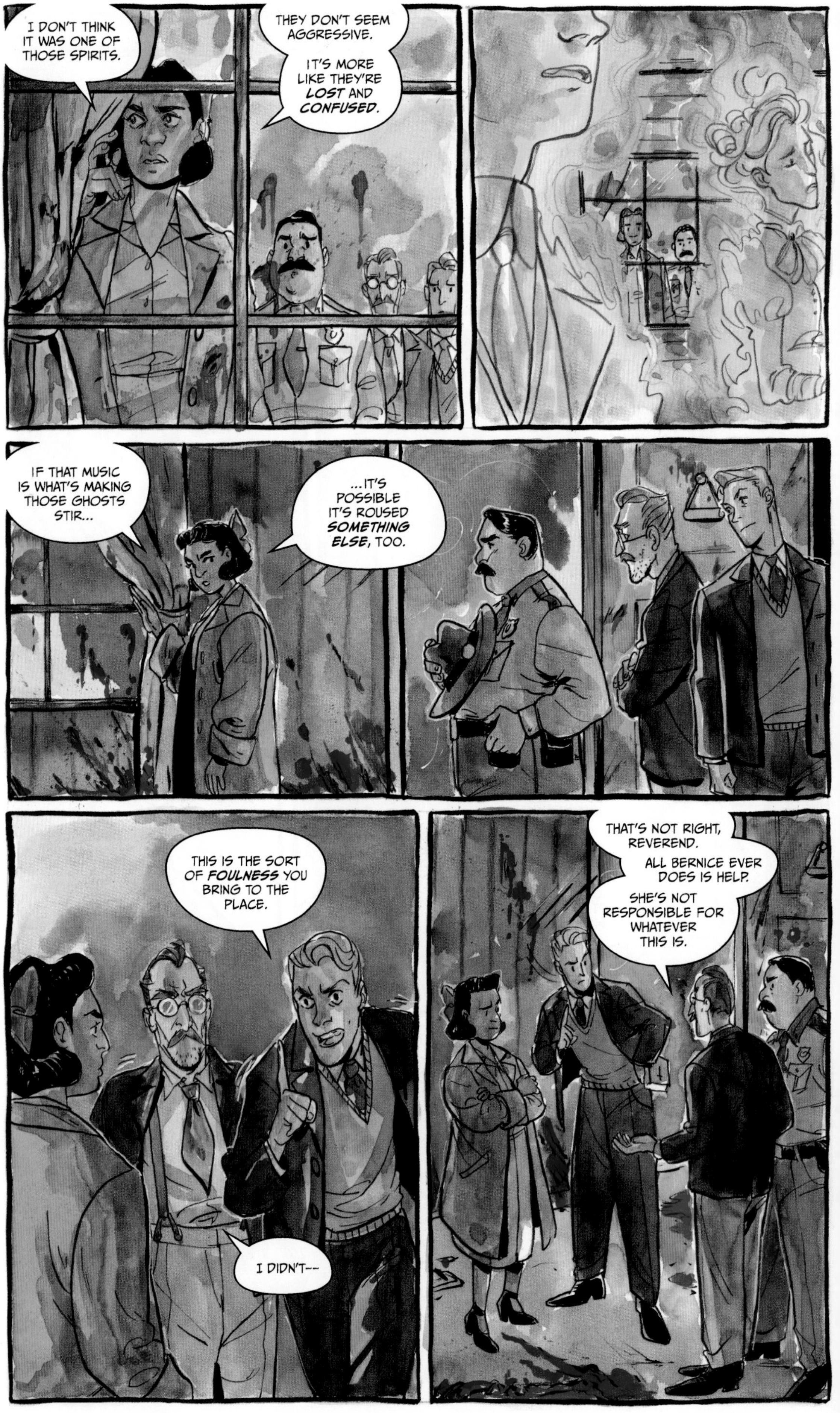

I DON'T THINK IT WAS ONE OF THOSE SPIRITS.
THEY DON'T SEEM AGGRESSIVE.
IT'S MORE LIKE THEY'RE *LOST* AND *CONFUSED*.
IF THAT MUSIC IS WHAT'S MAKING THOSE GHOSTS STIR...
...IT'S POSSIBLE IT'S ROUSED *SOMETHING ELSE*, TOO.
THIS IS THE SORT OF *FOULNESS* YOU BRING TO THE PLACE.
I DIDN'T--
THAT'S NOT RIGHT, REVEREND.
ALL BERNICE EVER DOES IS HELP.
SHE'S NOT RESPONSIBLE FOR WHATEVER THIS IS.

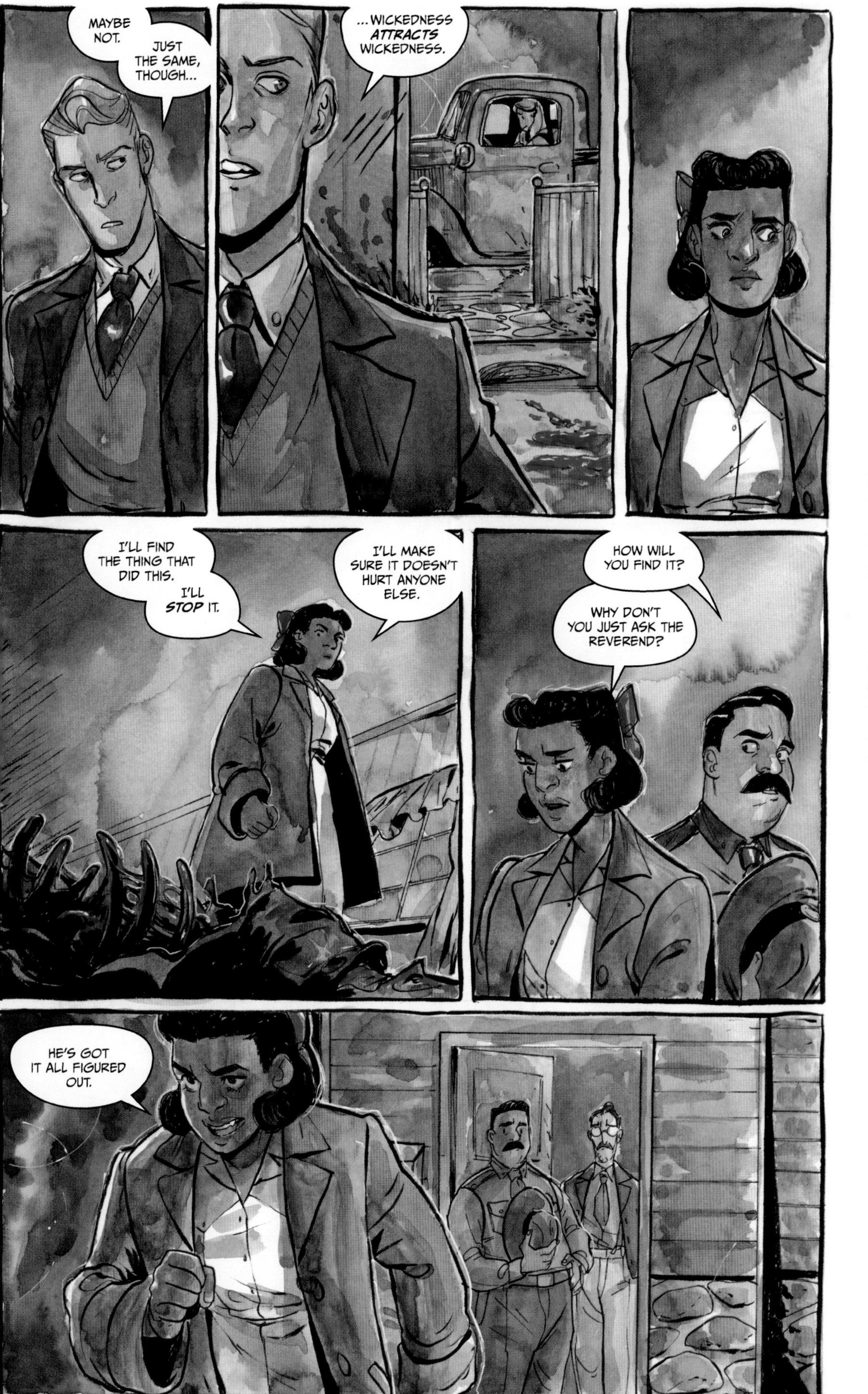
MAYBE NOT.
JUST THE SAME, THOUGH...
...WICKEDNESS ATTRACTS WICKEDNESS.
I'LL FIND THE THING THAT DID THIS.
I'LL STOP IT.
I'LL MAKE SURE IT DOESN'T HURT ANYONE ELSE.
HOW WILL YOU FIND IT?
WHY DON'T YOU JUST ASK THE REVEREND?
HE'S GOT IT ALL FIGURED OUT.

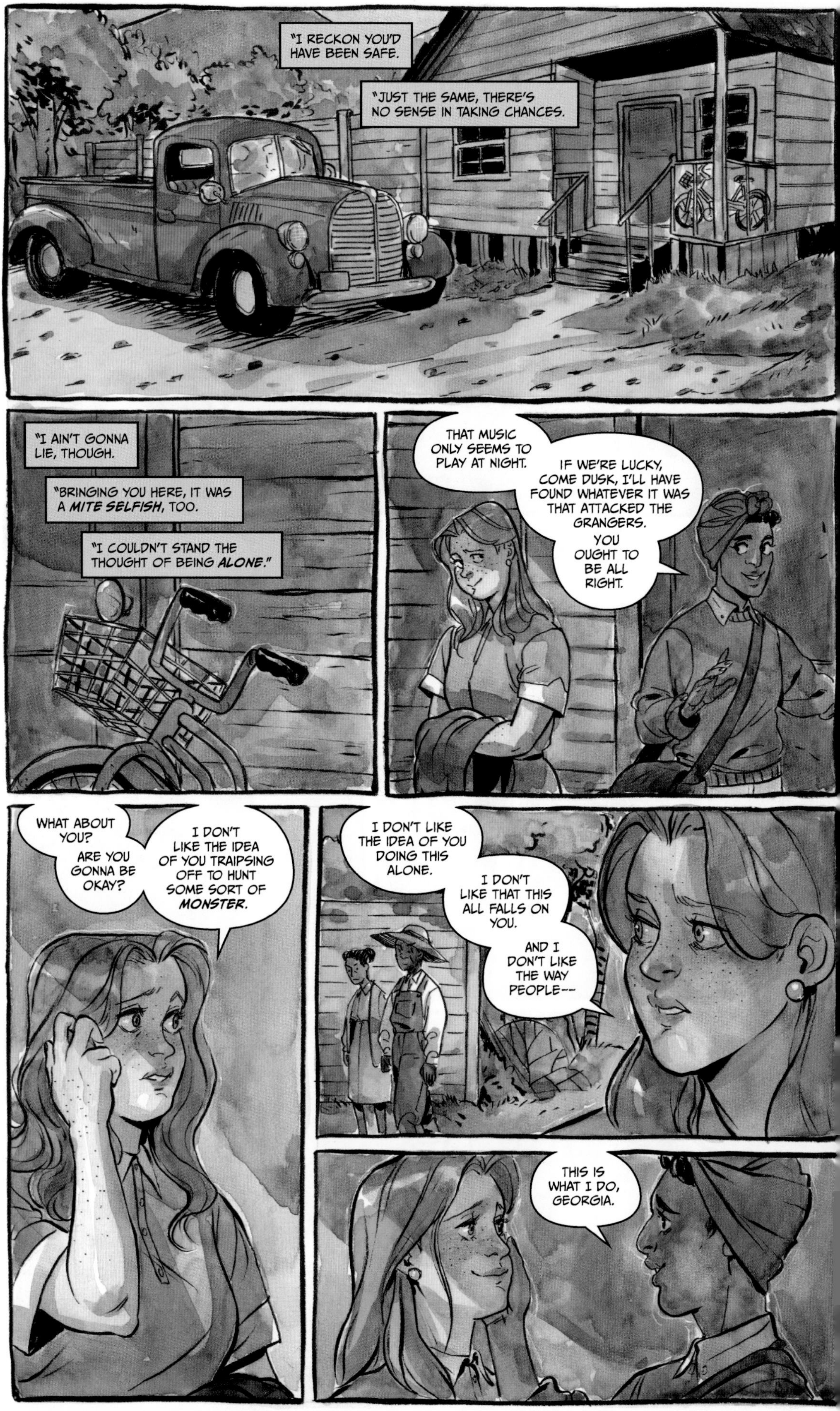

"I RECKON YOU'D HAVE BEEN SAFE.
"JUST THE SAME, THERE'S NO SENSE IN TAKING CHANCES.
"I AIN'T GONNA LIE, THOUGH.
"BRINGING YOU HERE, IT WAS A *MITE SELFISH*, TOO.
"I COULDN'T STAND THE THOUGHT OF BEING *ALONE*."
THAT MUSIC ONLY SEEMS TO PLAY AT NIGHT.
IF WE'RE LUCKY, COME DUSK, I'LL HAVE FOUND WHATEVER IT WAS THAT ATTACKED THE GRANGERS.
YOU OUGHT TO BE ALL RIGHT.
WHAT ABOUT YOU?
ARE YOU GONNA BE OKAY?
I DON'T LIKE THE IDEA OF YOU TRAIPSING OFF TO HUNT SOME SORT OF *MONSTER*.
I DON'T LIKE THE IDEA OF YOU DOING THIS ALONE.
I DON'T LIKE THAT THIS ALL FALLS ON YOU.
AND I DON'T LIKE THE WAY PEOPLE--
THIS IS WHAT I DO, GEORGIA.

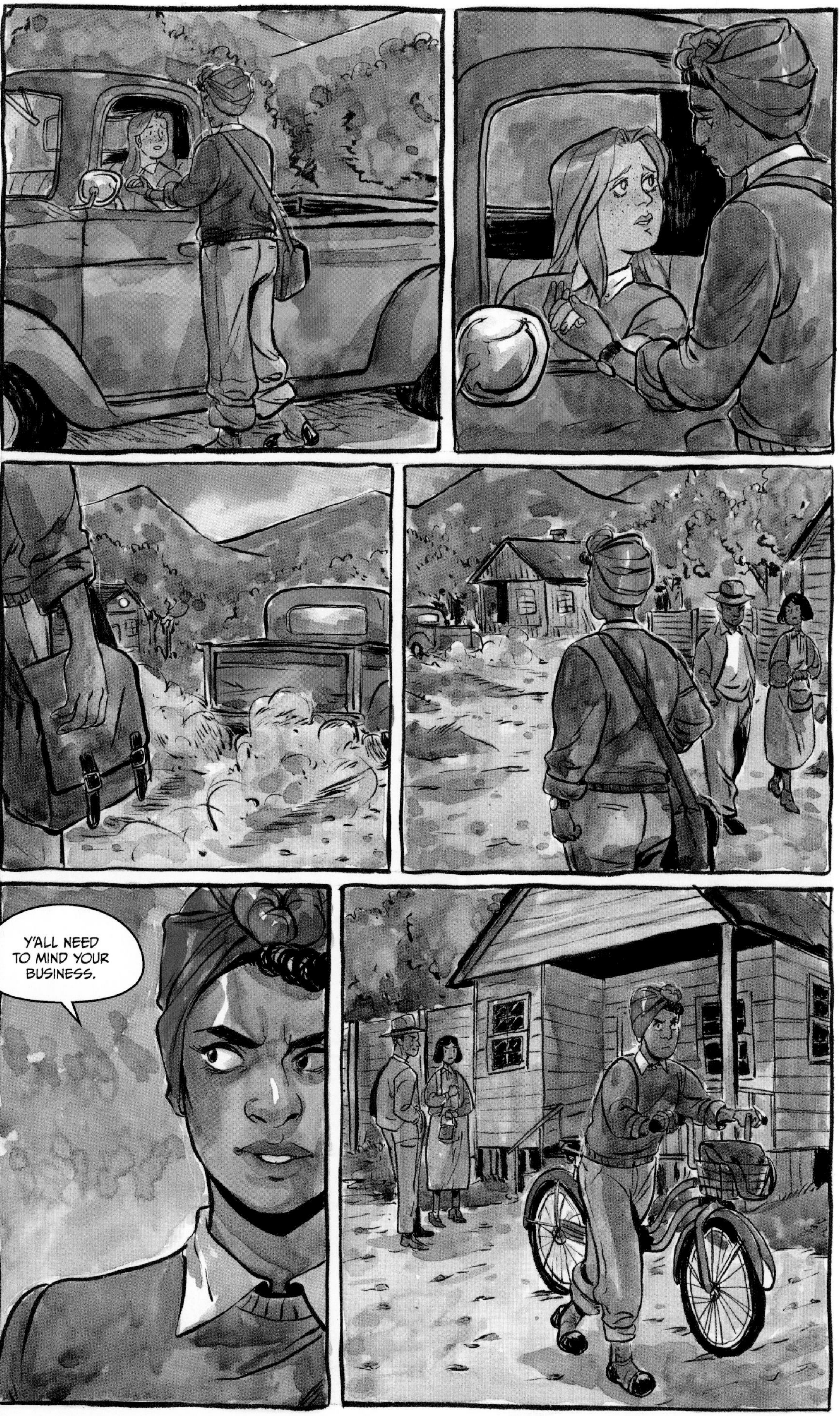
Y'ALL NEED TO MIND YOUR BUSINESS.

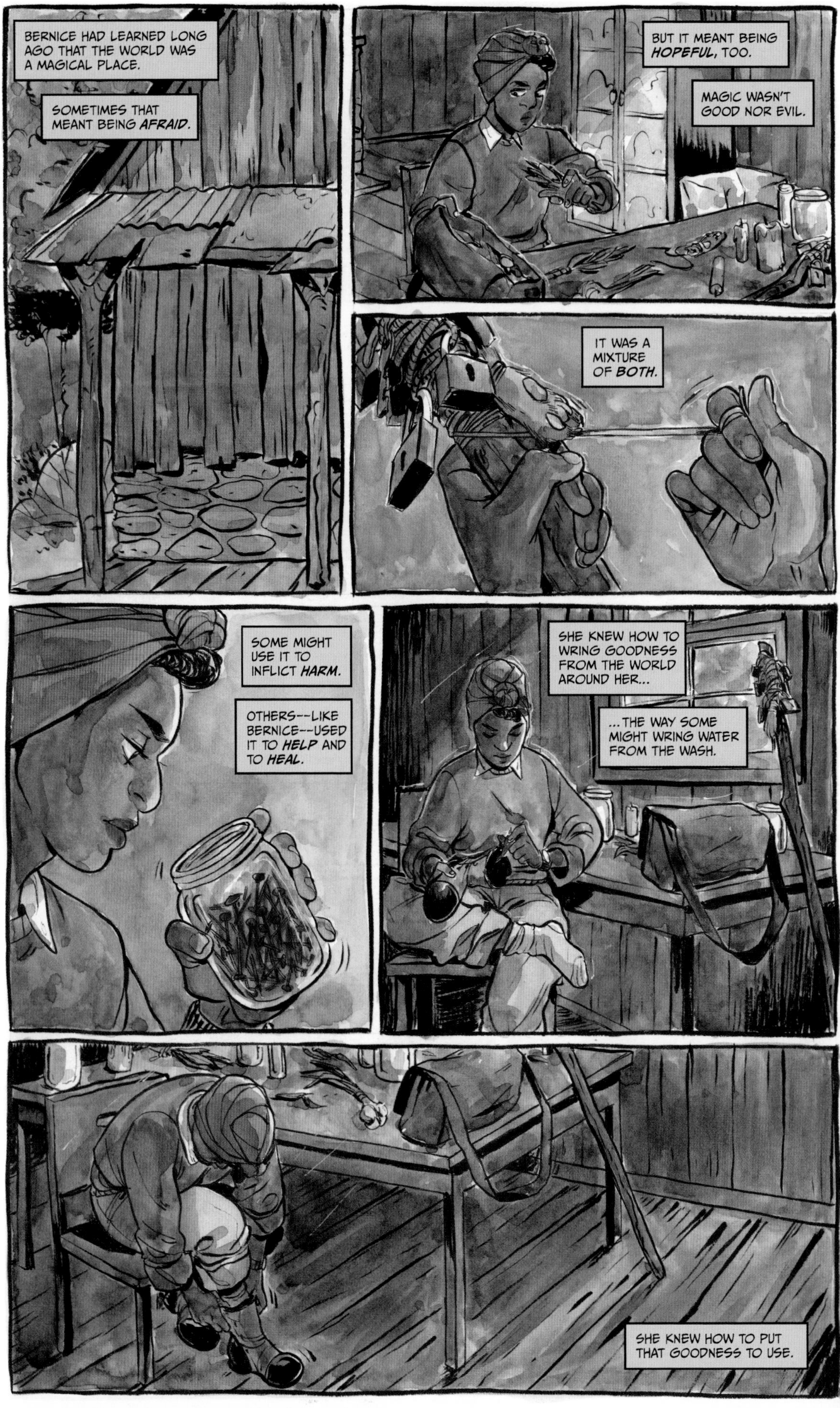
BERNICE HAD LEARNED LONG AGO THAT THE WORLD WAS A MAGICAL PLACE.
SOMETIMES THAT MEANT BEING *AFRAID*.
BUT IT MEANT BEING *HOPEFUL*, TOO.
MAGIC WASN'T GOOD NOR EVIL.
IT WAS A MIXTURE OF *BOTH*.
SOME MIGHT USE IT TO INFLICT *HARM*.
OTHERS--LIKE BERNICE--USED IT TO *HELP* AND TO *HEAL*.
SHE KNEW HOW TO WRING GOODNESS FROM THE WORLD AROUND HER...
...THE WAY SOME MIGHT WRING WATER FROM THE WASH.
SHE KNEW HOW TO PUT THAT GOODNESS TO USE.

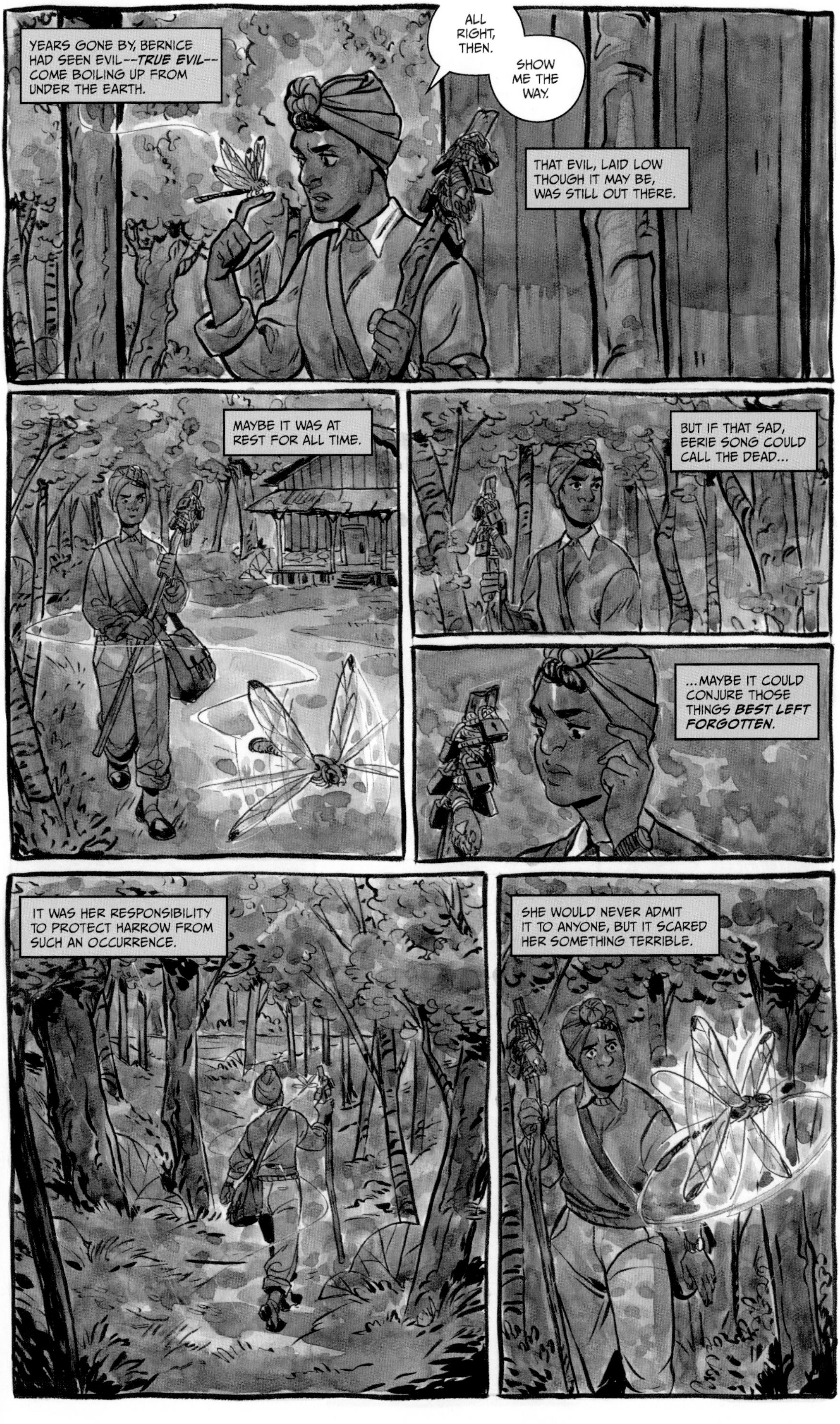

YEARS GONE BY, BERNICE HAD SEEN EVIL--TRUE EVIL--COME BOILING UP FROM UNDER THE EARTH.
ALL RIGHT, THEN.
SHOW ME THE WAY.
THAT EVIL, LAID LOW THOUGH IT MAY BE, WAS STILL OUT THERE.
MAYBE IT WAS AT REST FOR ALL TIME.
BUT IF THAT SAD, EERIE SONG COULD CALL THE DEAD...
...MAYBE IT COULD CONJURE THOSE THINGS BEST LEFT FORGOTTEN.
IT WAS HER RESPONSIBILITY TO PROTECT HARROW FROM SUCH AN OCCURRENCE.
SHE WOULD NEVER ADMIT IT TO ANYONE, BUT IT SCARED HER SOMETHING TERRIBLE.

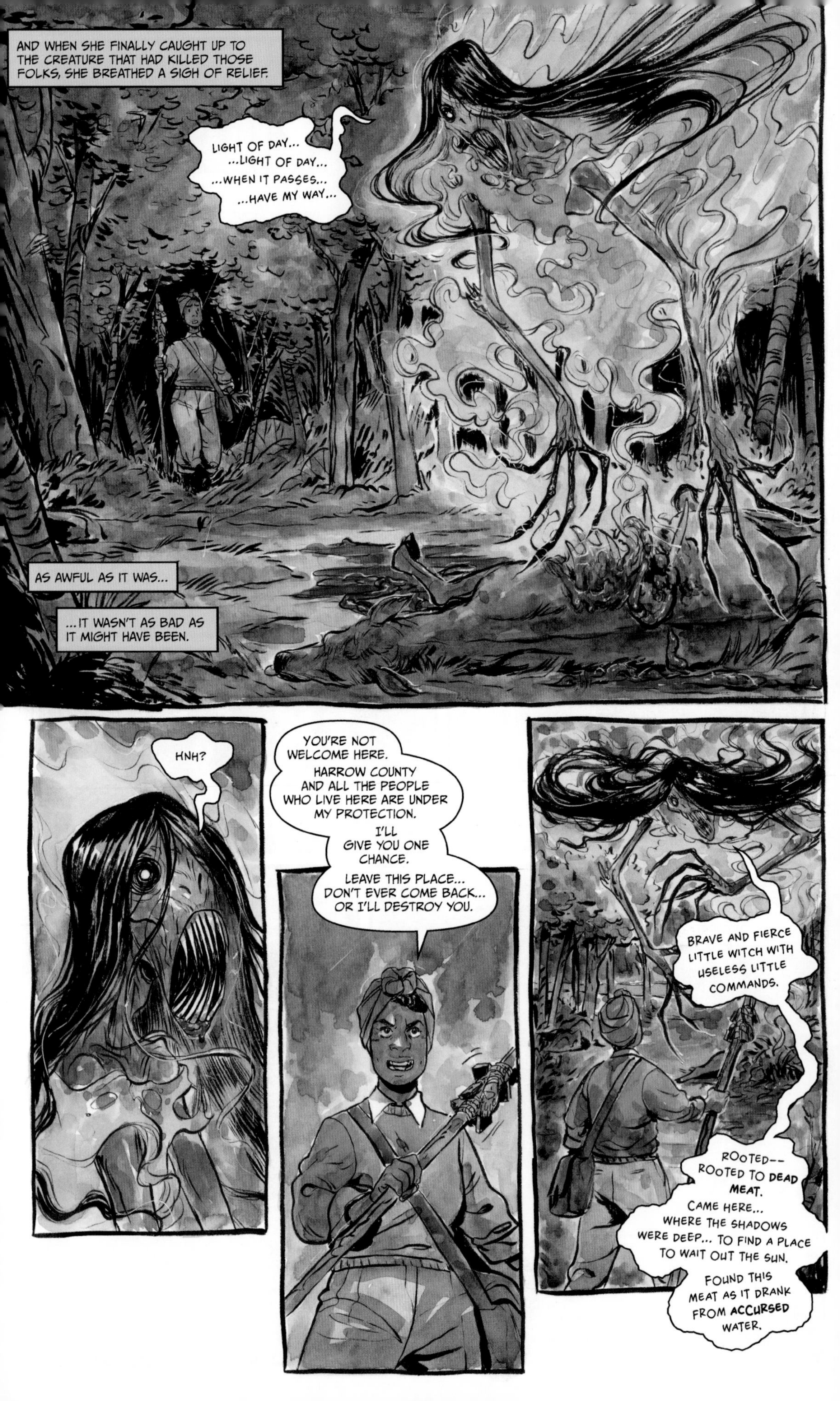
AND WHEN SHE FINALLY CAUGHT UP TO THE CREATURE THAT HAD KILLED THOSE FOLKS, SHE BREATHED A SIGH OF RELIEF.
LIGHT OF DAY... ...LIGHT OF DAY... ...WHEN IT PASSES... ...HAVE MY WAY...
AS AWFUL AS IT WAS...
...IT WASN'T AS BAD AS IT MIGHT HAVE BEEN.
HNH?
YOU'RE NOT WELCOME HERE.
HARROW COUNTY AND ALL THE PEOPLE WHO LIVE HERE ARE UNDER MY PROTECTION.
I'LL GIVE YOU ONE CHANCE.
LEAVE THIS PLACE... DON'T EVER COME BACK... OR I'LL DESTROY YOU.
BRAVE AND FIERCE LITTLE WITCH WITH USELESS LITTLE COMMANDS.
ROOTED-- ROOTED TO DEAD MEAT.
CAME HERE... WHERE THE SHADOWS WERE DEEP... TO FIND A PLACE TO WAIT OUT THE SUN.
FOUND THIS MEAT AS IT DRANK FROM ACCURSED WATER.

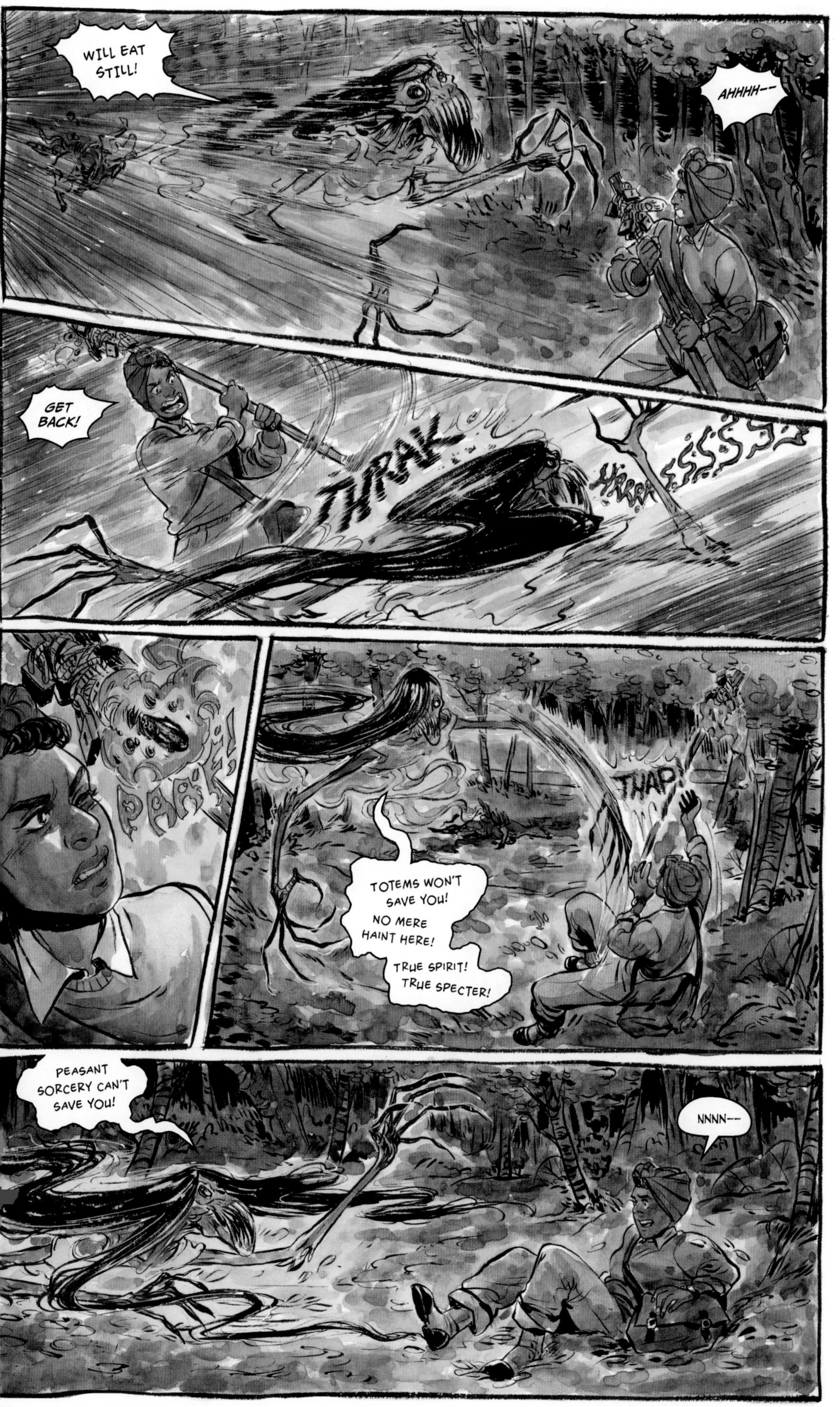
WILL EAT STILL!
AHHHH--
GET BACK!
THRAK
HRRRA
SSSSSS
PAAH!
THAP!
TOTEMS WON'T SAVE YOU!
NO MERE HAINT HERE!
TRUE SPIRIT! TRUE SPECTER!
PEASANT SORCERY CAN'T SAVE YOU!
NNNN--

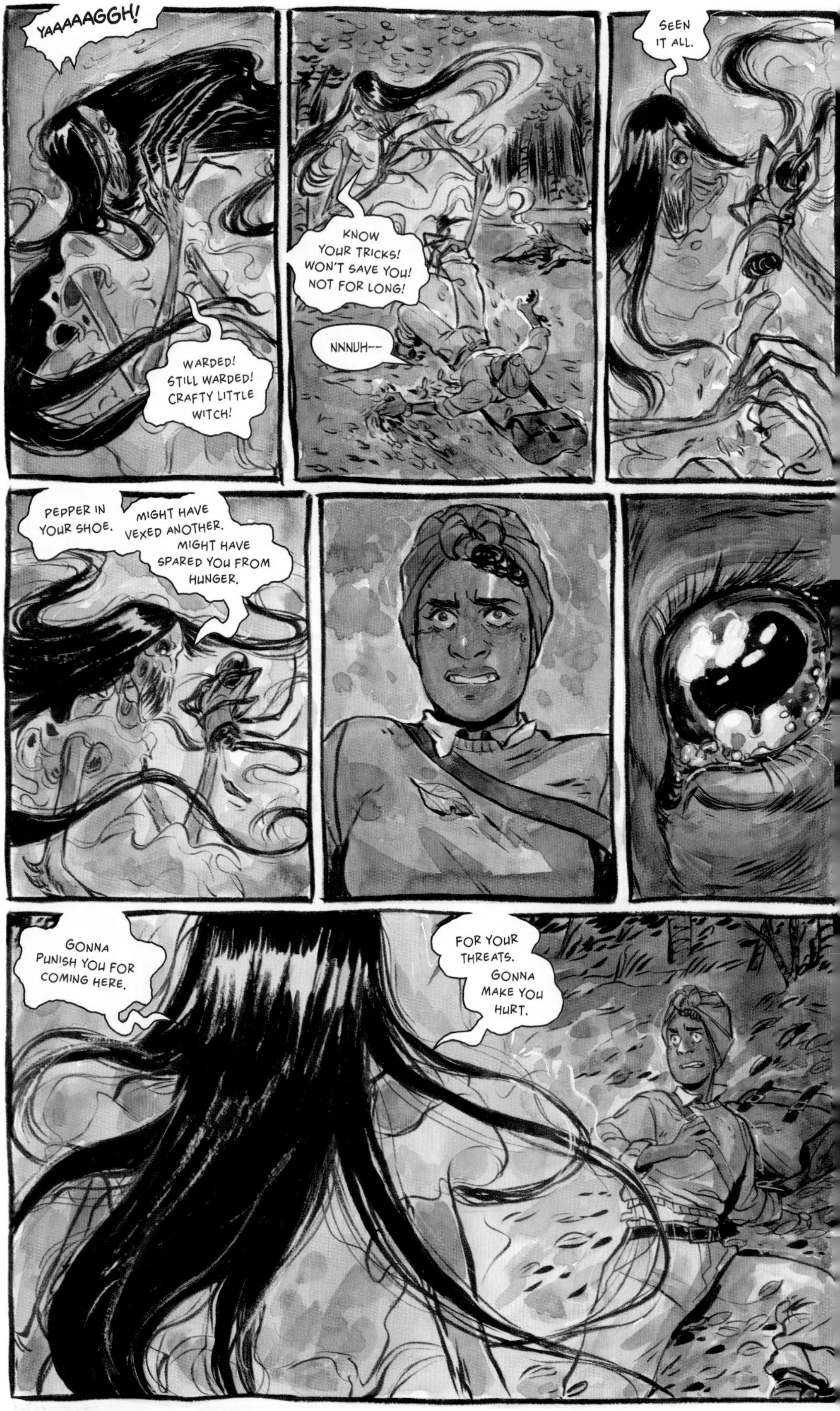
YAAAAAGGH!
WARDED! STILL WARDED! CRAFTY LITTLE WITCH!
KNOW YOUR TRICKS! WON'T SAVE YOU! NOT FOR LONG!
NNNUH--
SEEN IT ALL.
PEPPER IN YOUR SHOE.
MIGHT HAVE VEXED ANOTHER.
MIGHT HAVE SPARED YOU FROM HUNGER.
GONNA PUNISH YOU FOR COMING HERE.
FOR YOUR THREATS.
GONNA MAKE YOU HURT.

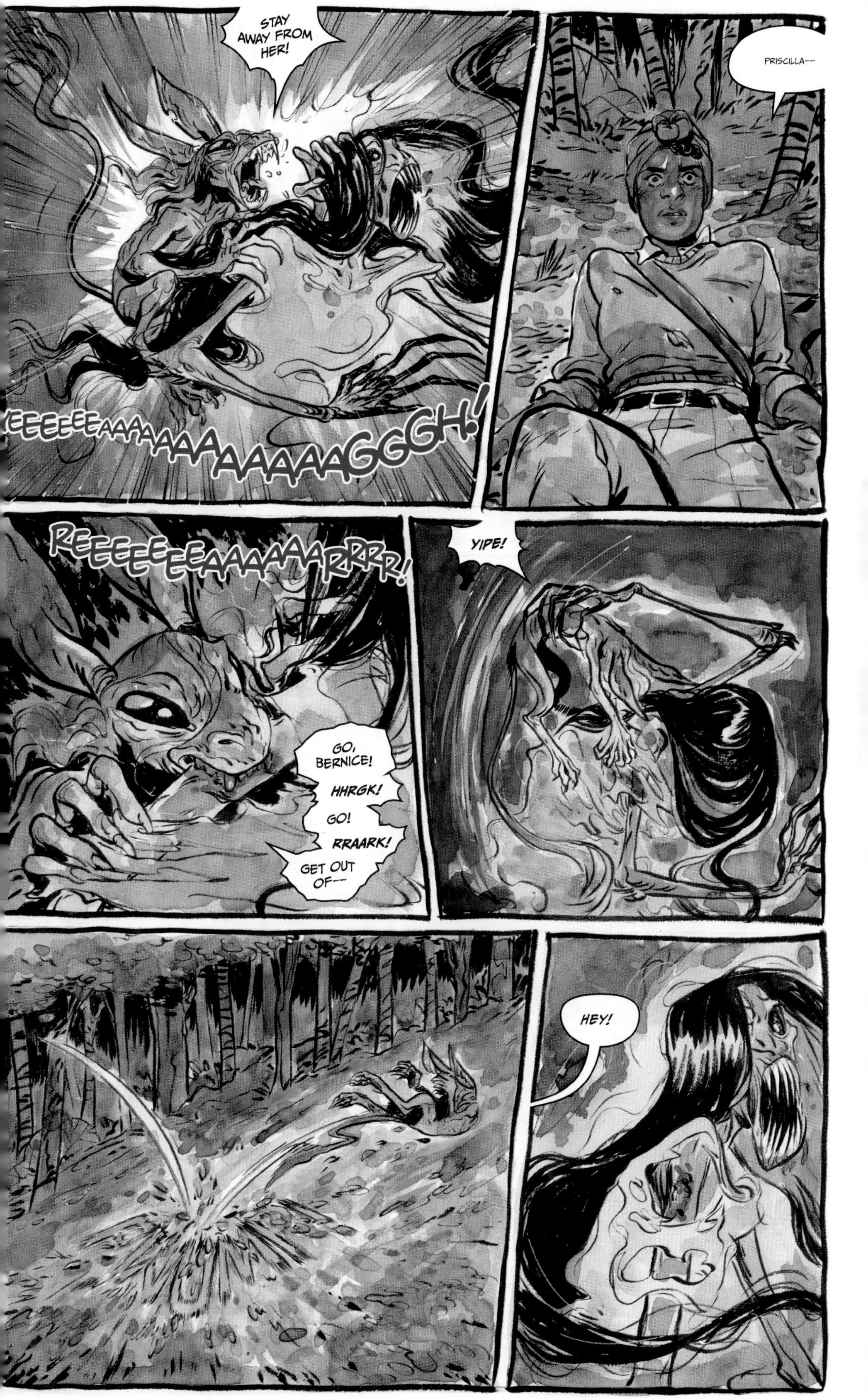
STAY AWAY FROM HER!
KEEEEEEAAAAAAAAAAAAAAGGGH!
PRISCILLA--
REEEEEEEEAAAAAARRRR!
GO, BERNICE!
HHRGK!
GO!
RRAARK!
GET OUT OF--
YIPE!
HEY!

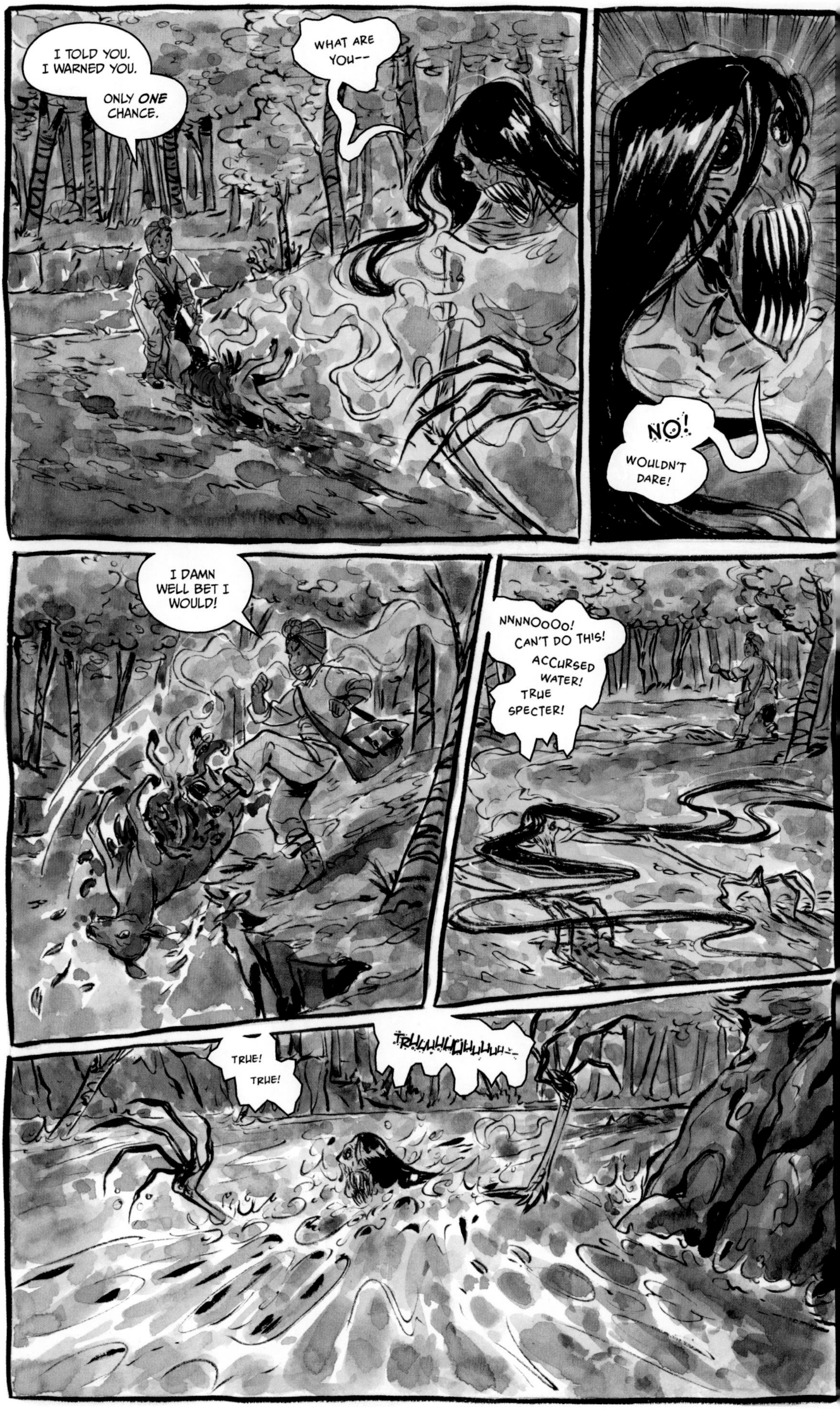
I TOLD YOU. I WARNED YOU.
ONLY ONE CHANCE.
WHAT ARE YOU--
NO! WOULDN'T DARE!
I DAMN WELL BET I WOULD!
NNNNOOOOo! CAN'T DO THIS! ACCURSED WATER! TRUE SPECTER!
TRUE! TRUE!
TRUUUUUUUUUUUUU--

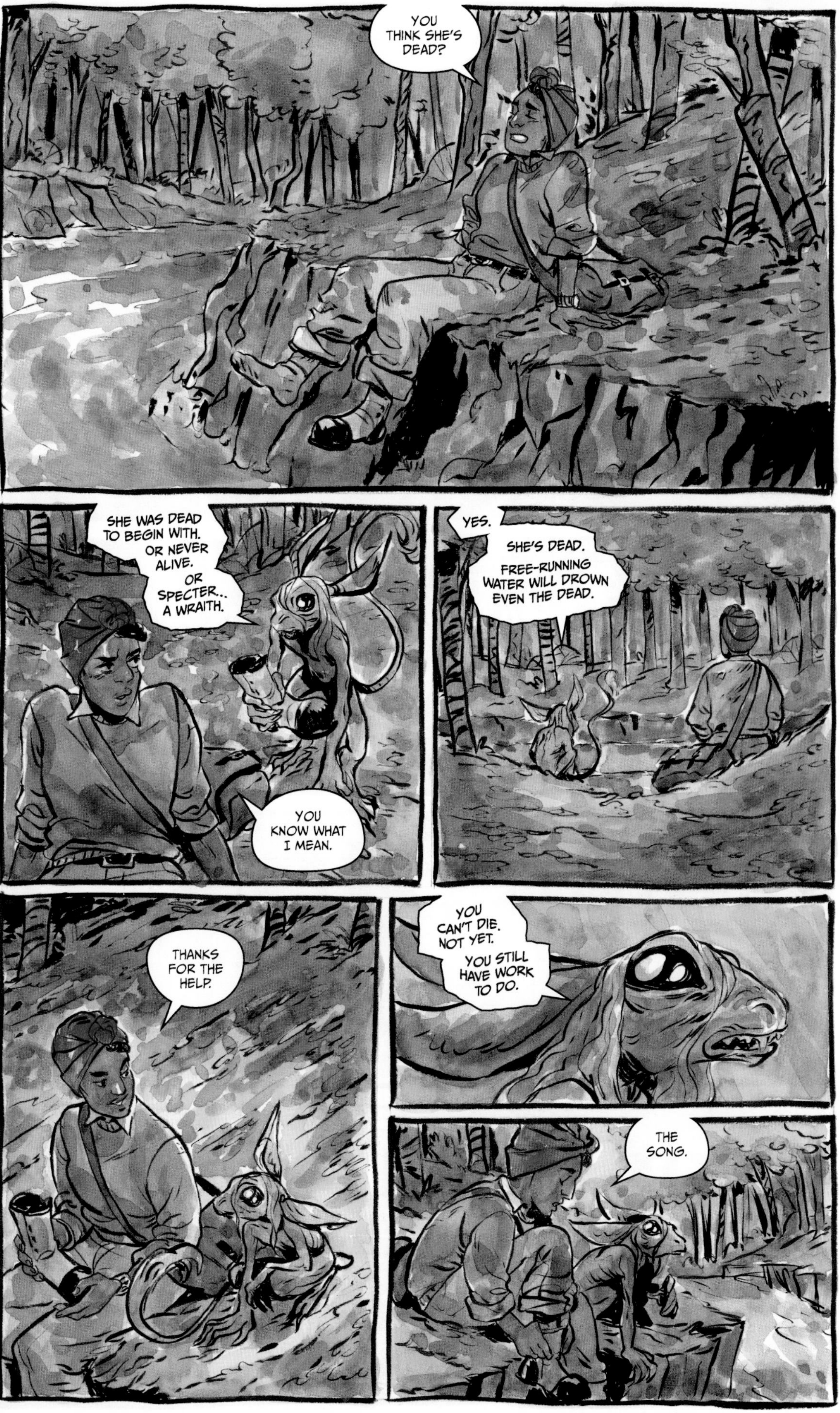
YOU THINK SHE'S DEAD?
SHE WAS DEAD TO BEGIN WITH.
OR NEVER ALIVE.
OR SPECTER... A WRAITH.
YOU KNOW WHAT I MEAN.
YES.
SHE'S DEAD.
FREE-RUNNING WATER WILL DROWN EVEN THE DEAD.
THANKS FOR THE HELP.
YOU CAN'T DIE. NOT YET.
YOU STILL HAVE WORK TO DO.
THE SONG.

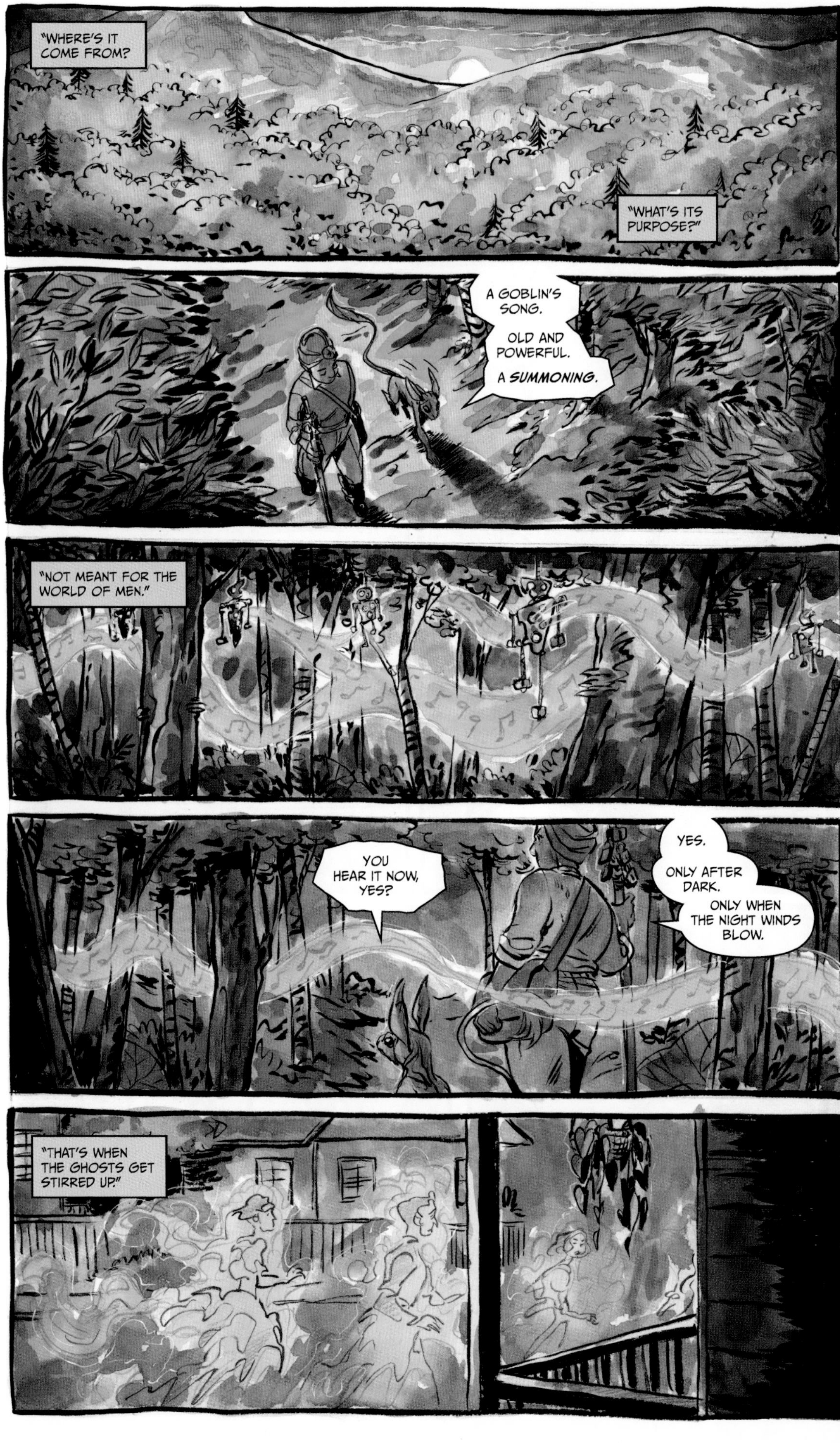
"WHERE'S IT COME FROM?
"WHAT'S ITS PURPOSE?"
A GOBLIN'S SONG.
OLD AND POWERFUL.
A SUMMONING.
"NOT MEANT FOR THE WORLD OF MEN."
YOU HEAR IT NOW, YES?
YES.
ONLY AFTER DARK.
ONLY WHEN THE NIGHT WINDS BLOW.
"THAT'S WHEN THE GHOSTS GET STIRRED UP."

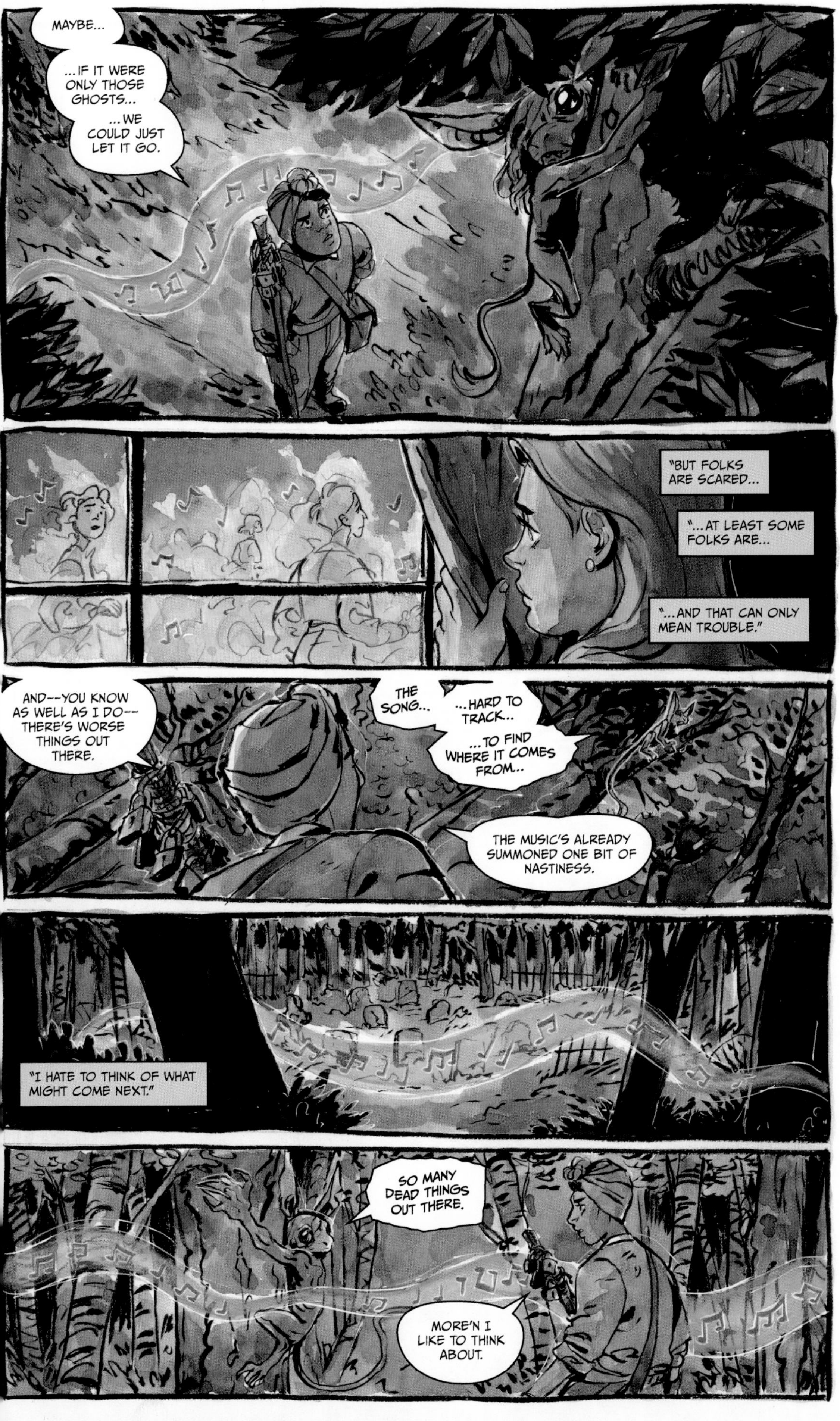
MAYBE...
...IF IT WERE ONLY THOSE GHOSTS...
...WE COULD JUST LET IT GO.
"BUT FOLKS ARE SCARED...
"...AT LEAST SOME FOLKS ARE...
"...AND THAT CAN ONLY MEAN TROUBLE."
AND--YOU KNOW AS WELL AS I DO--THERE'S WORSE THINGS OUT THERE.
THE SONG...
...HARD TO TRACK...
...TO FIND WHERE IT COMES FROM...
THE MUSIC'S ALREADY SUMMONED ONE BIT OF NASTINESS.
"I HATE TO THINK OF WHAT MIGHT COME NEXT."
SO MANY DEAD THINGS OUT THERE.
MORE'N I LIKE TO THINK ABOUT.

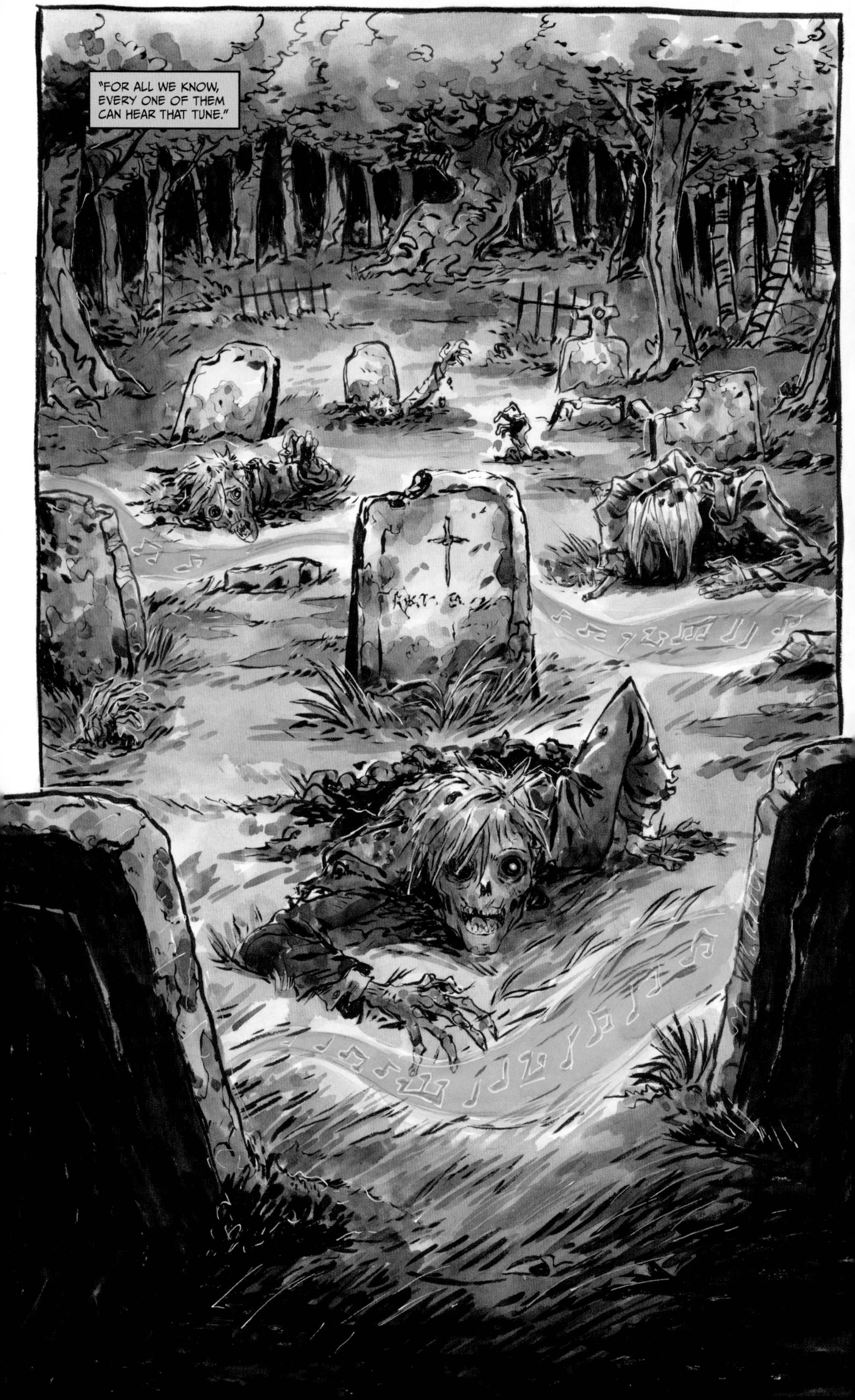
"FOR ALL WE KNOW, EVERY ONE OF THEM CAN HEAR THAT TUNE."

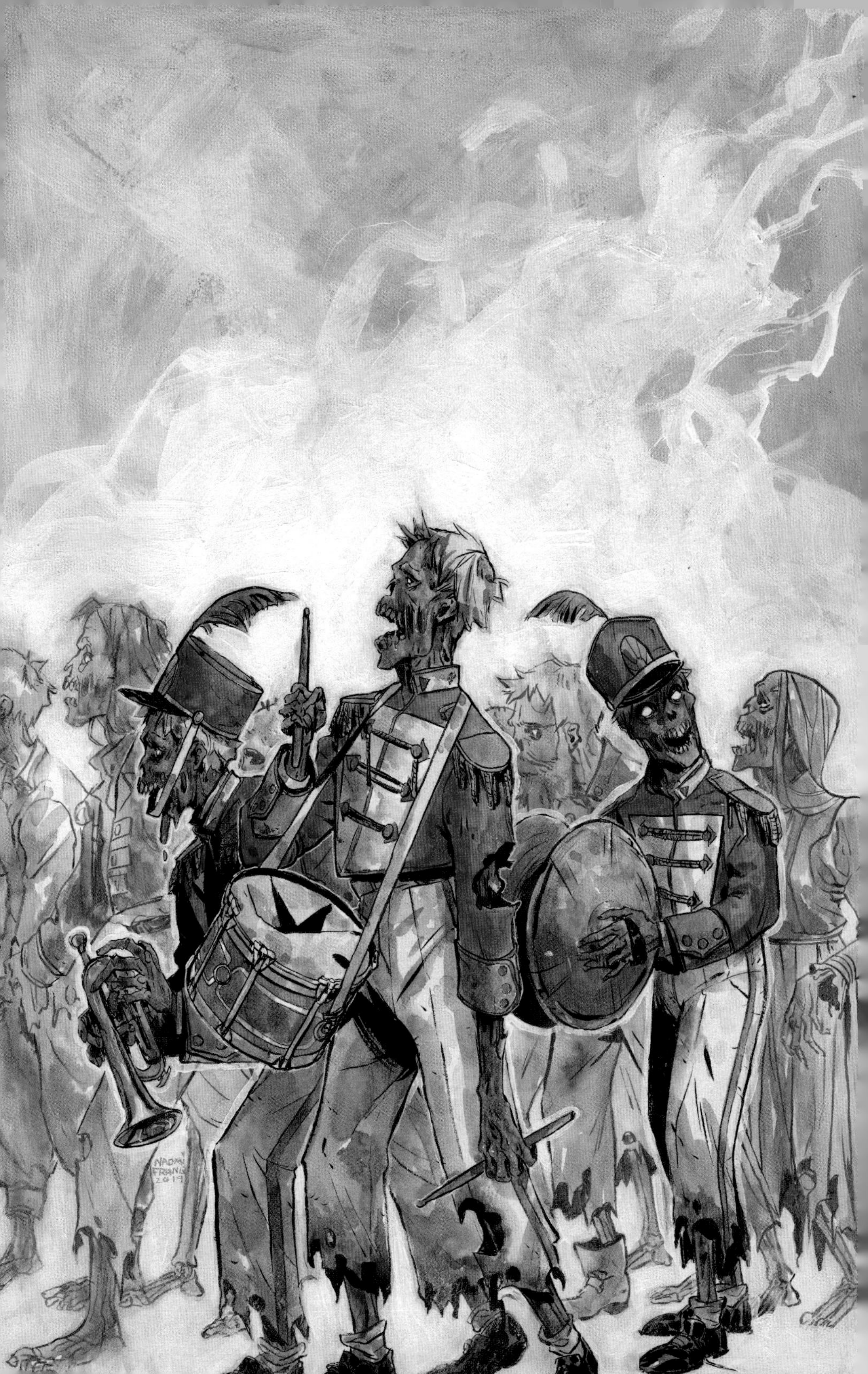
NAOMI
FRANQ
2019

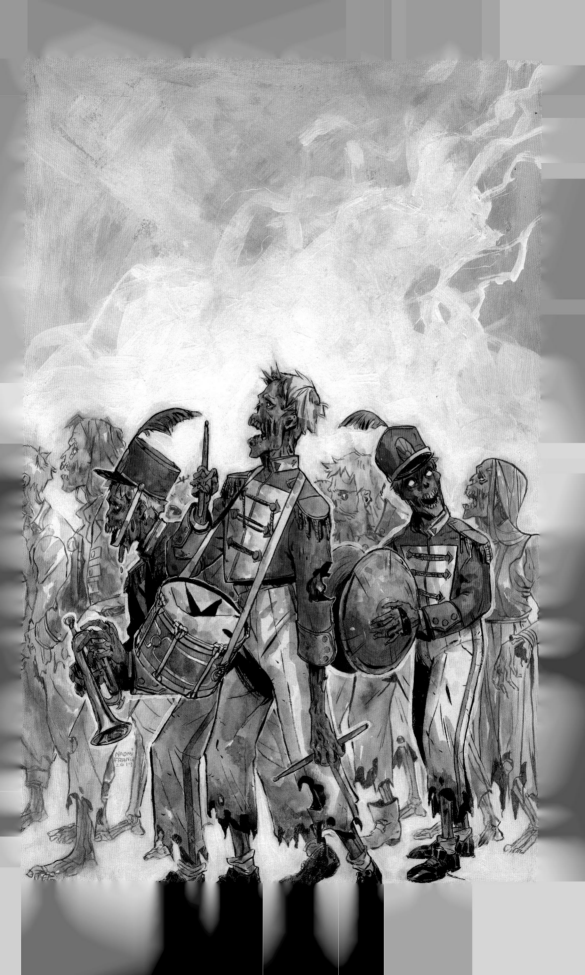

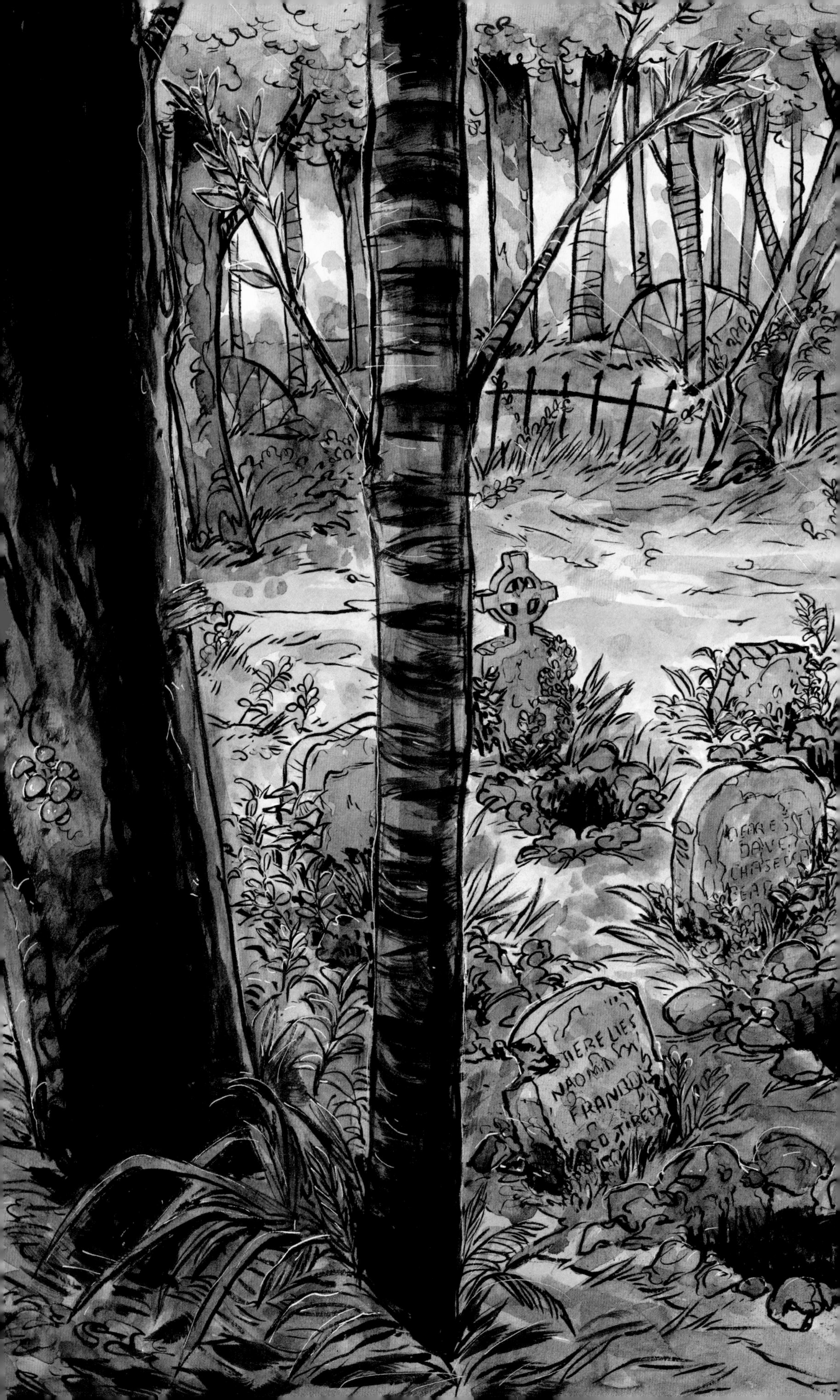

DAVE
SO TIRED

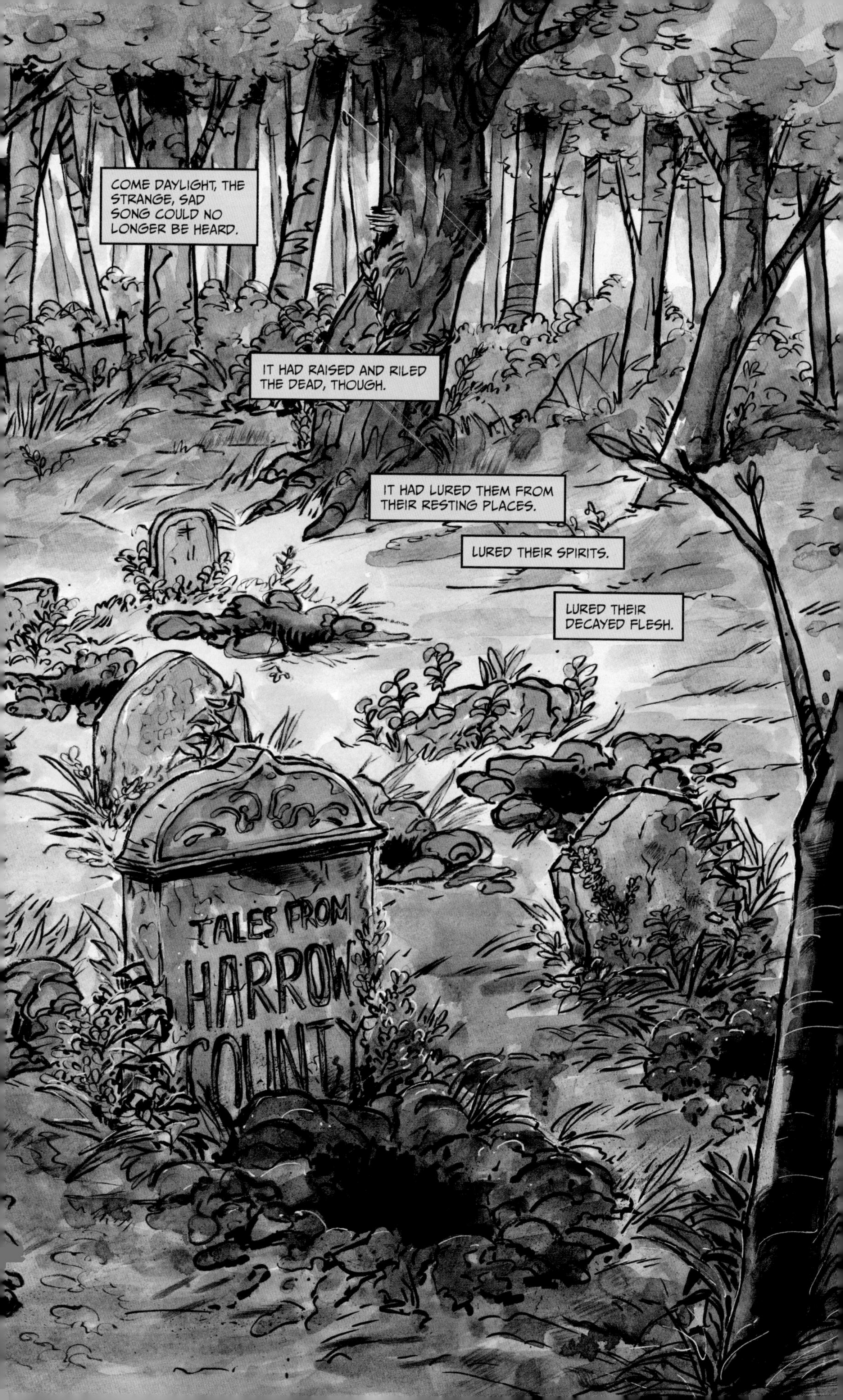
COME DAYLIGHT, THE STRANGE, SAD SONG COULD NO LONGER BE HEARD.
IT HAD RAISED AND RILED THE DEAD, THOUGH.
IT HAD LURED THEM FROM THEIR RESTING PLACES.
LURED THEIR SPIRITS.
LURED THEIR DECAYED FLESH.
TALES FROM HARROW COUNTY

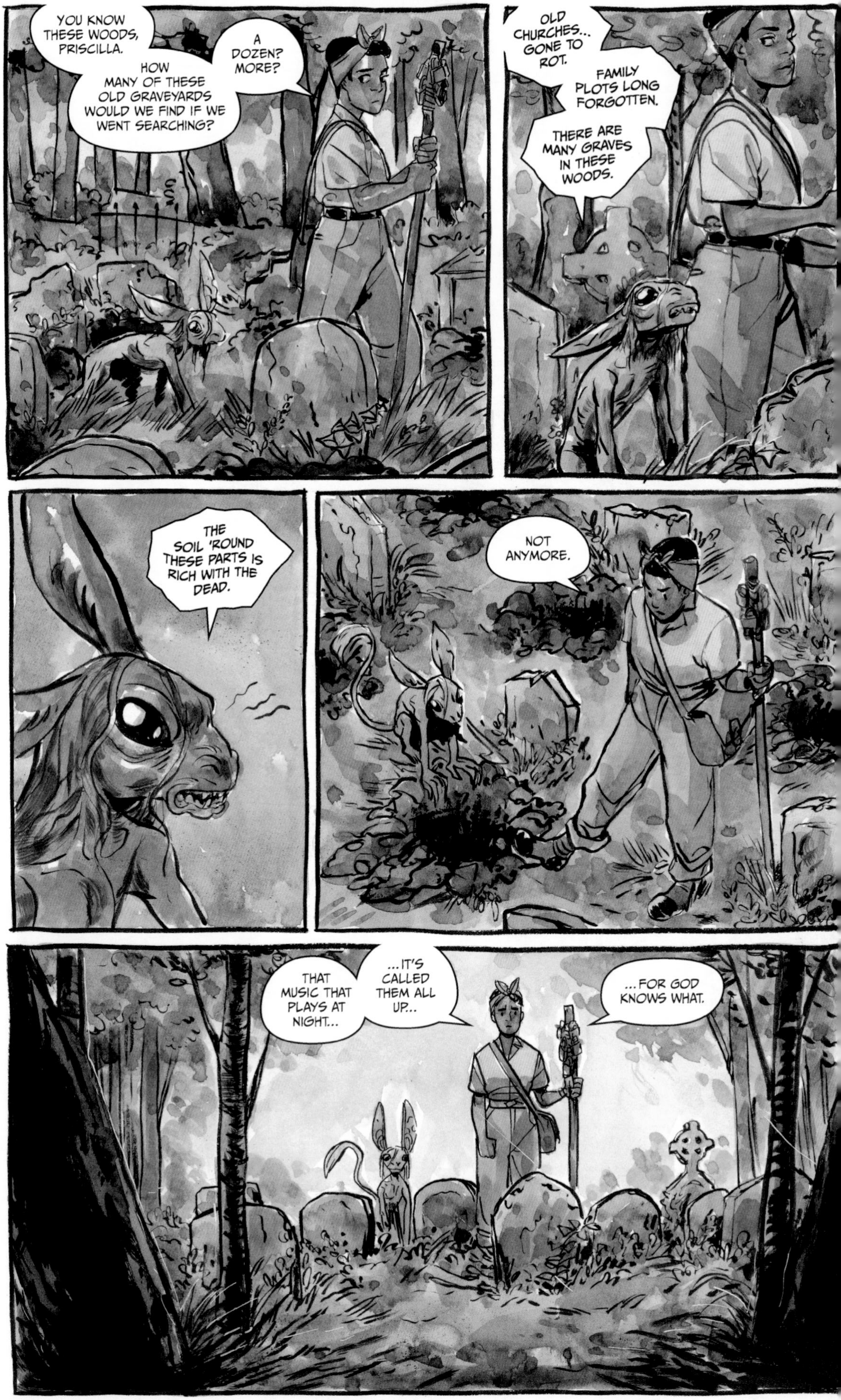

YOU KNOW THESE WOODS, PRISCILLA.
HOW MANY OF THESE OLD GRAVEYARDS WOULD WE FIND IF WE WENT SEARCHING?
A DOZEN? MORE?
OLD CHURCHES... GONE TO ROT.
FAMILY PLOTS LONG FORGOTTEN.
THERE ARE MANY GRAVES IN THESE WOODS.
THE SOIL 'ROUND THESE PARTS IS RICH WITH THE DEAD.
NOT ANYMORE.
THAT MUSIC THAT PLAYS AT NIGHT...
...IT'S CALLED THEM ALL UP...
...FOR GOD KNOWS WHAT.

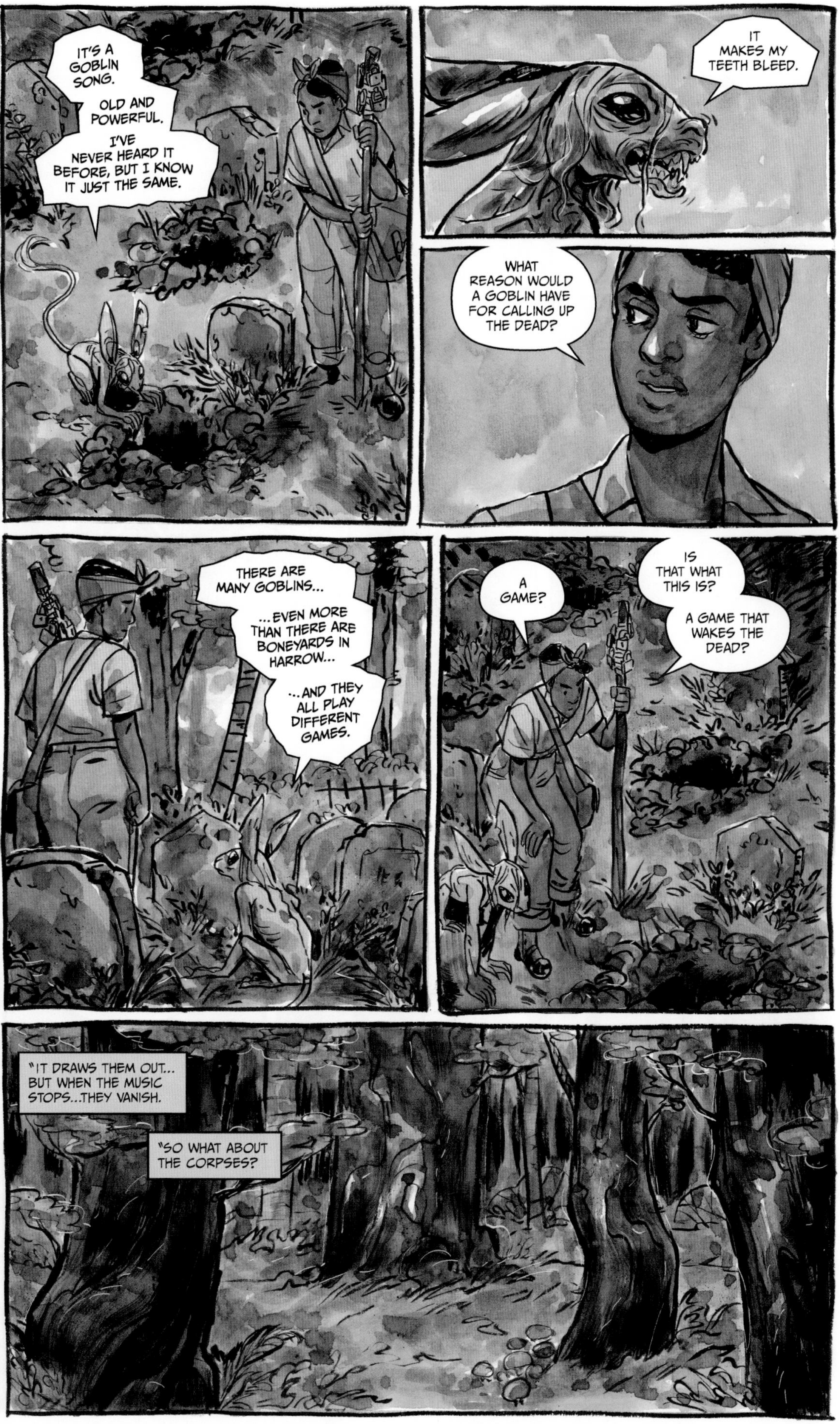

IT'S A GOBLIN SONG.
OLD AND POWERFUL.
I'VE NEVER HEARD IT BEFORE, BUT I KNOW IT JUST THE SAME.
IT MAKES MY TEETH BLEED.
WHAT REASON WOULD A GOBLIN HAVE FOR CALLING UP THE DEAD?
THERE ARE MANY GOBLINS...
...EVEN MORE THAN THERE ARE BONEYARDS IN HARROW...
...AND THEY ALL PLAY DIFFERENT GAMES.
A GAME?
IS THAT WHAT THIS IS?
A GAME THAT WAKES THE DEAD?
"IT DRAWS THEM OUT... BUT WHEN THE MUSIC STOPS...THEY VANISH.
"SO WHAT ABOUT THE CORPSES?

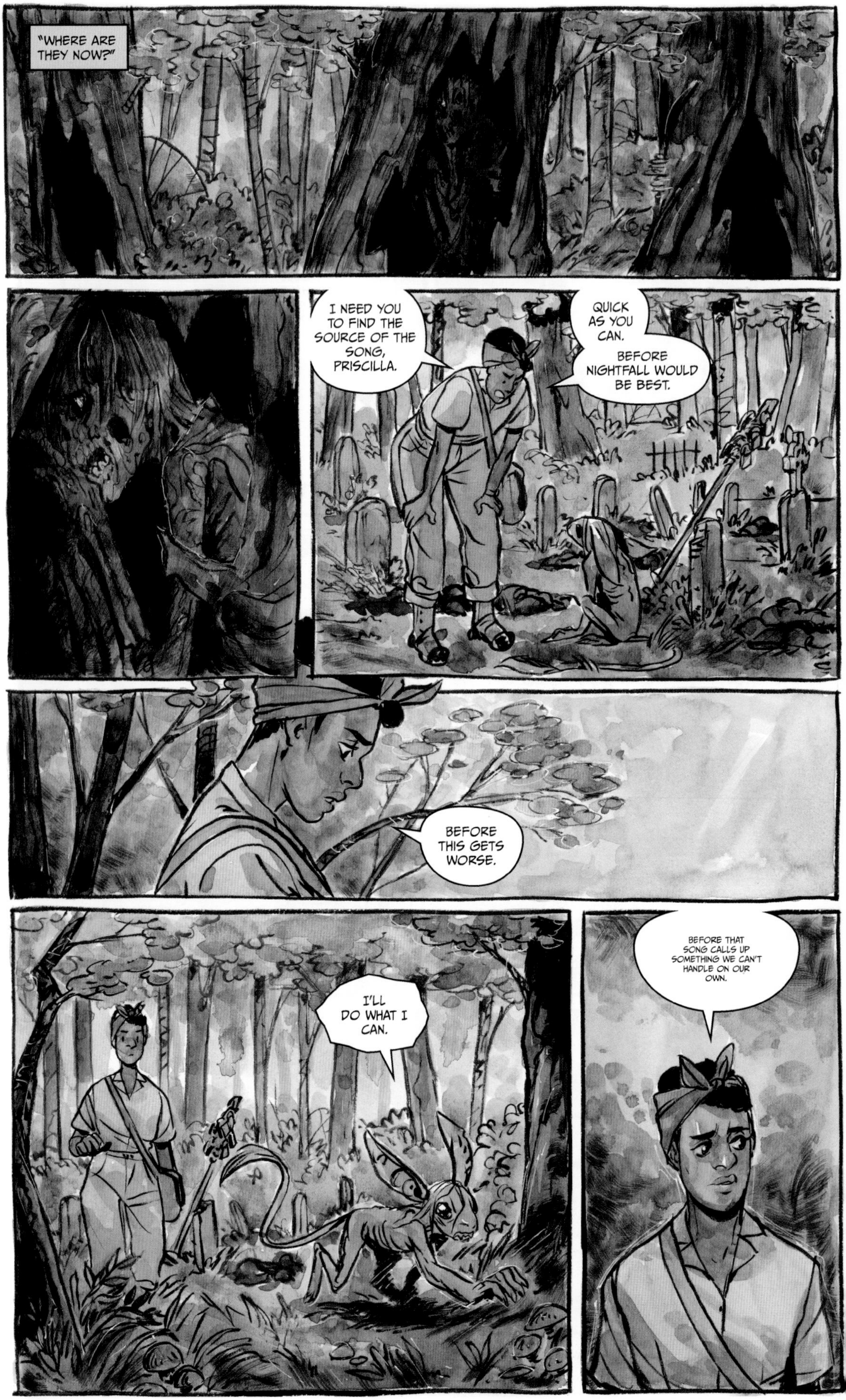
"WHERE ARE THEY NOW?"
I NEED YOU TO FIND THE SOURCE OF THE SONG, PRISCILLA.
QUICK AS YOU CAN.
BEFORE NIGHTFALL WOULD BE BEST.
BEFORE THIS GETS WORSE.
I'LL DO WHAT I CAN.
BEFORE THAT SONG CALLS UP SOMETHING WE CAN'T HANDLE ON OUR OWN.

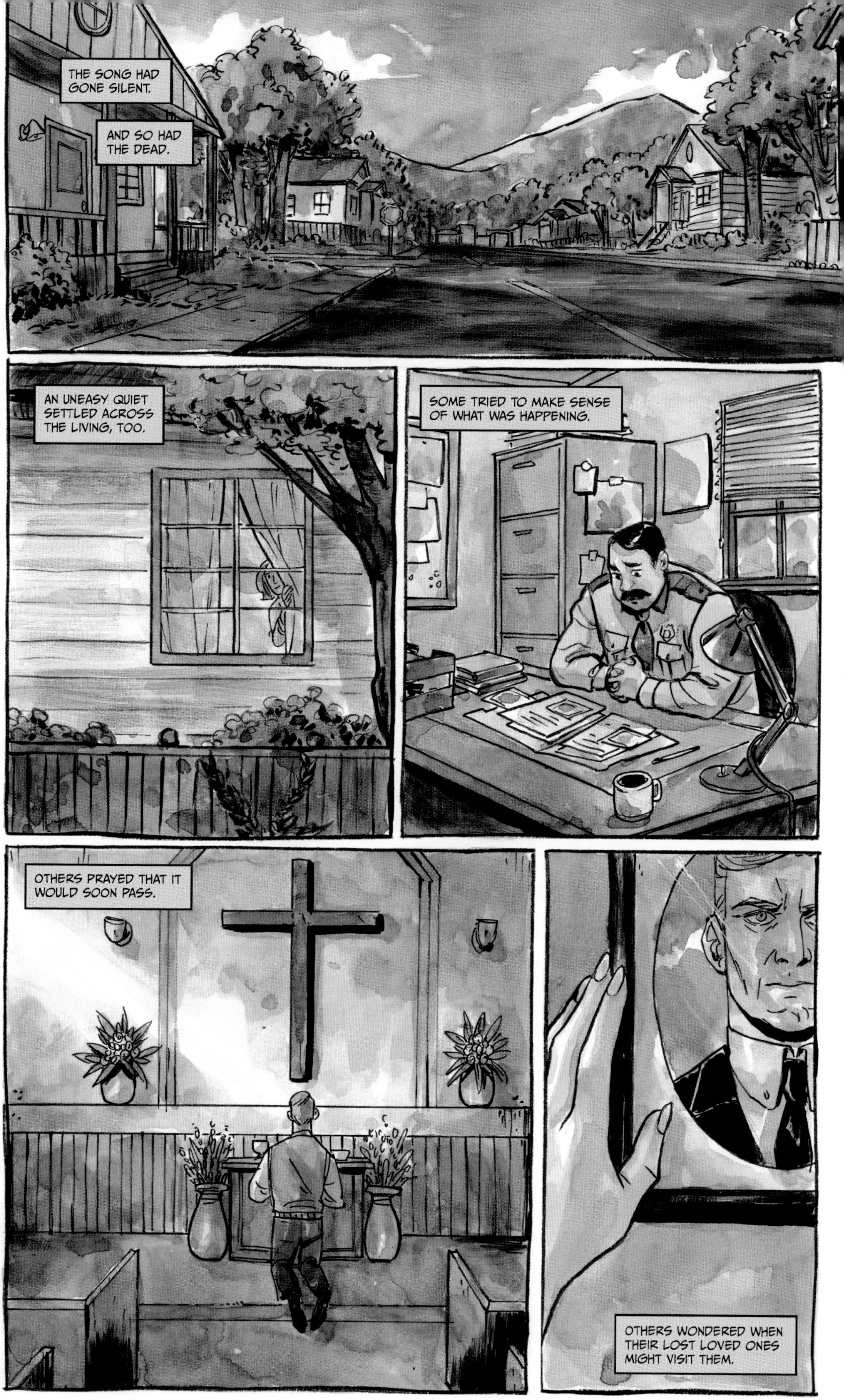
THE SONG HAD GONE SILENT.
AND SO HAD THE DEAD.
AN UNEASY QUIET SETTLED ACROSS THE LIVING, TOO.
SOME TRIED TO MAKE SENSE OF WHAT WAS HAPPENING.
OTHERS PRAYED THAT IT WOULD SOON PASS.
OTHERS WONDERED WHEN THEIR LOST LOVED ONES MIGHT VISIT THEM.

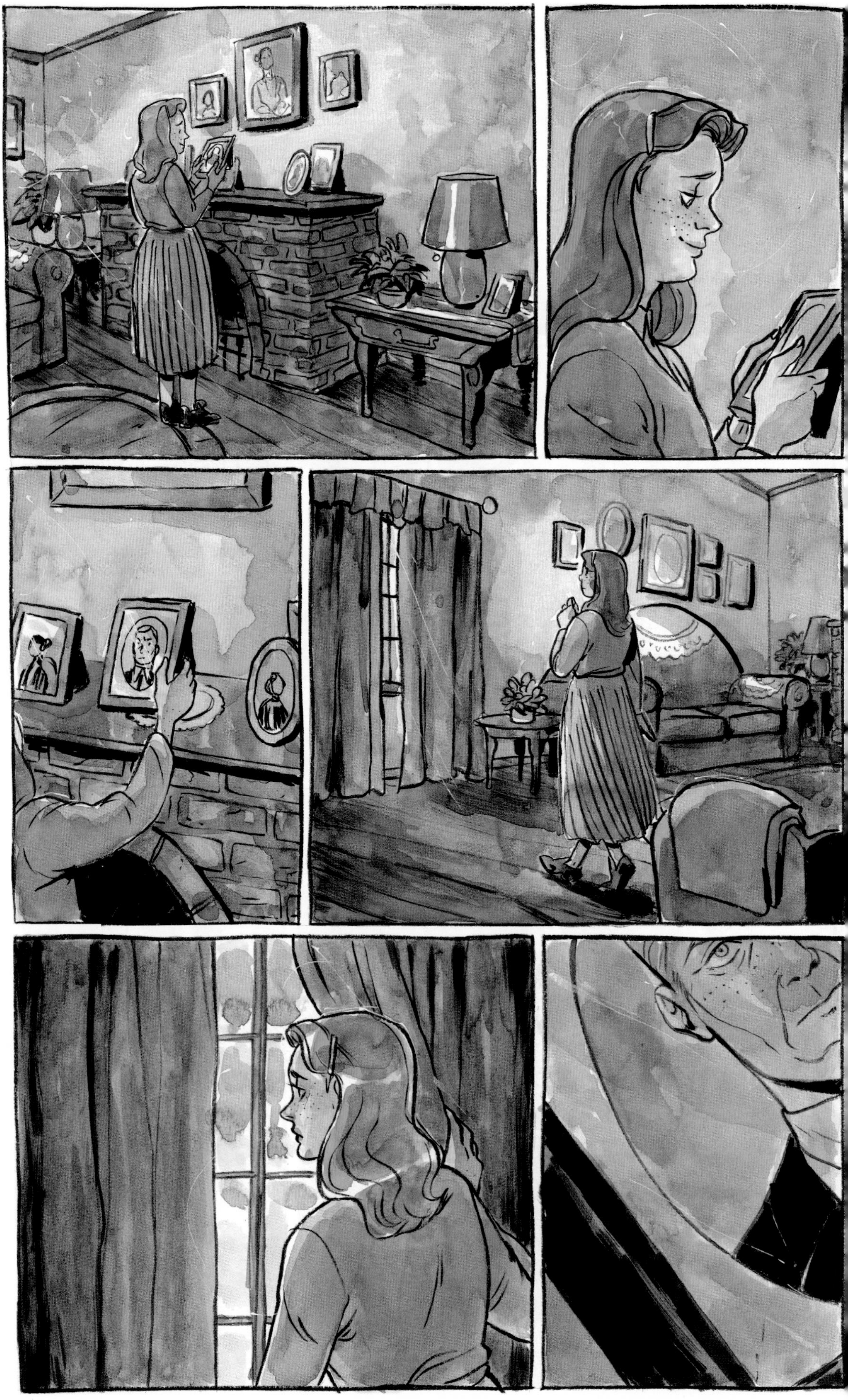

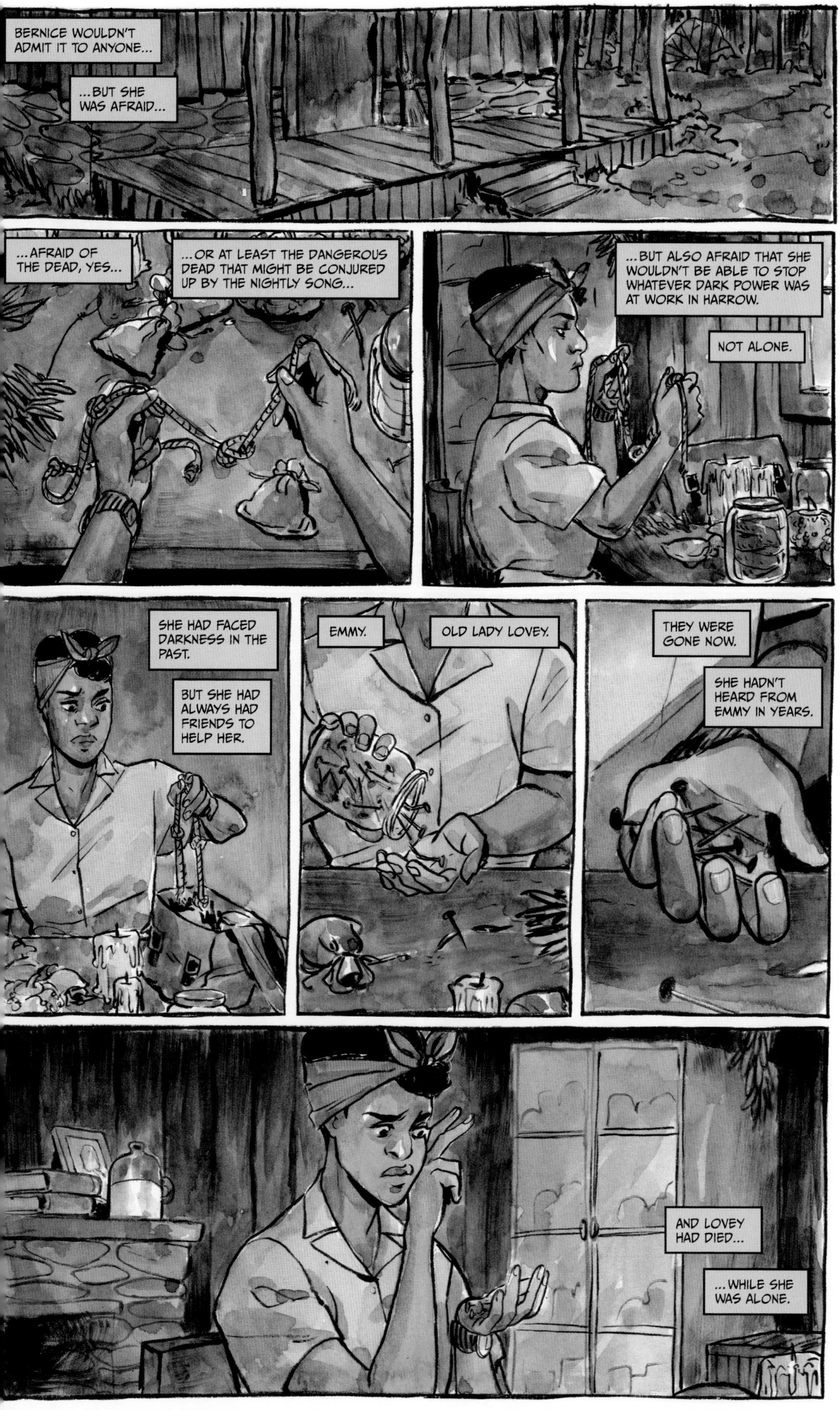
BERNICE WOULDN'T ADMIT IT TO ANYONE...
...BUT SHE WAS AFRAID...
...AFRAID OF THE DEAD, YES...
...OR AT LEAST THE DANGEROUS DEAD THAT MIGHT BE CONJURED UP BY THE NIGHTLY SONG...
...BUT ALSO AFRAID THAT SHE WOULDN'T BE ABLE TO STOP WHATEVER DARK POWER WAS AT WORK IN HARROW.
NOT ALONE.
SHE HAD FACED DARKNESS IN THE PAST.
BUT SHE HAD ALWAYS HAD FRIENDS TO HELP HER.
EMMY.
OLD LADY LOVEY.
THEY WERE GONE NOW.
SHE HADN'T HEARD FROM EMMY IN YEARS.
AND LOVEY HAD DIED...
...WHILE SHE WAS ALONE.

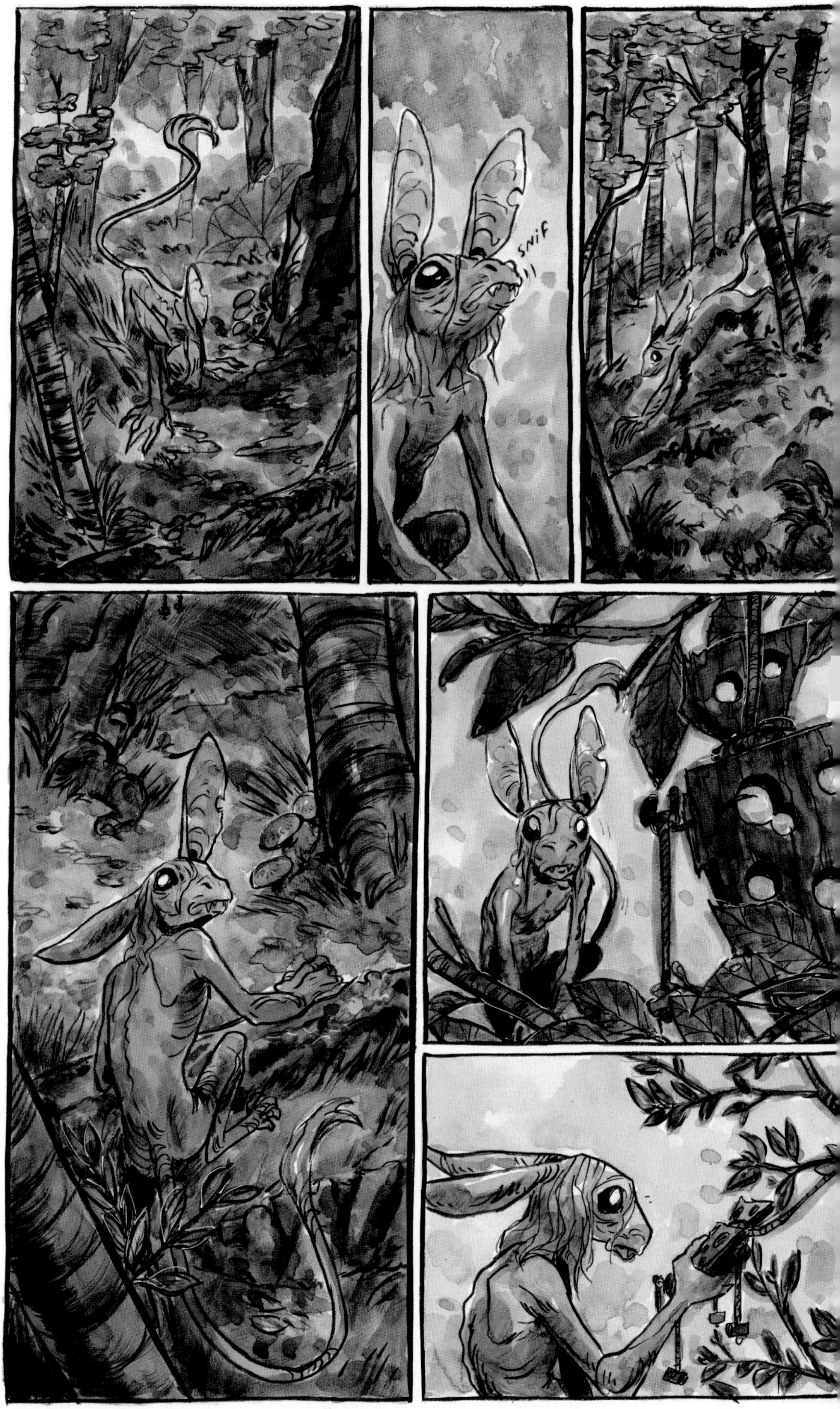
SNIF

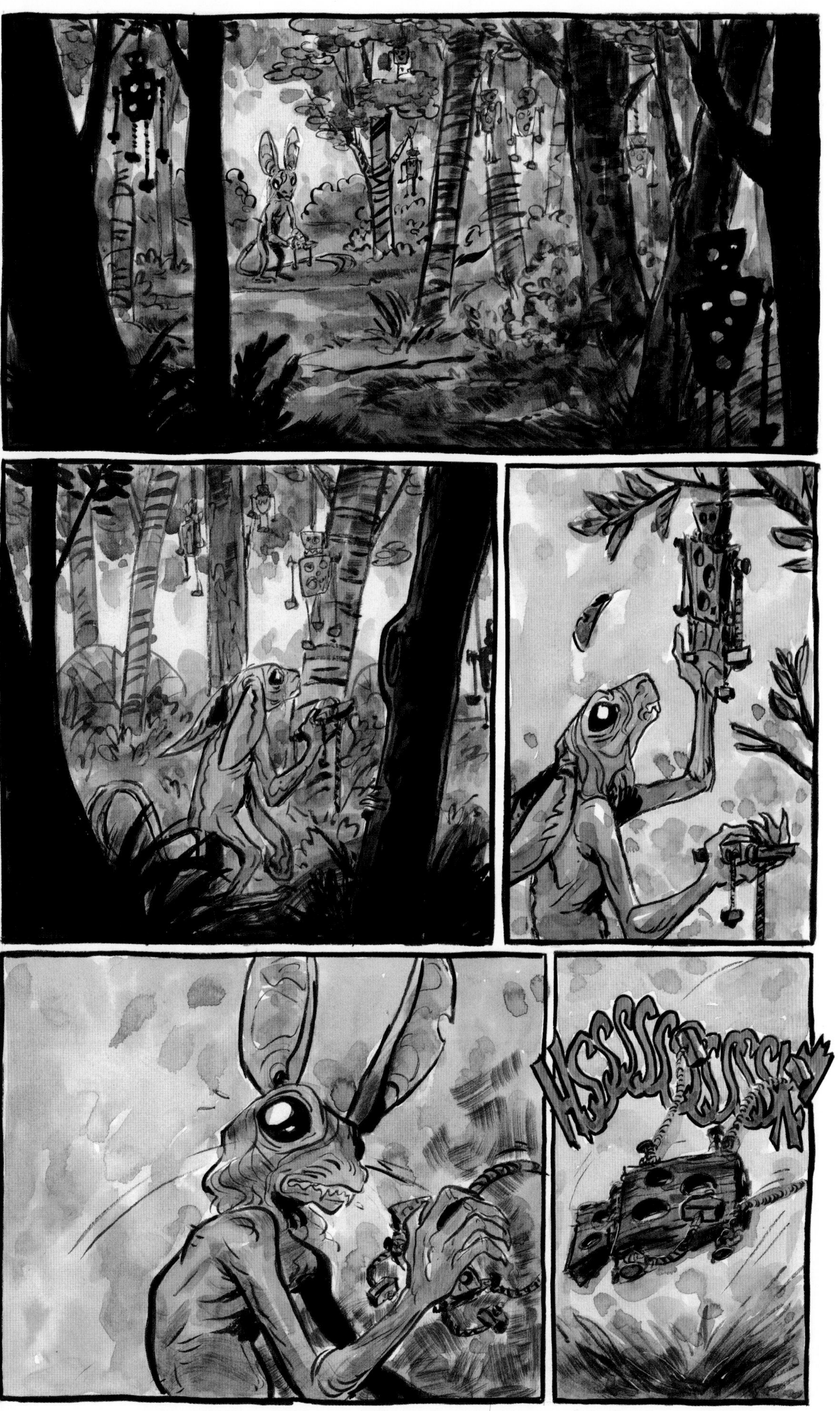

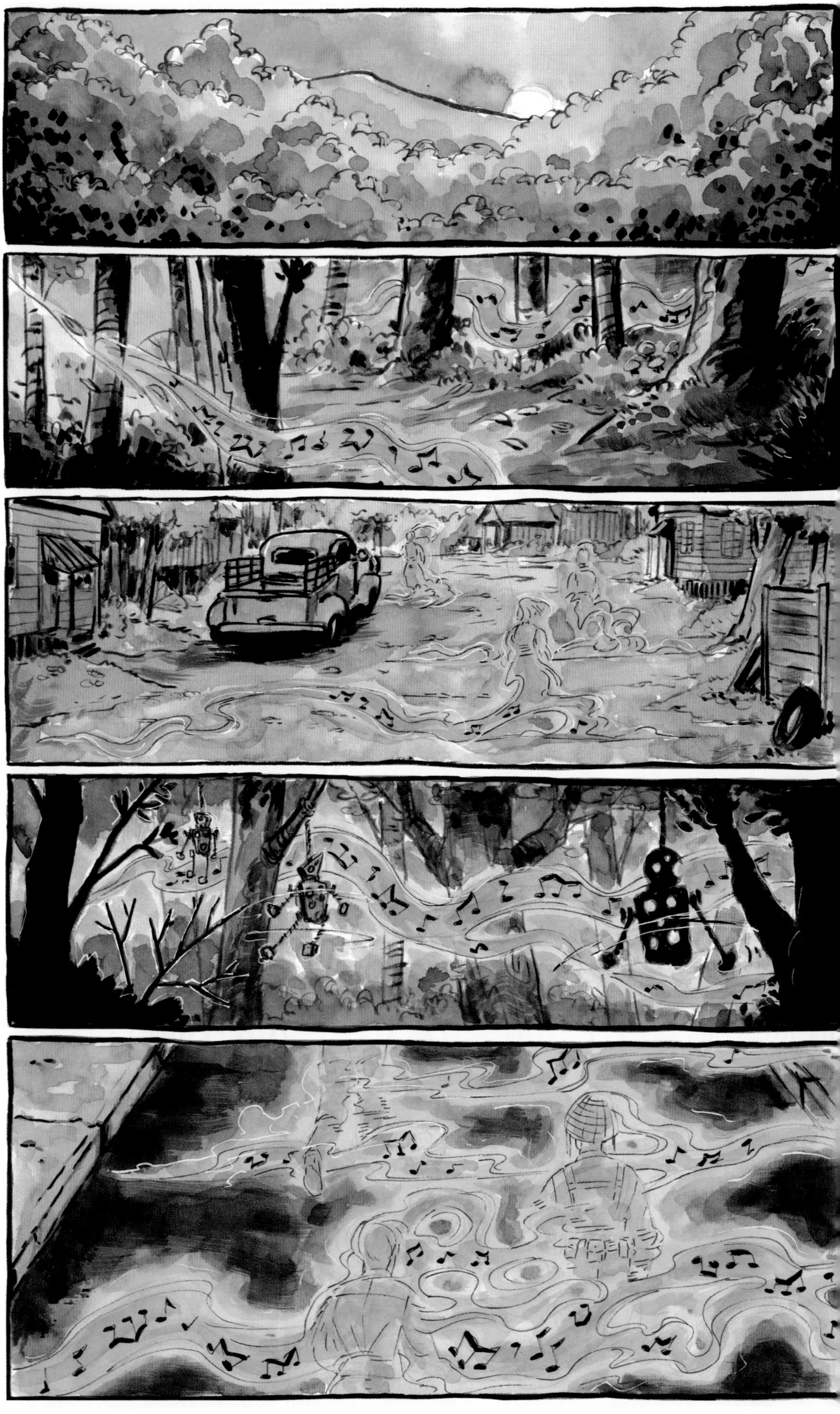

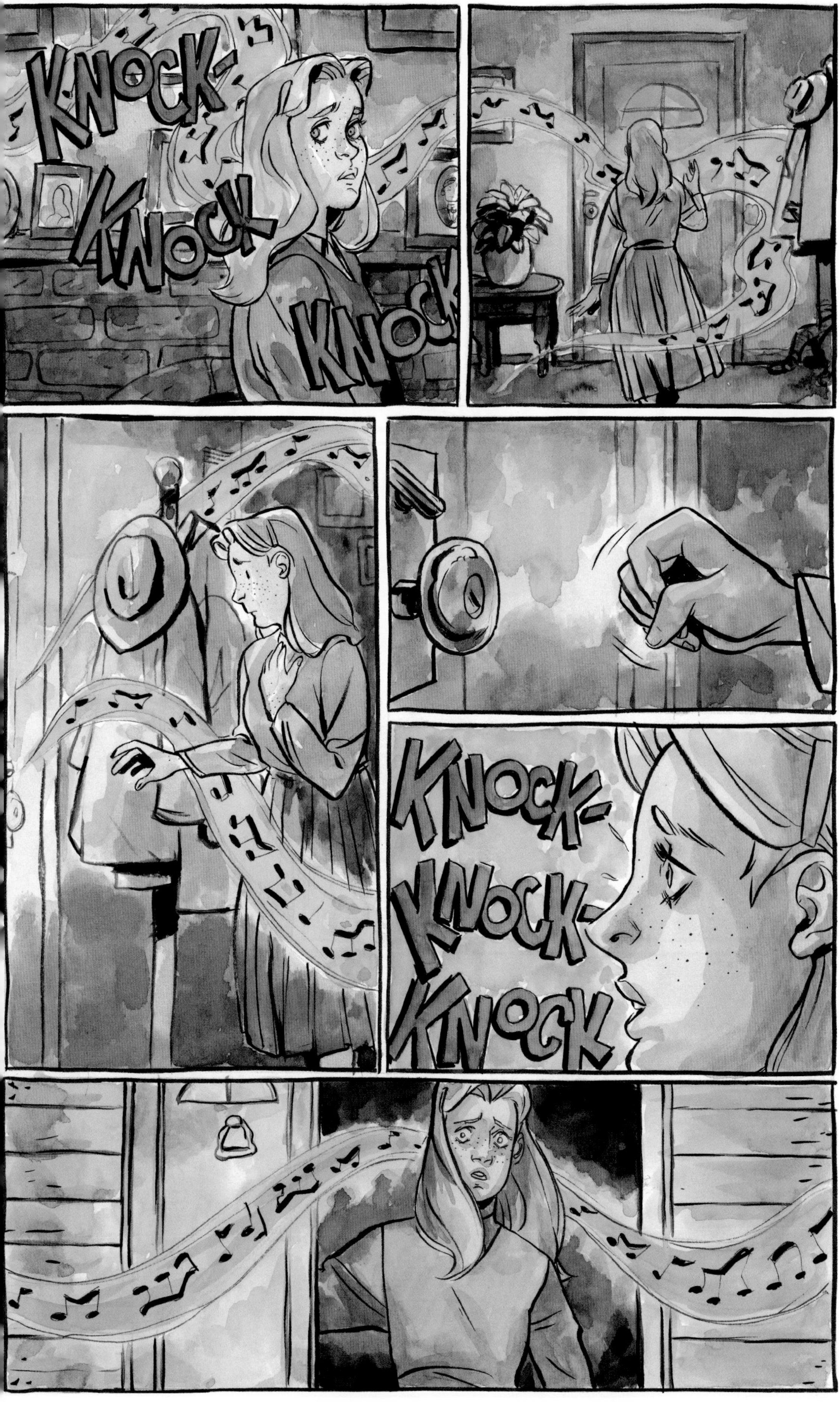

KNOCK-
KNOCK
KNOCK
KNOCK-
KNOCK-
KNOCK

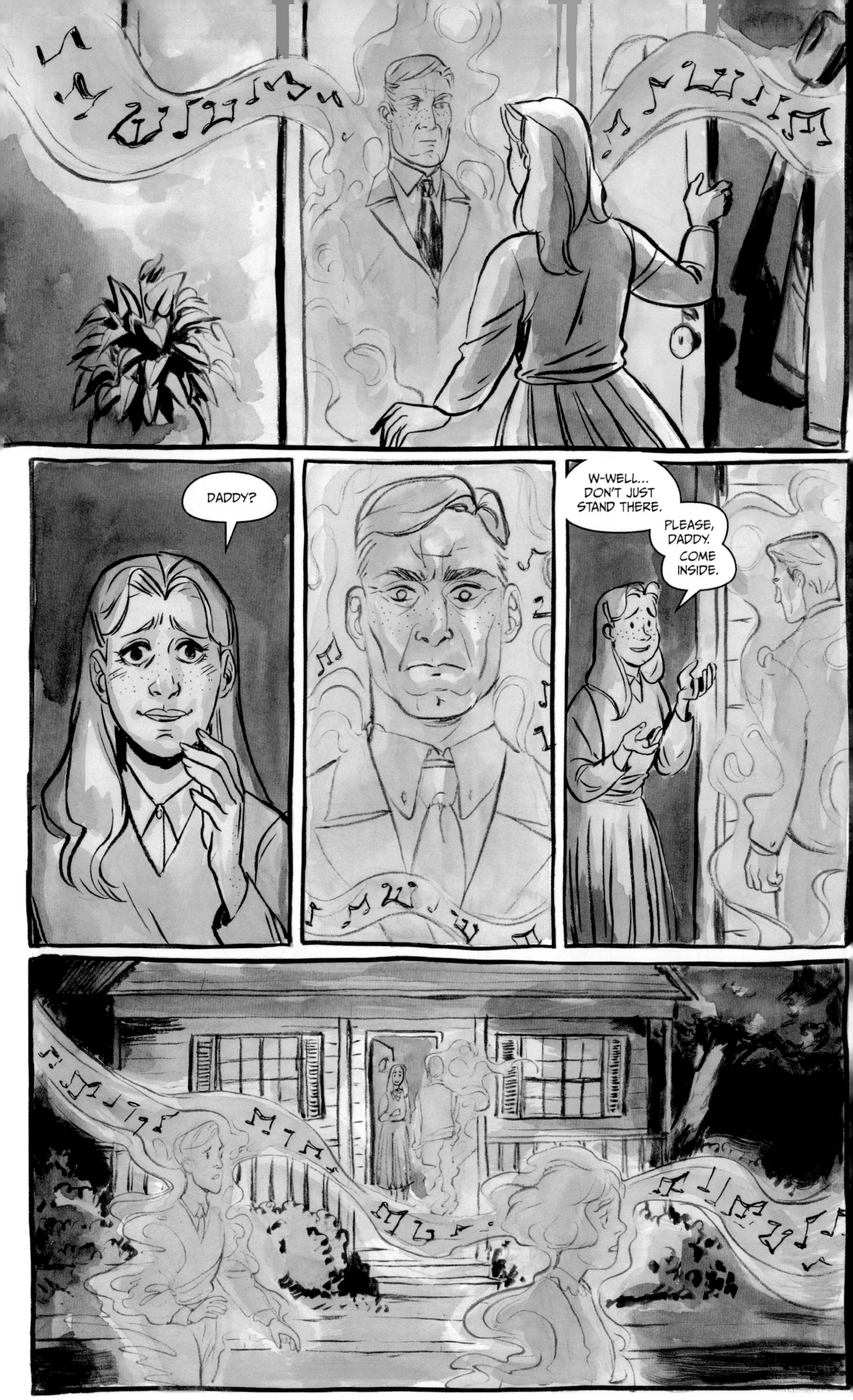
DADDY?
W-WELL... DON'T JUST STAND THERE.
PLEASE, DADDY. COME INSIDE.

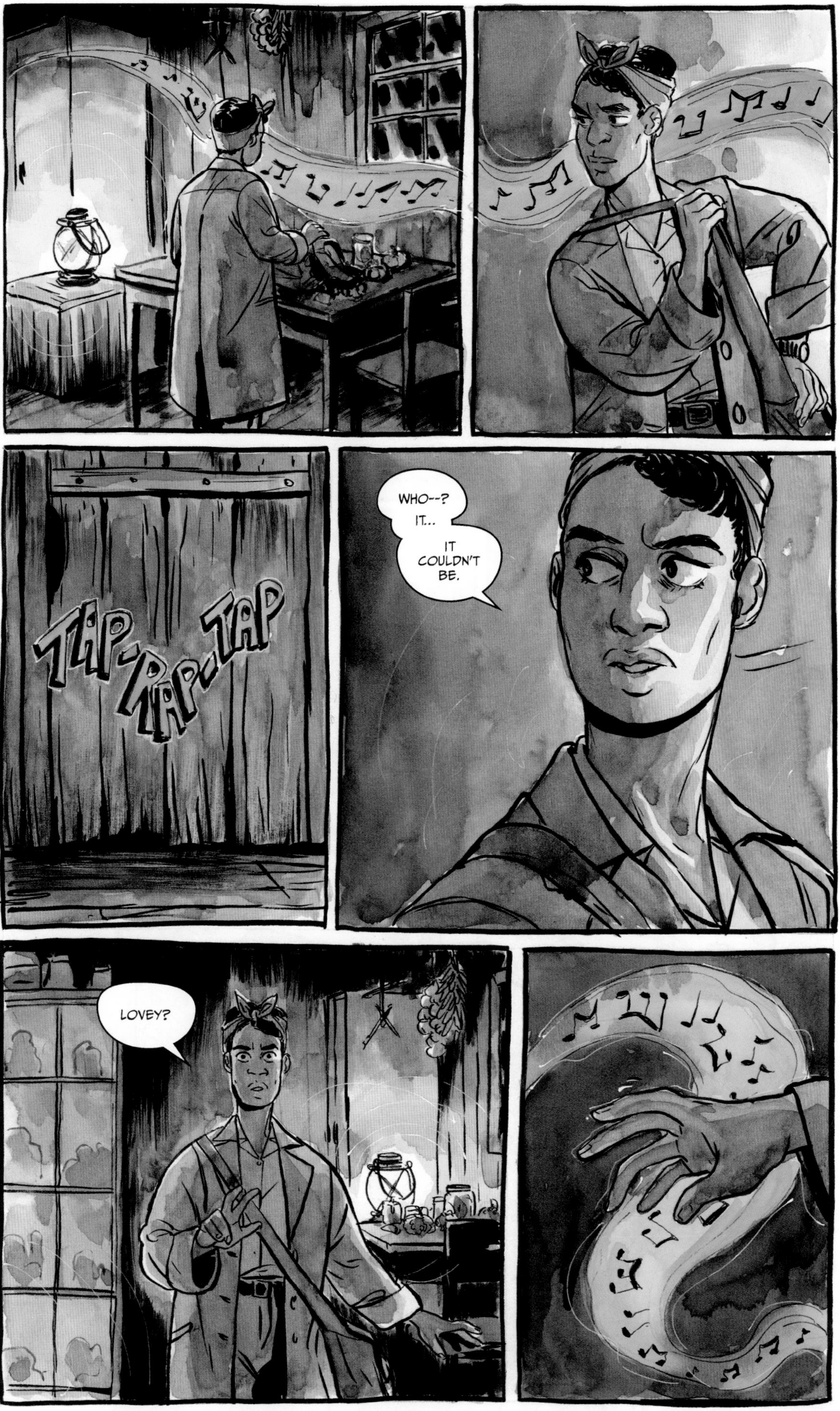
TAP-RAP-TAP
WHO--?
IT...
IT COULDN'T BE.
LOVEY?

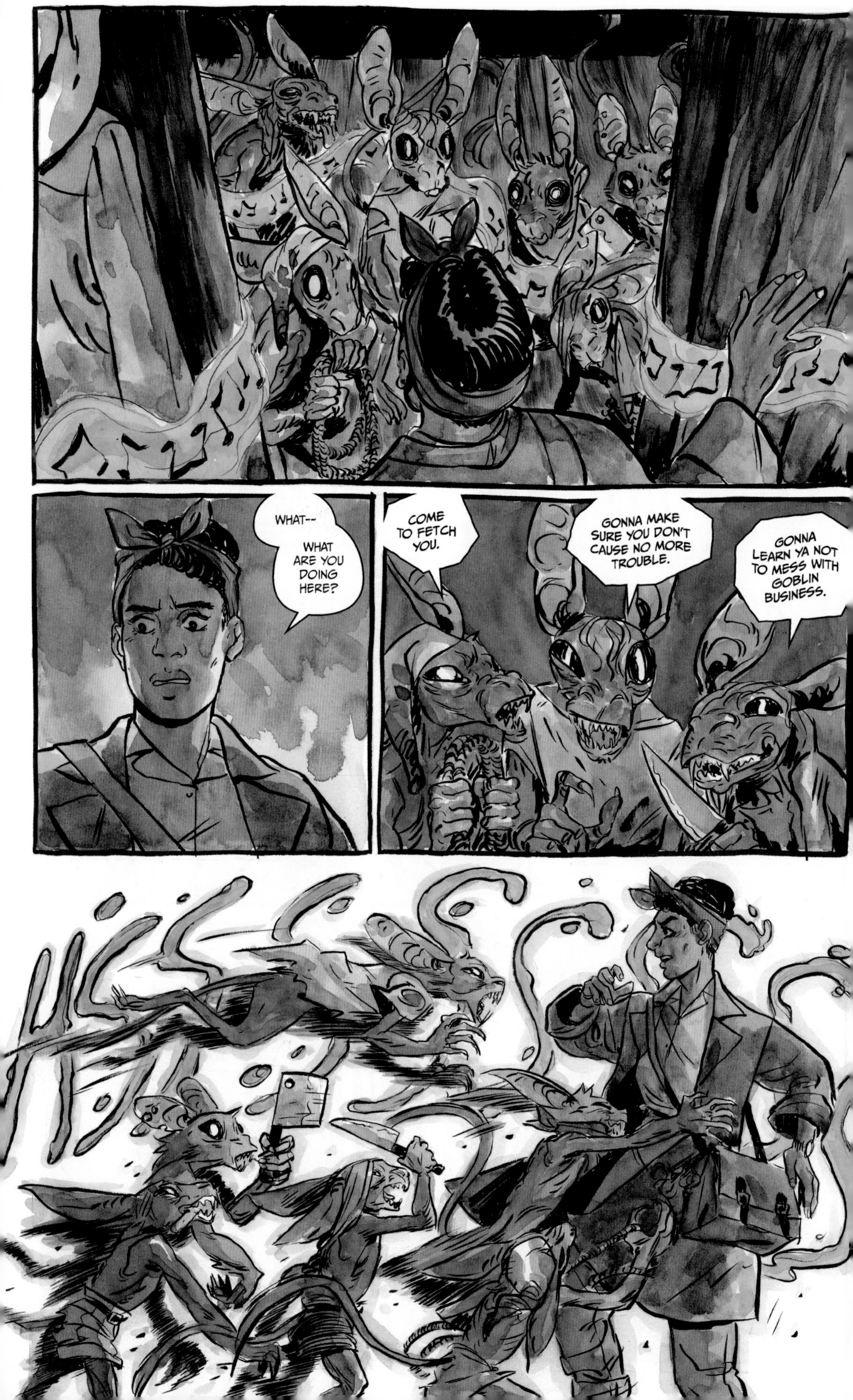
WHAT--
WHAT ARE YOU DOING HERE?
COME TO FETCH YOU.
GONNA MAKE SURE YOU DON'T CAUSE NO MORE TROUBLE.
GONNA LEARN YA NOT TO MESS WITH GOBLIN BUSINESS.

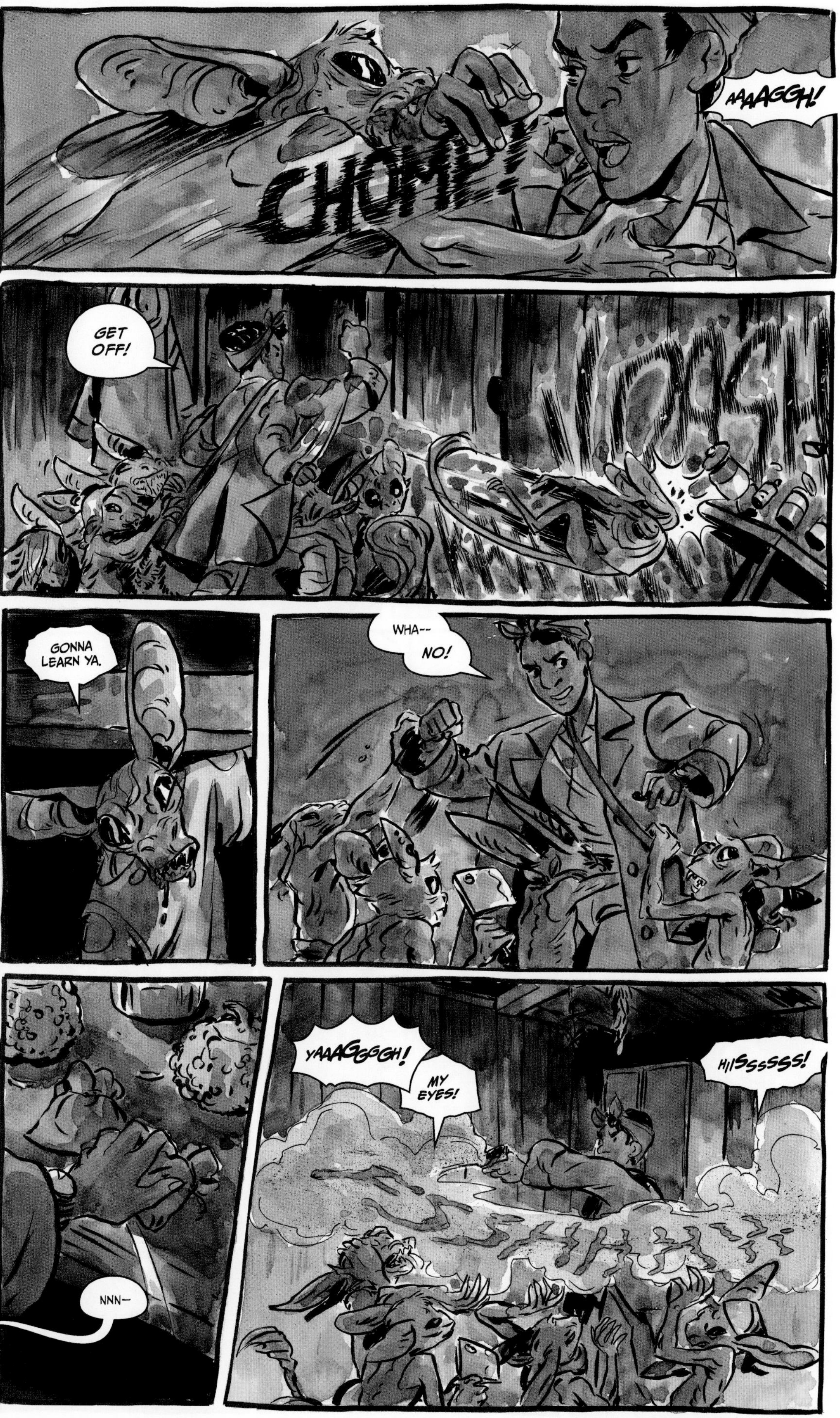
CHOMP!
AAAAAGGH!
GET OFF!
WOOSH!
GONNA LEARN YA.
WHA-- NO!
NNN--
YAAAGGGGH!
MY EYES!
HISSSSSS!

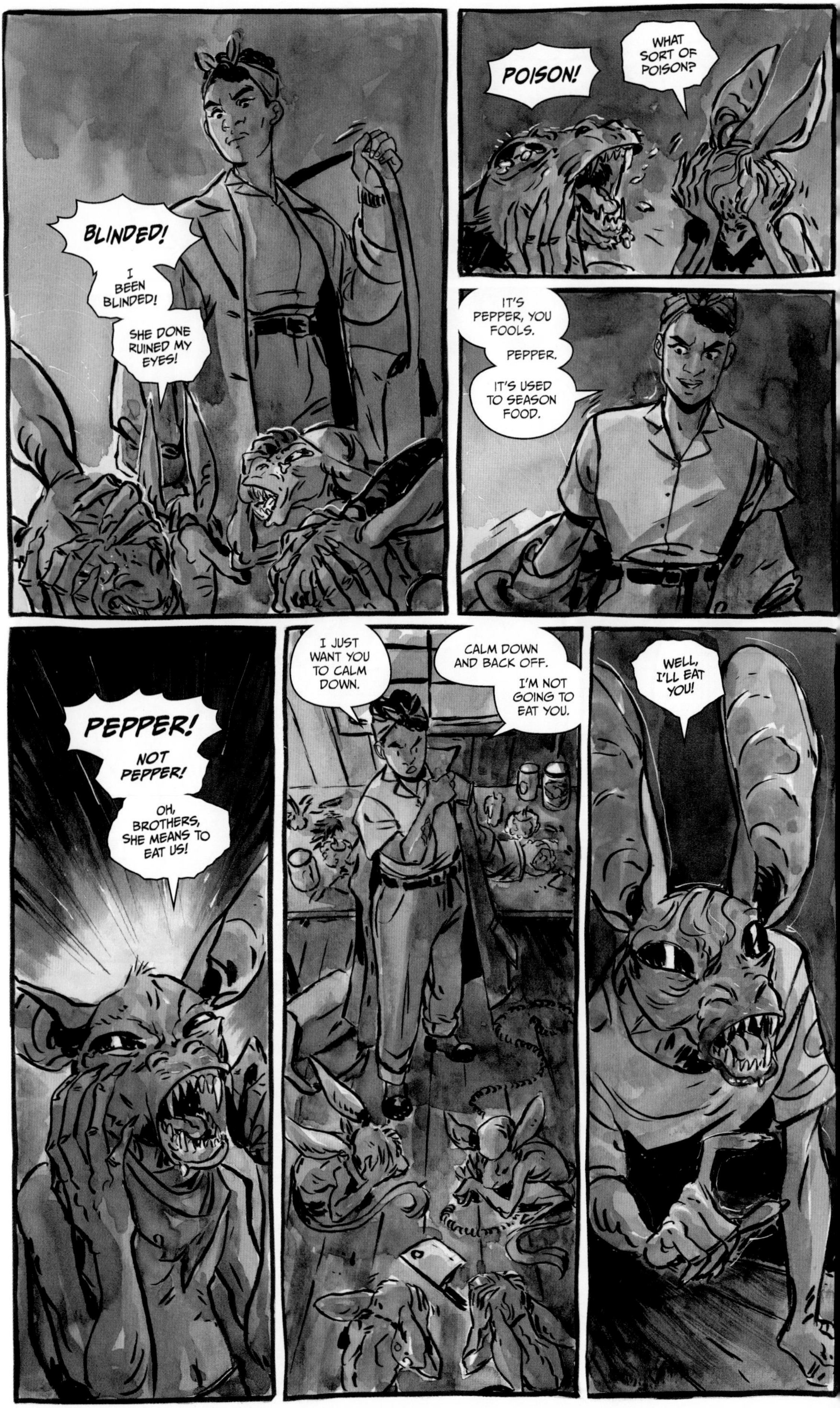
BLINDED!
I BEEN BLINDED!
SHE DONE RUINED MY EYES!
POISON!
WHAT SORT OF POISON?
IT'S PEPPER, YOU FOOLS.
PEPPER.
IT'S USED TO SEASON FOOD.
PEPPER!
NOT PEPPER!
OH, BROTHERS, SHE MEANS TO EAT US!
I JUST WANT YOU TO CALM DOWN.
CALM DOWN AND BACK OFF.
I'M NOT GOING TO EAT YOU.
WELL, I'LL EAT YOU!

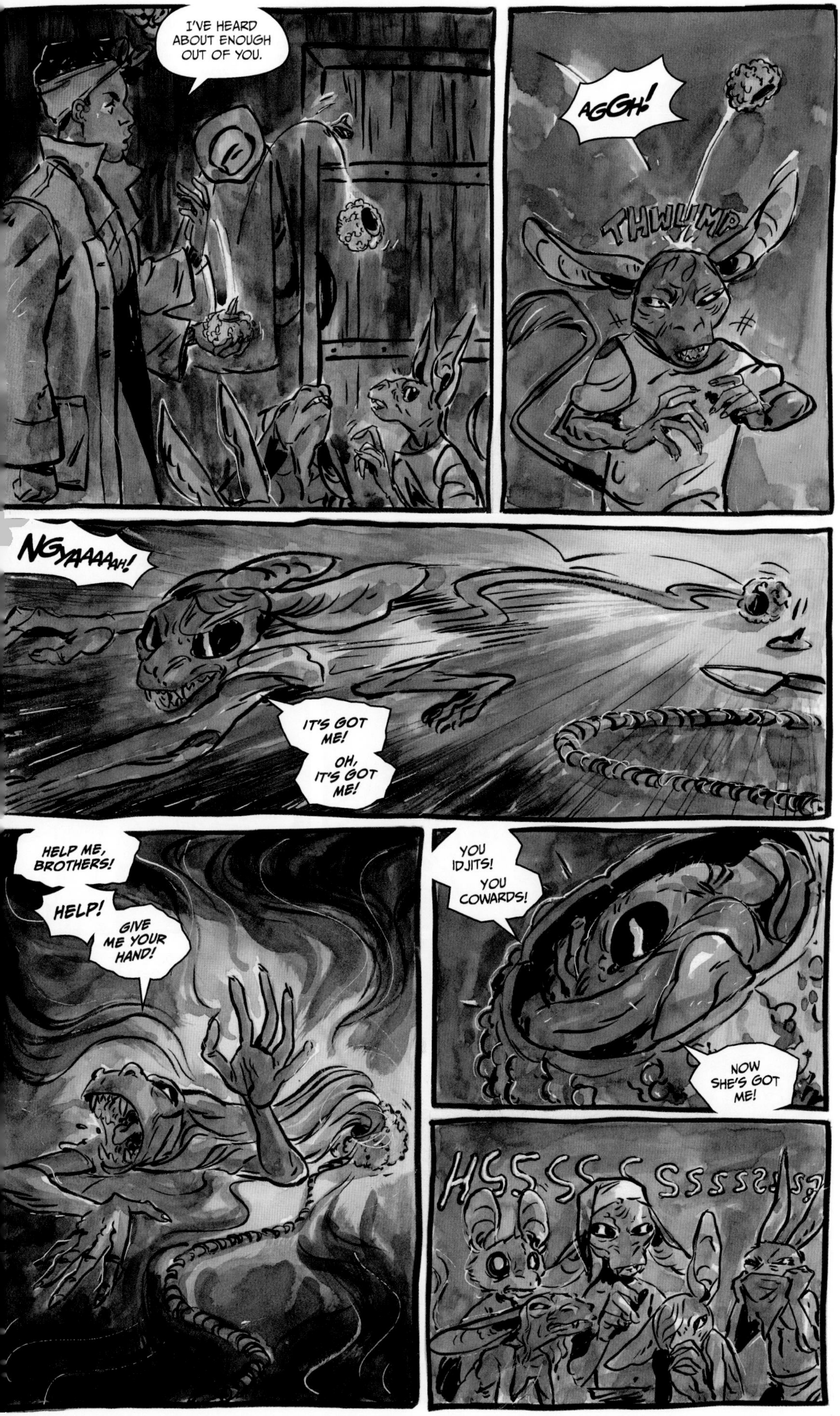
I'VE HEARD ABOUT ENOUGH OUT OF YOU.
AGGH!
THWUMP
NGYAAAAAH!
IT'S GOT ME!
OH, IT'S GOT ME!
HELP ME, BROTHERS!
HELP!
GIVE ME YOUR HAND!
YOU IDJITS!
YOU COWARDS!
NOW SHE'S GOT ME!
HSSSSSSSSSSS

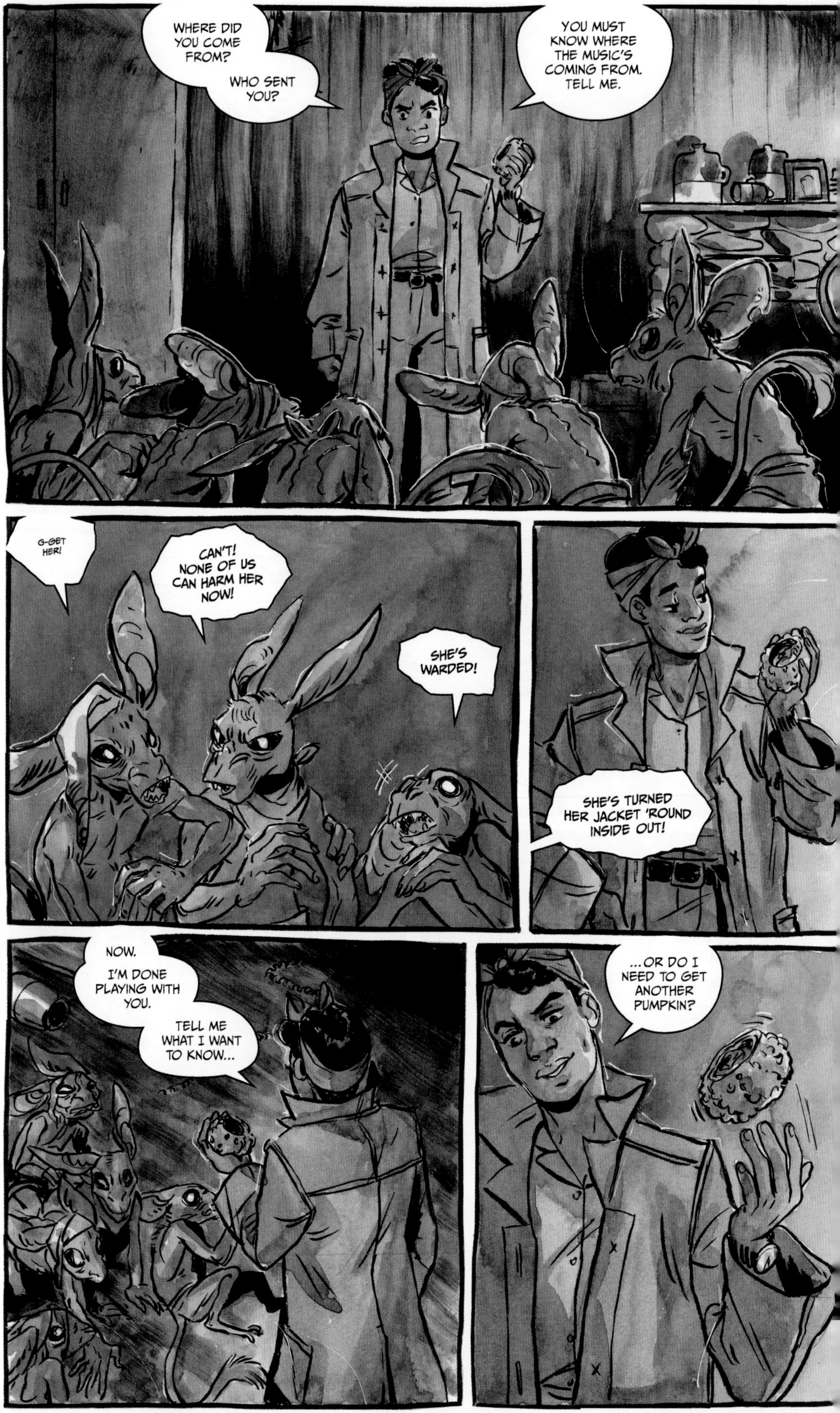

WHERE DID YOU COME FROM?
WHO SENT YOU?
YOU MUST KNOW WHERE THE MUSIC'S COMING FROM. TELL ME.
G-GET HER!
CAN'T! NONE OF US CAN HARM HER NOW!
SHE'S WARDED!
SHE'S TURNED HER JACKET 'ROUND INSIDE OUT!
NOW.
I'M DONE PLAYING WITH YOU.
TELL ME WHAT I WANT TO KNOW...
...OR DO I NEED TO GET ANOTHER PUMPKIN?

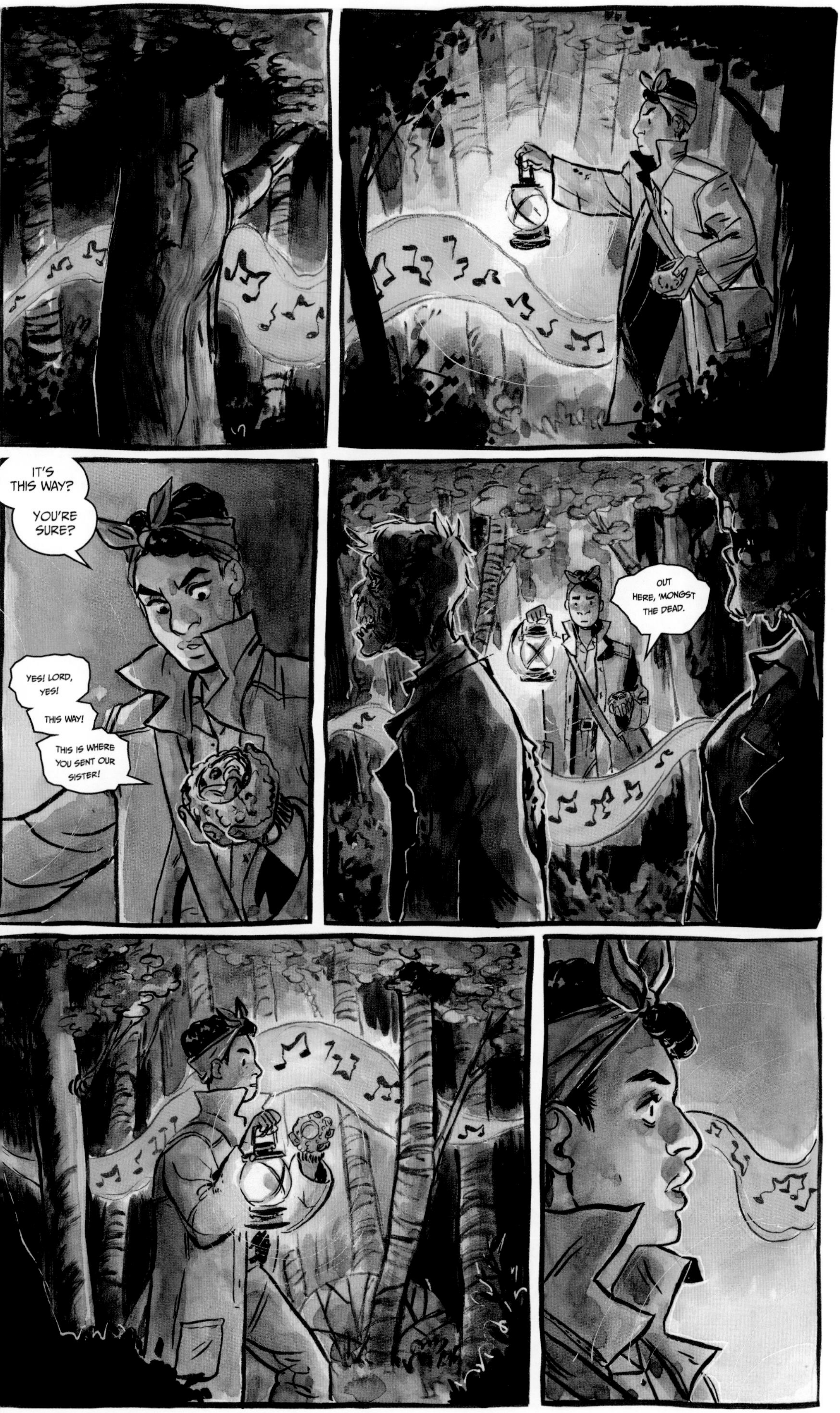
IT'S THIS WAY?
YOU'RE SURE?
YES! LORD, YES!
THIS WAY!
THIS IS WHERE YOU SENT OUR SISTER!
OUT HERE, 'MONGST THE DEAD.

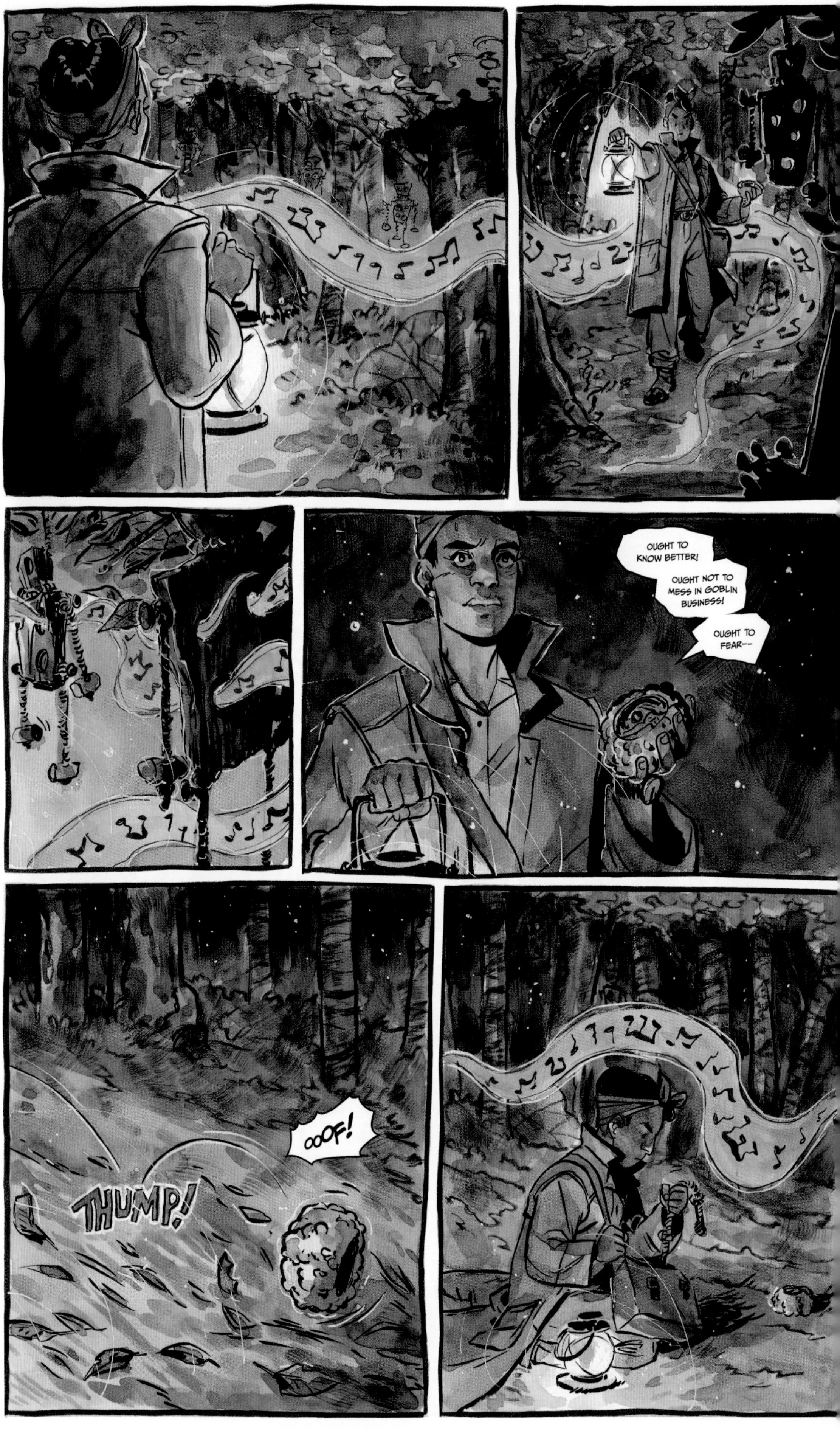
OUGHT TO KNOW BETTER!
OUGHT NOT TO MESS IN GOBLIN BUSINESS!
OUGHT TO FEAR--
THUMP!
OOOF!

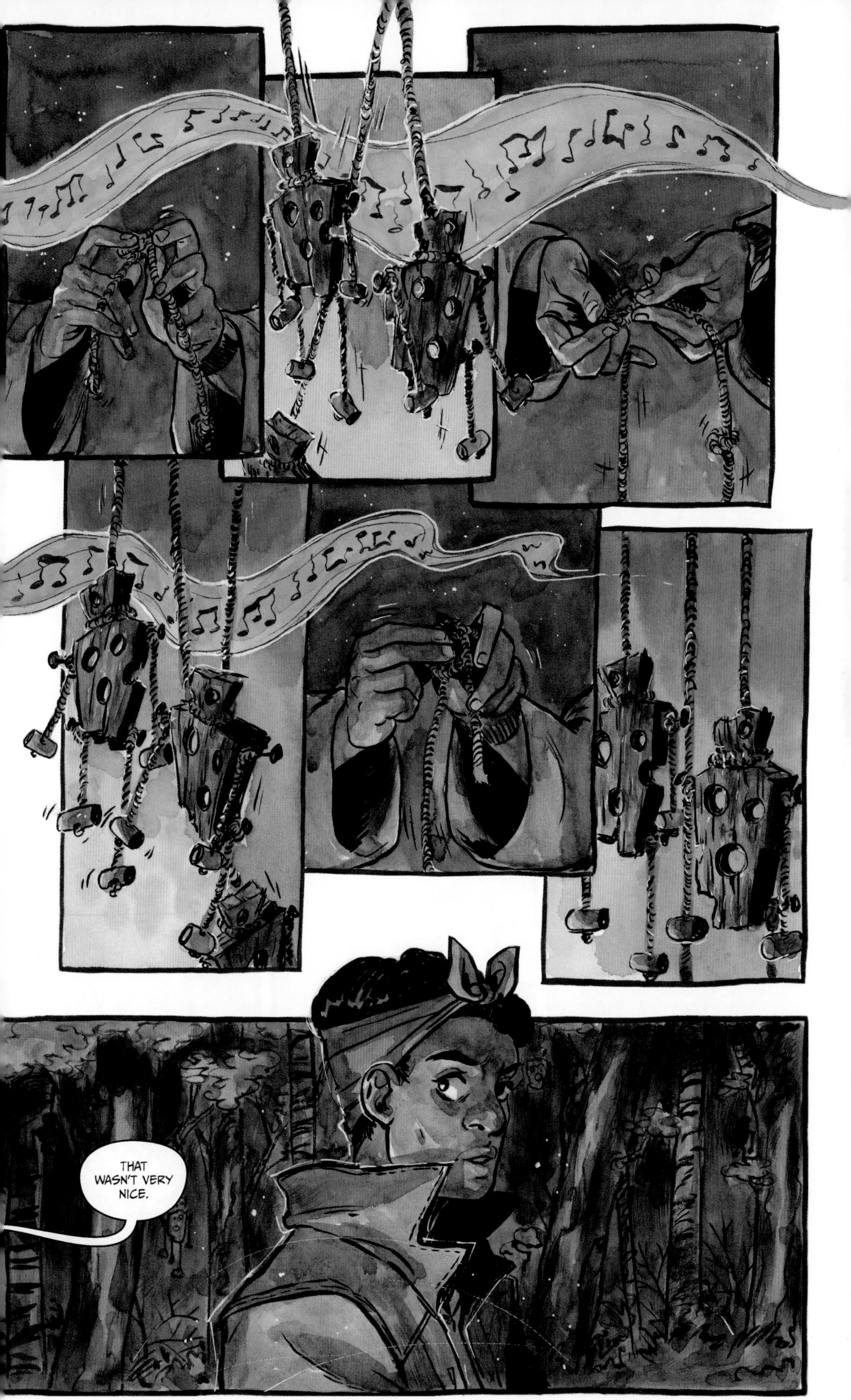
THAT WASN'T VERY NICE.

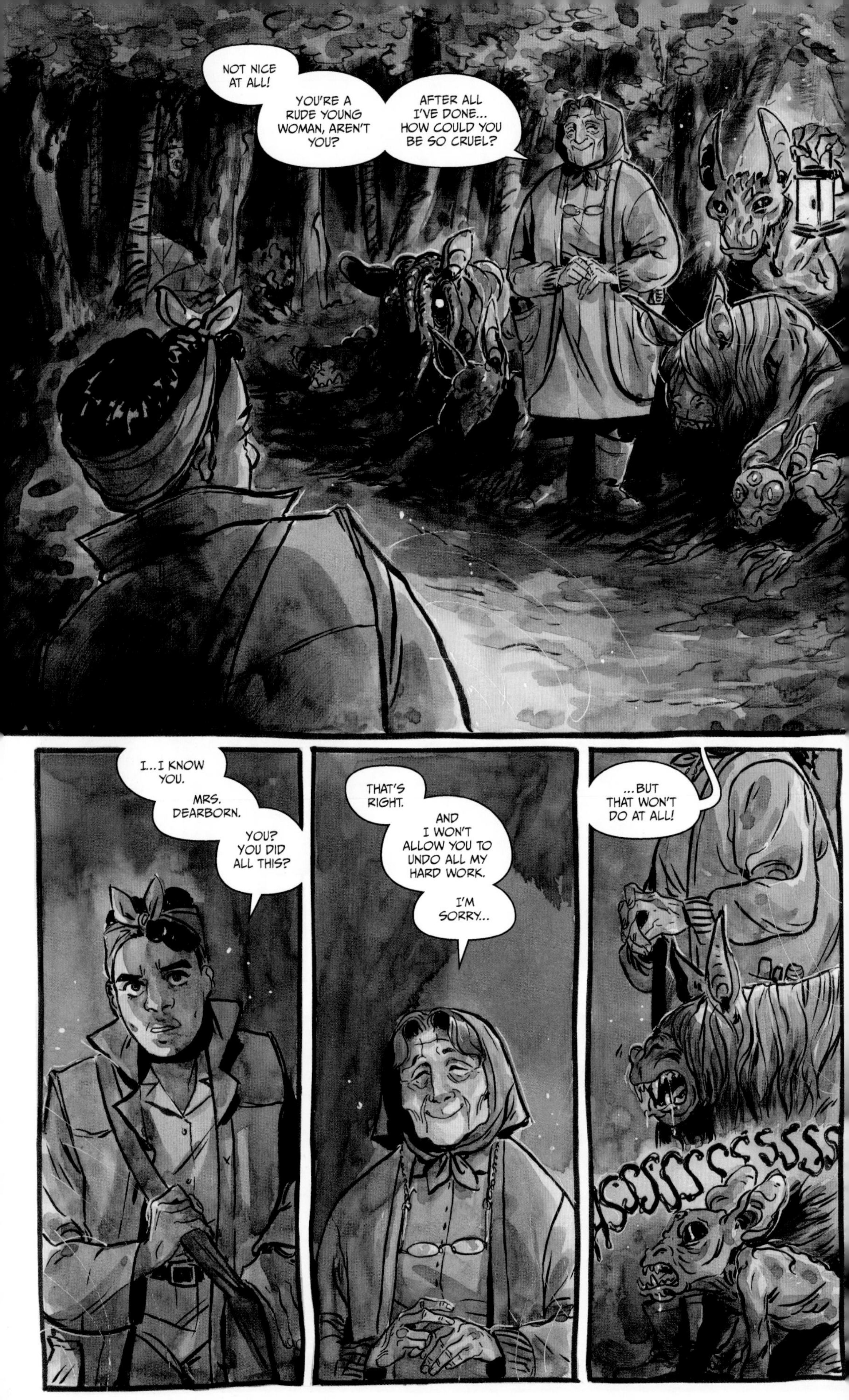
NOT NICE AT ALL!
YOU'RE A RUDE YOUNG WOMAN, AREN'T YOU?
AFTER ALL I'VE DONE... HOW COULD YOU BE SO CRUEL?
I...I KNOW YOU.
MRS. DEARBORN.
YOU? YOU DID ALL THIS?
THAT'S RIGHT.
AND I WON'T ALLOW YOU TO UNDO ALL MY HARD WORK.
I'M SORRY...
...BUT THAT WON'T DO AT ALL!

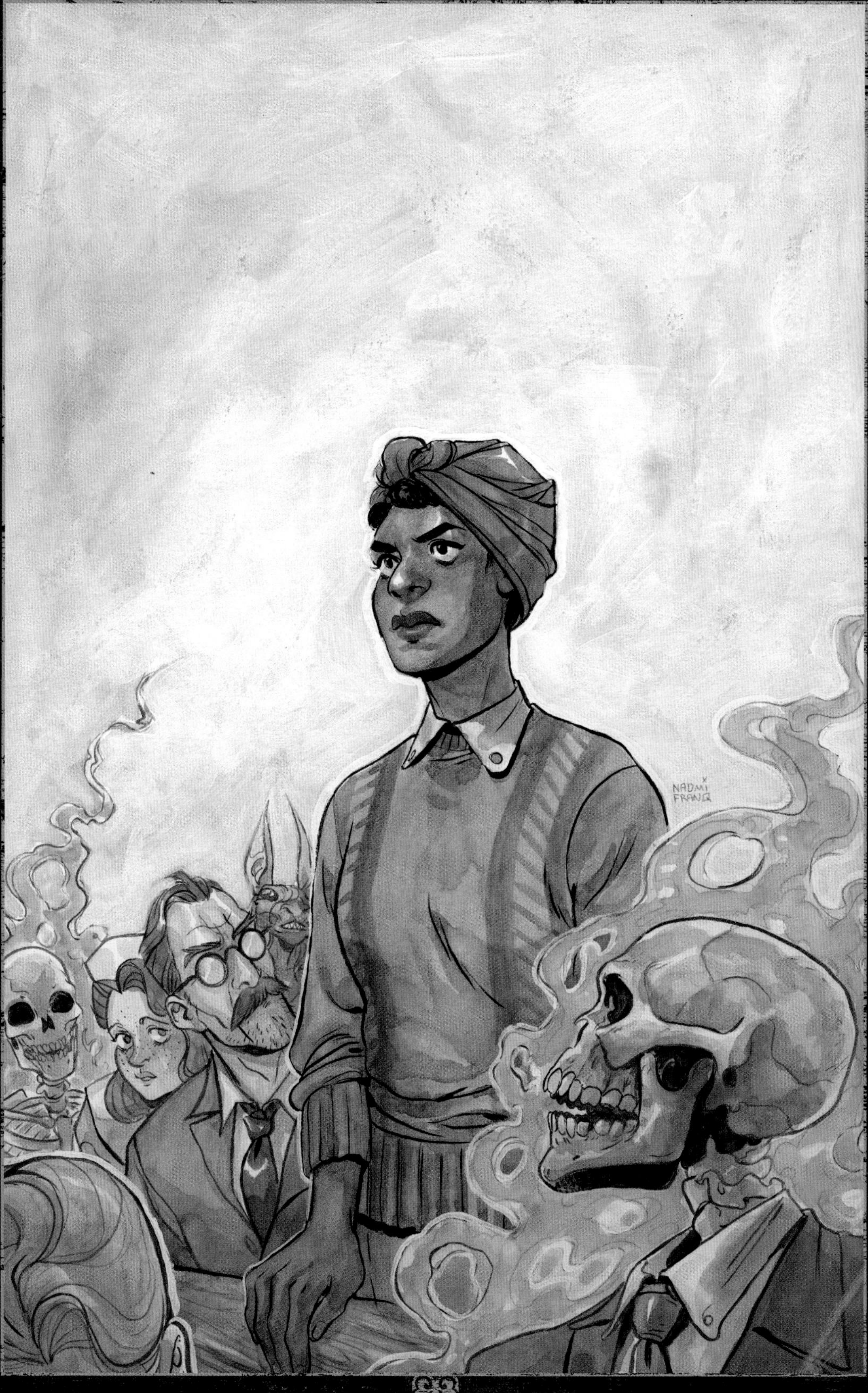
NADMI FRANQ

FOUR

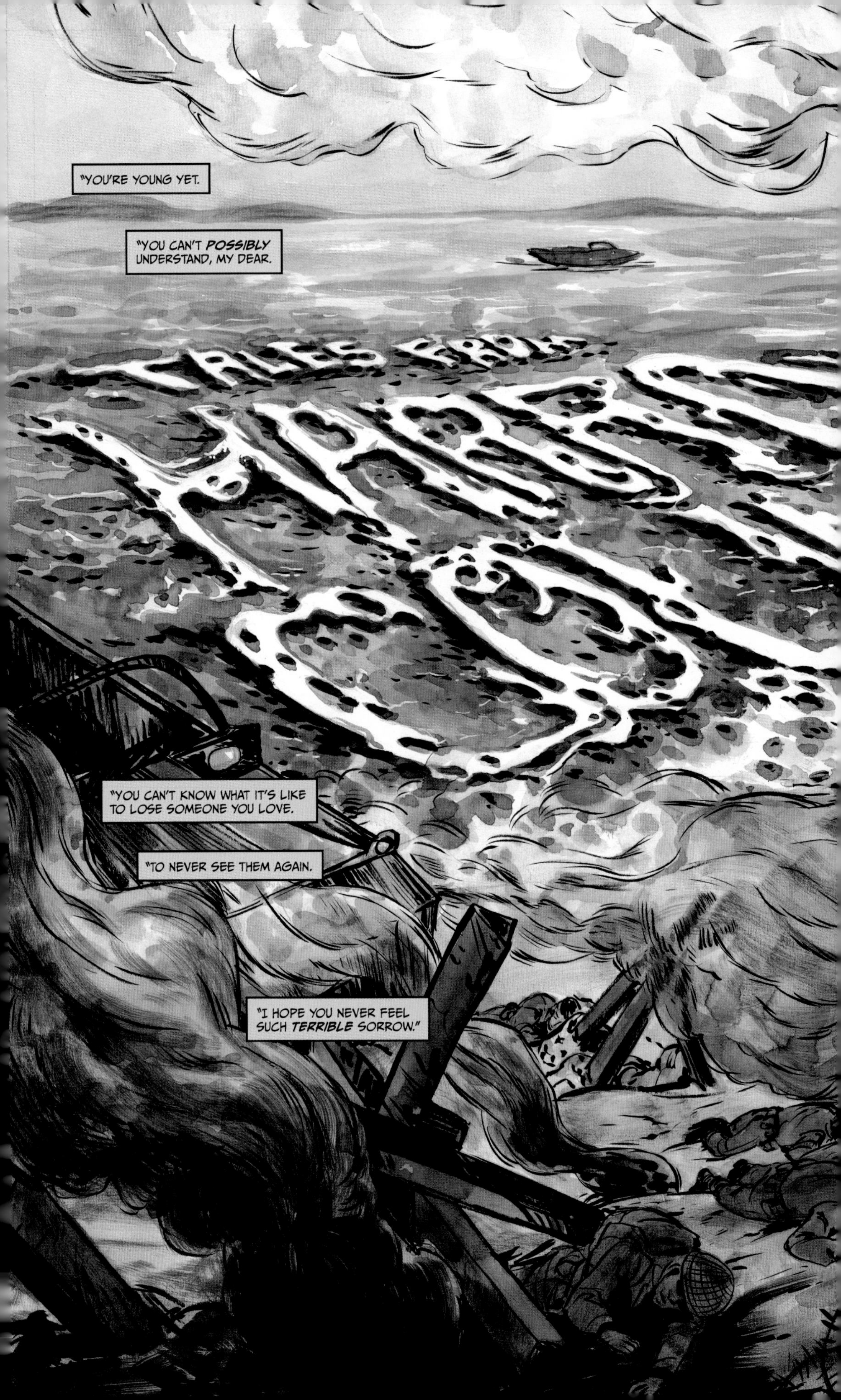

"YOU'RE YOUNG YET.
"YOU CAN'T *POSSIBLY* UNDERSTAND, MY DEAR.
"YOU CAN'T KNOW WHAT IT'S LIKE TO LOSE SOMEONE YOU LOVE.
"TO NEVER SEE THEM AGAIN.
"I HOPE YOU NEVER FEEL SUCH *TERRIBLE* SORROW."

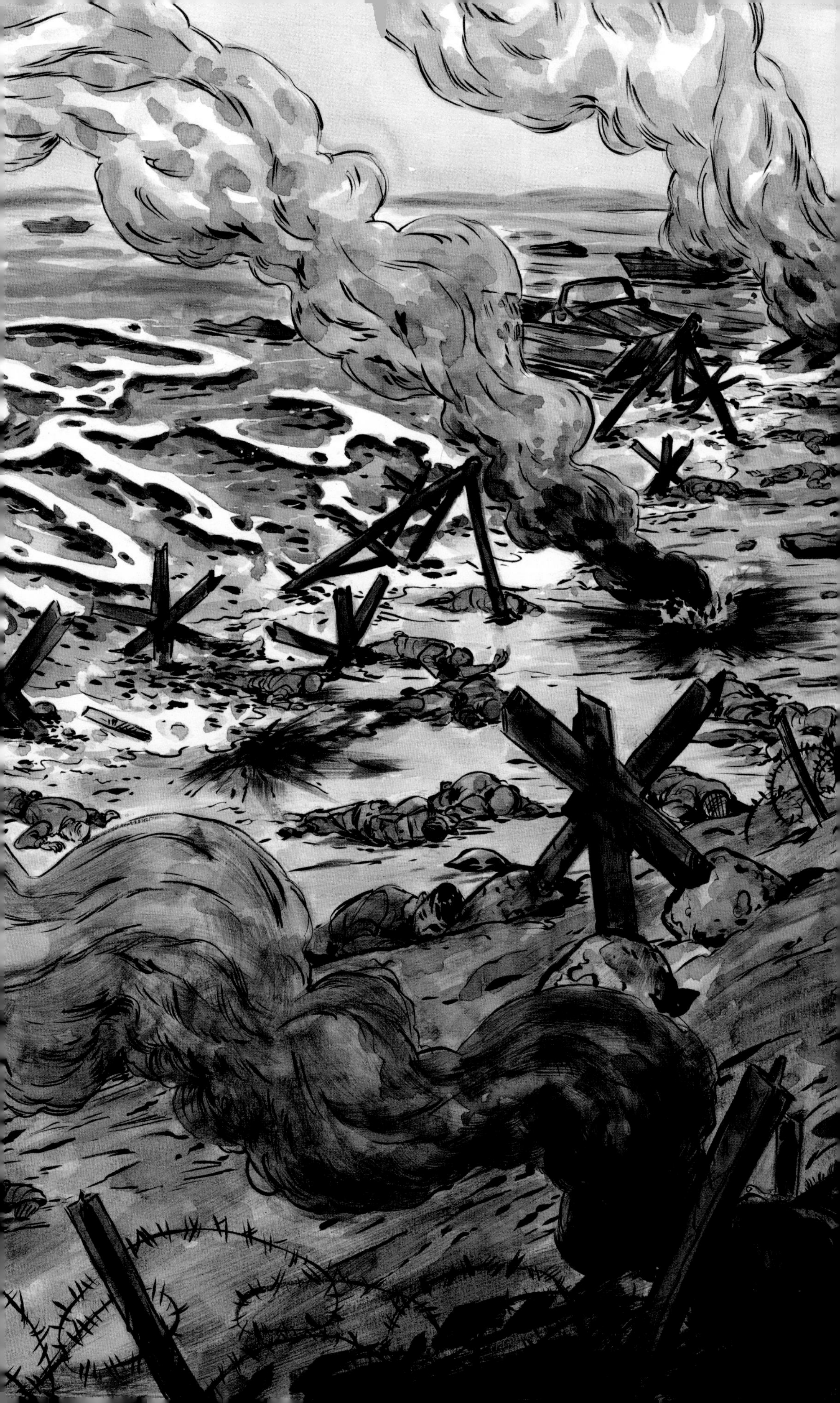

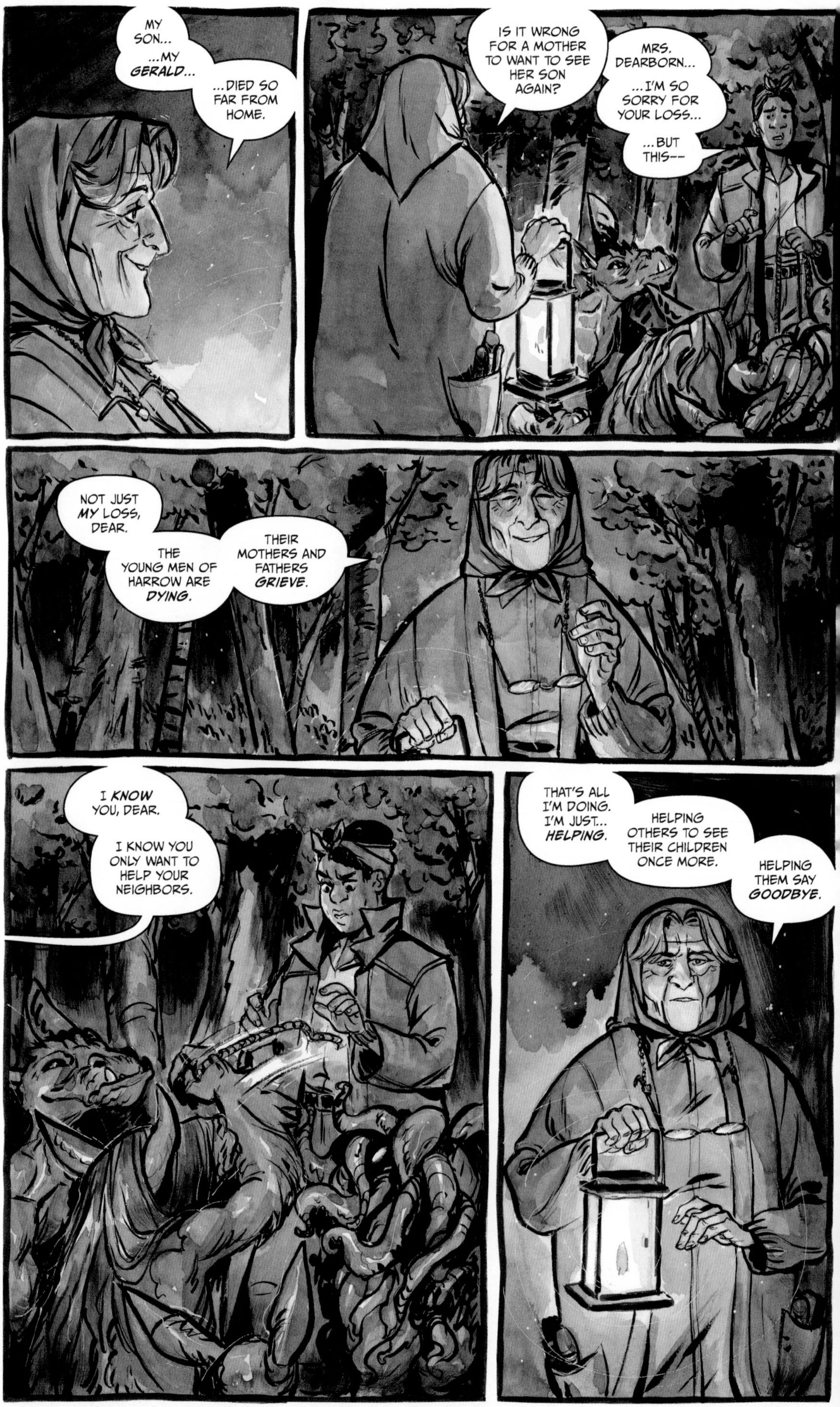
MY SON...
...MY *GERALD*...
...DIED SO FAR FROM HOME.
IS IT WRONG FOR A MOTHER TO WANT TO SEE HER SON AGAIN?
MRS. DEARBORN...
...I'M SO SORRY FOR YOUR LOSS...
...BUT THIS--
NOT JUST *MY* LOSS, DEAR.
THE YOUNG MEN OF HARROW ARE *DYING*.
THEIR MOTHERS AND FATHERS *GRIEVE*.
I *KNOW* YOU, DEAR.
I KNOW YOU ONLY WANT TO HELP YOUR NEIGHBORS.
THAT'S ALL I'M DOING. I'M JUST... *HELPING*.
HELPING OTHERS TO SEE THEIR CHILDREN ONCE MORE.
HELPING THEM SAY *GOODBYE*.

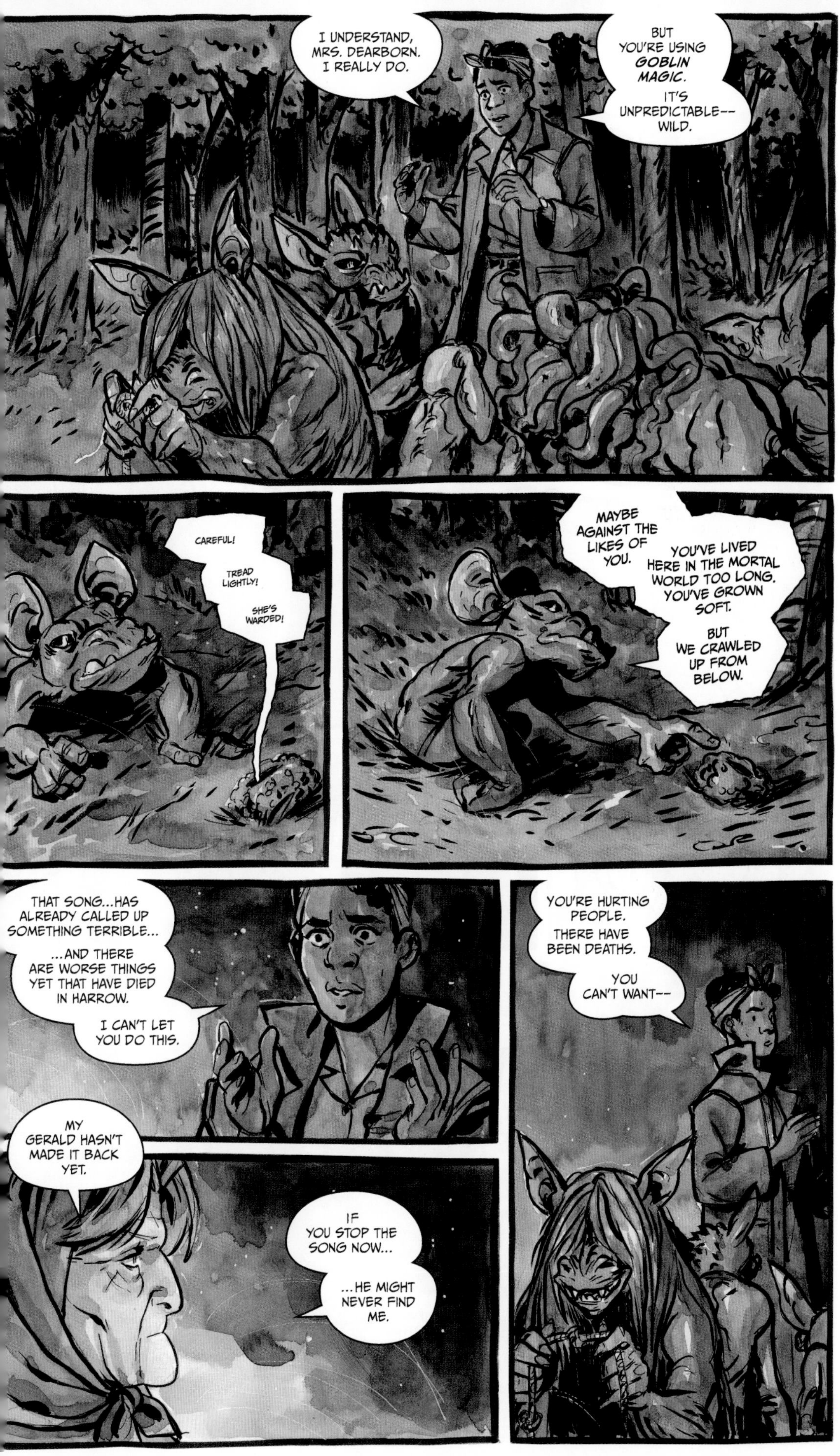

I UNDERSTAND, MRS. DEARBORN. I REALLY DO.
BUT YOU'RE USING GOBLIN MAGIC.
IT'S UNPREDICTABLE-- WILD.
CAREFUL!
TREAD LIGHTLY!
SHE'S WARDED!
MAYBE AGAINST THE LIKES OF YOU.
YOU'VE LIVED HERE IN THE MORTAL WORLD TOO LONG. YOU'VE GROWN SOFT.
BUT WE CRAWLED UP FROM BELOW.
THAT SONG...HAS ALREADY CALLED UP SOMETHING TERRIBLE...
...AND THERE ARE WORSE THINGS YET THAT HAVE DIED IN HARROW.
I CAN'T LET YOU DO THIS.
YOU'RE HURTING PEOPLE.
THERE HAVE BEEN DEATHS.
YOU CAN'T WANT--
MY GERALD HASN'T MADE IT BACK YET.
IF YOU STOP THE SONG NOW...
...HE MIGHT NEVER FIND ME.

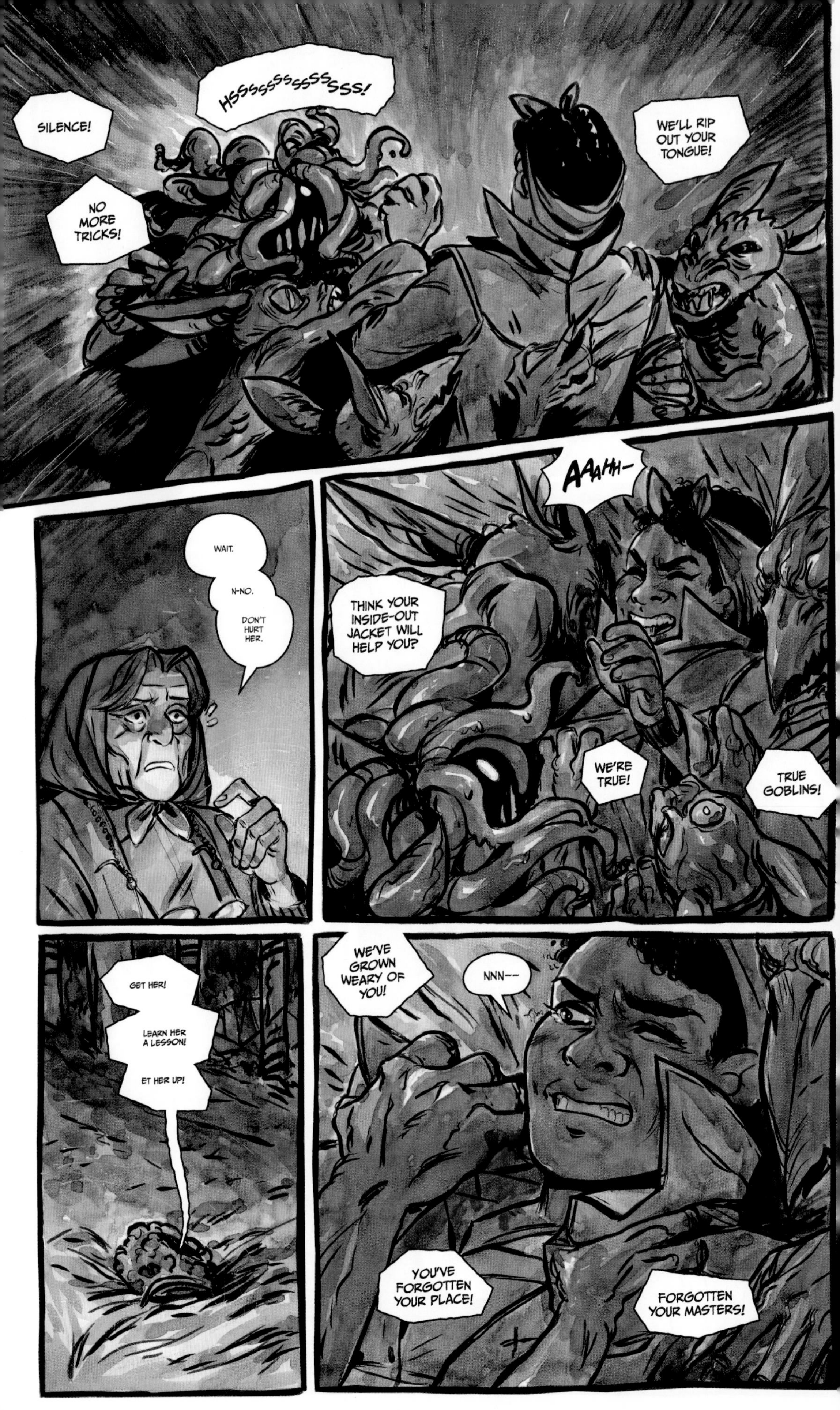
SILENCE!
HSSSSSSSSSSSSS!
NO MORE TRICKS!
WE'LL RIP OUT YOUR TONGUE!
WAIT.
N-NO.
DON'T HURT HER.
AAAHH-
THINK YOUR INSIDE-OUT JACKET WILL HELP YOU?
WE'RE TRUE!
TRUE GOBLINS!
GET HER!
LEARN HER A LESSON!
ET HER UP!
WE'VE GROWN WEARY OF YOU!
NNN--
YOU'VE FORGOTTEN YOUR PLACE!
FORGOTTEN YOUR MASTERS!

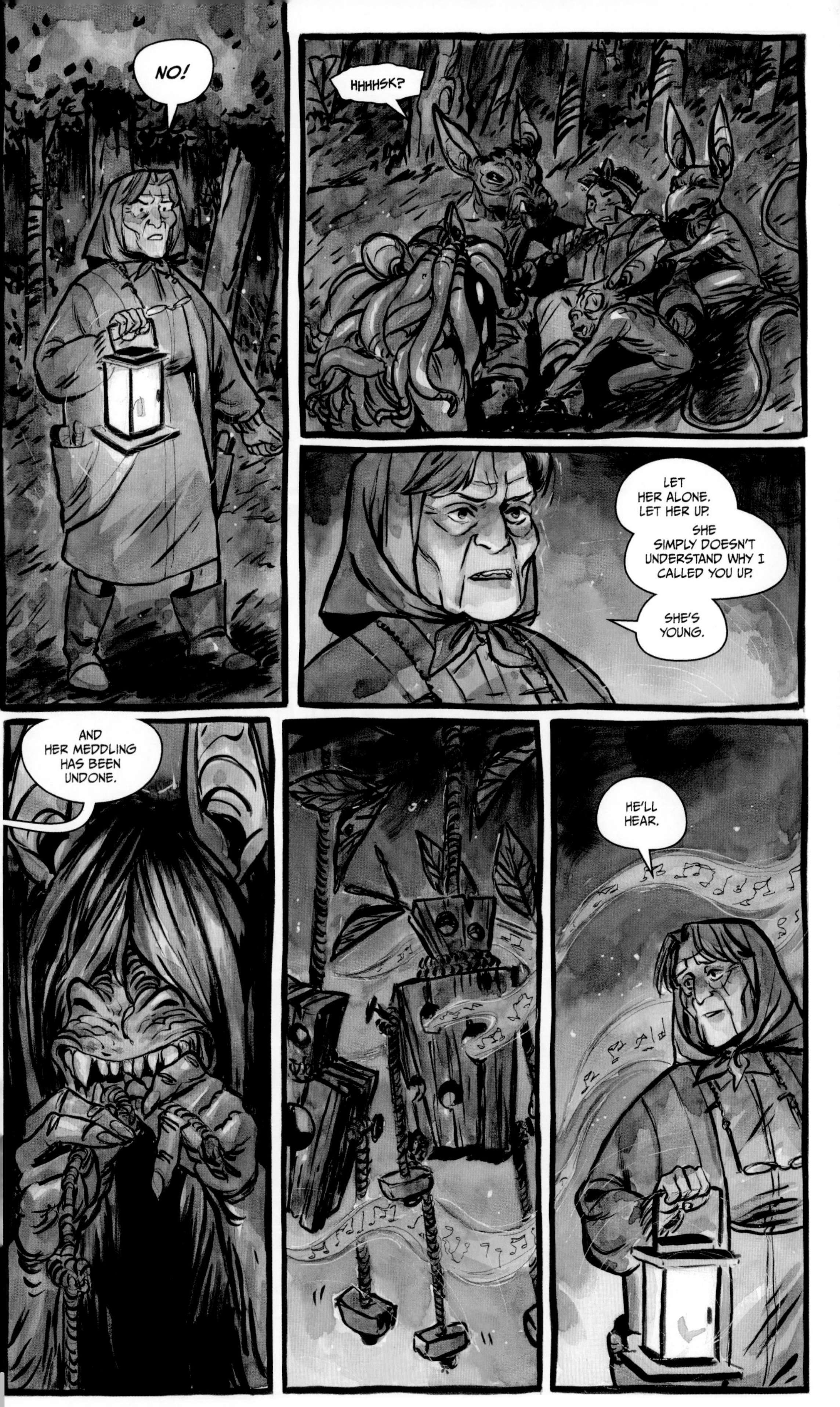
NO!
HHHHSK?
LET HER ALONE. LET HER UP.
SHE SIMPLY DOESN'T UNDERSTAND WHY I CALLED YOU UP.
SHE'S YOUNG.
AND HER MEDDLING HAS BEEN UNDONE.
HE'LL HEAR.

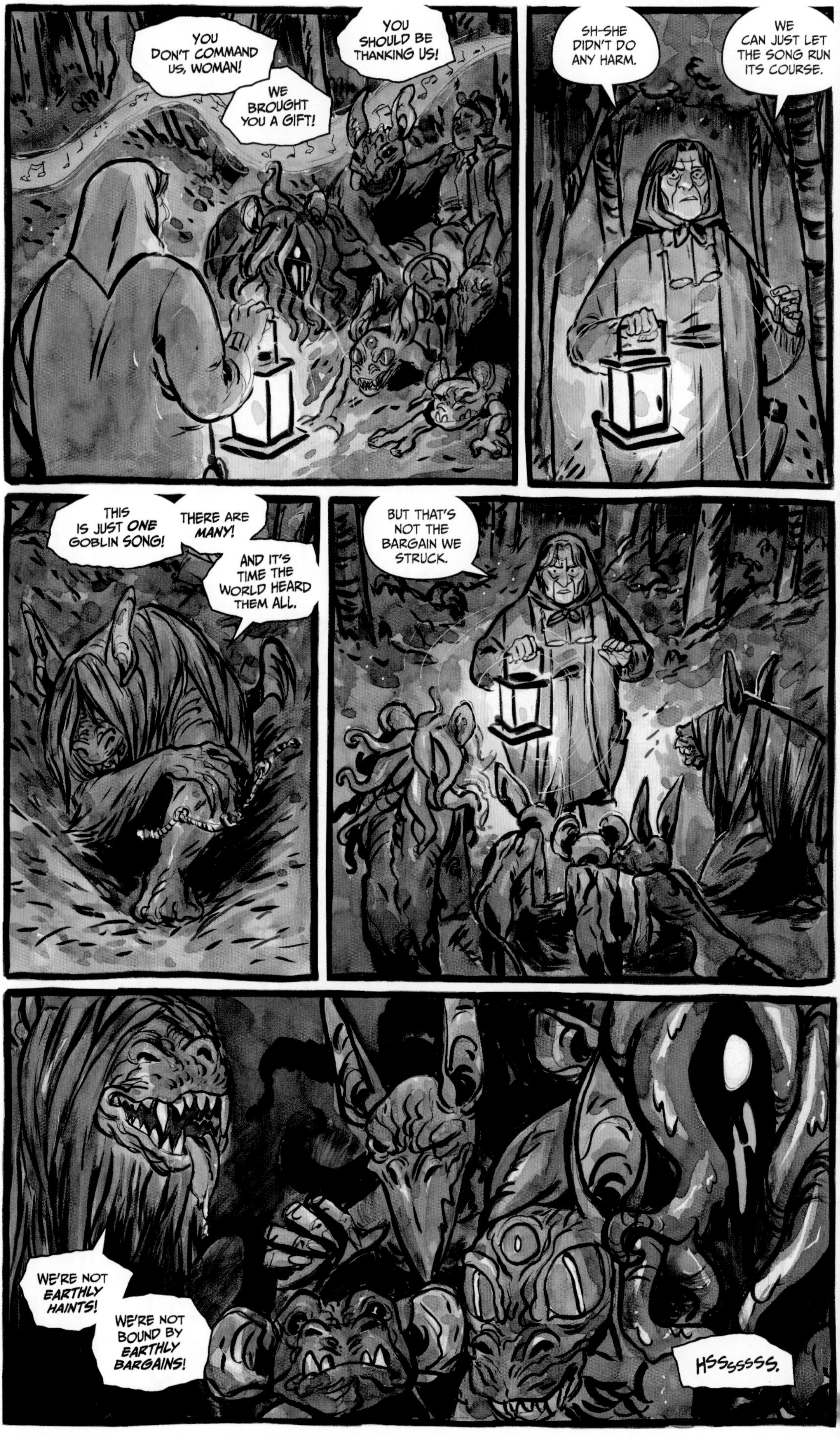
YOU DON'T COMMAND US, WOMAN!
WE BROUGHT YOU A GIFT!
YOU SHOULD BE THANKING US!
SH-SHE DIDN'T DO ANY HARM.
WE CAN JUST LET THE SONG RUN ITS COURSE.
THIS IS JUST ONE GOBLIN SONG!
THERE ARE MANY!
AND IT'S TIME THE WORLD HEARD THEM ALL.
BUT THAT'S NOT THE BARGAIN WE STRUCK.
WE'RE NOT EARTHLY HAINTS!
WE'RE NOT BOUND BY EARTHLY BARGAINS!
HSSsssss.

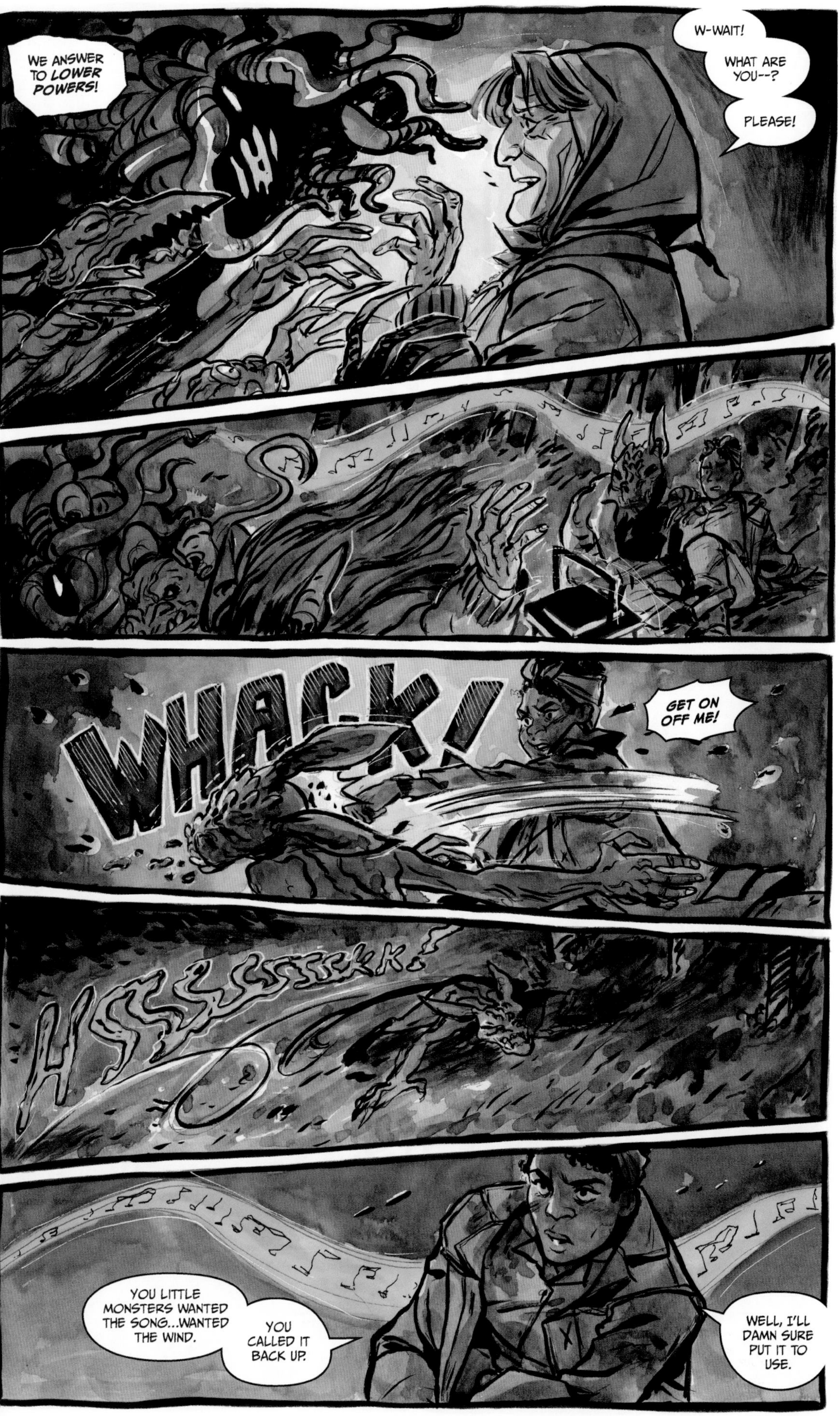
WE ANSWER TO LOWER POWERS!
W-WAIT!
WHAT ARE YOU--?
PLEASE!
WHACK!
GET ON OFF ME!
HSSSSSSKK!
YOU LITTLE MONSTERS WANTED THE SONG...WANTED THE WIND.
YOU CALLED IT BACK UP.
WELL, I'LL DAMN SURE PUT IT TO USE.

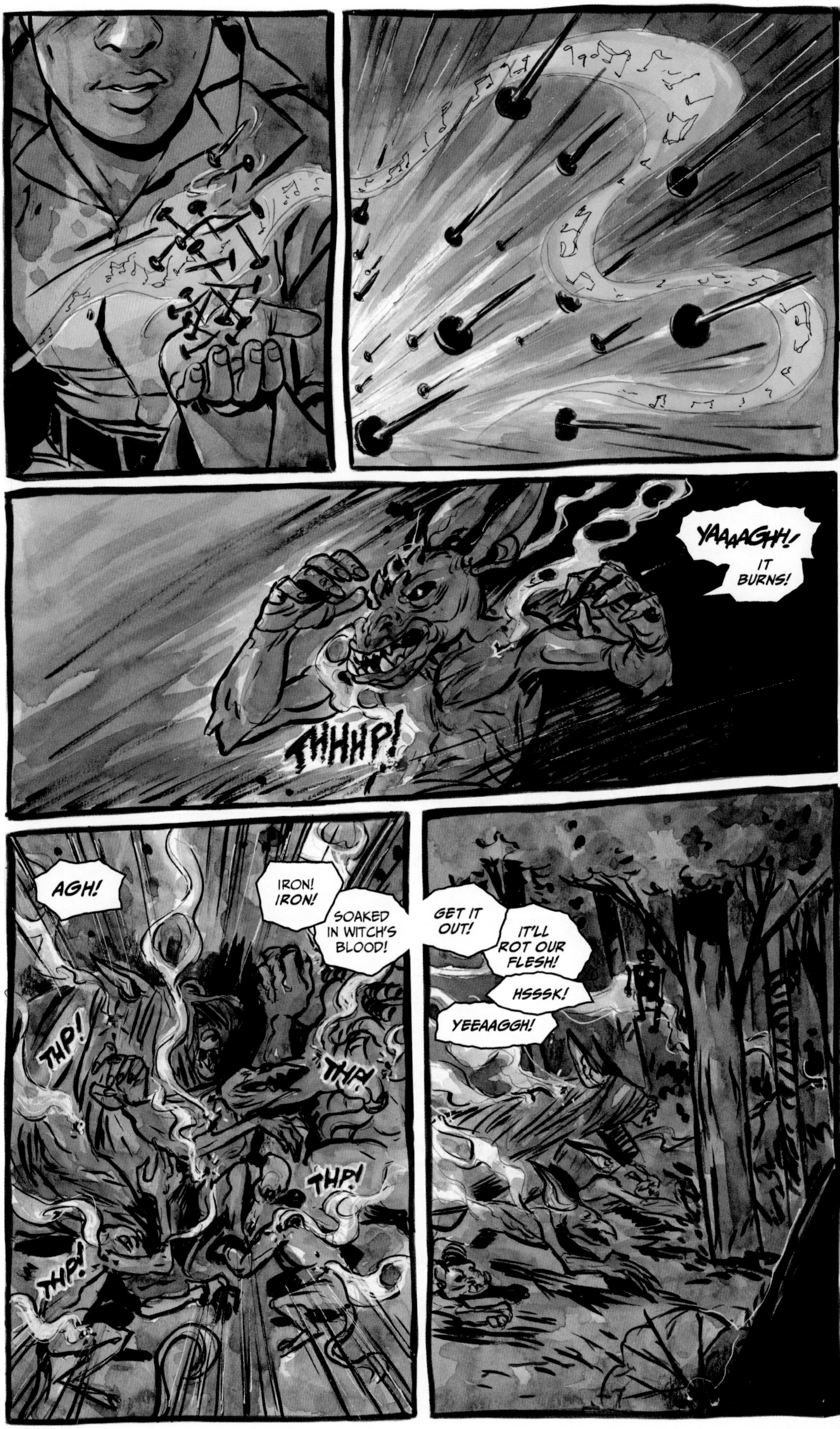
YAAAAGH! IT BURNS!
THHHP!
AGH!
IRON! IRON!
SOAKED IN WITCH'S BLOOD!
THP!
THP!
THP!
THP!
GET IT OUT!
IT'LL ROT OUR FLESH!
HSSSK!
YEEAAGGH!

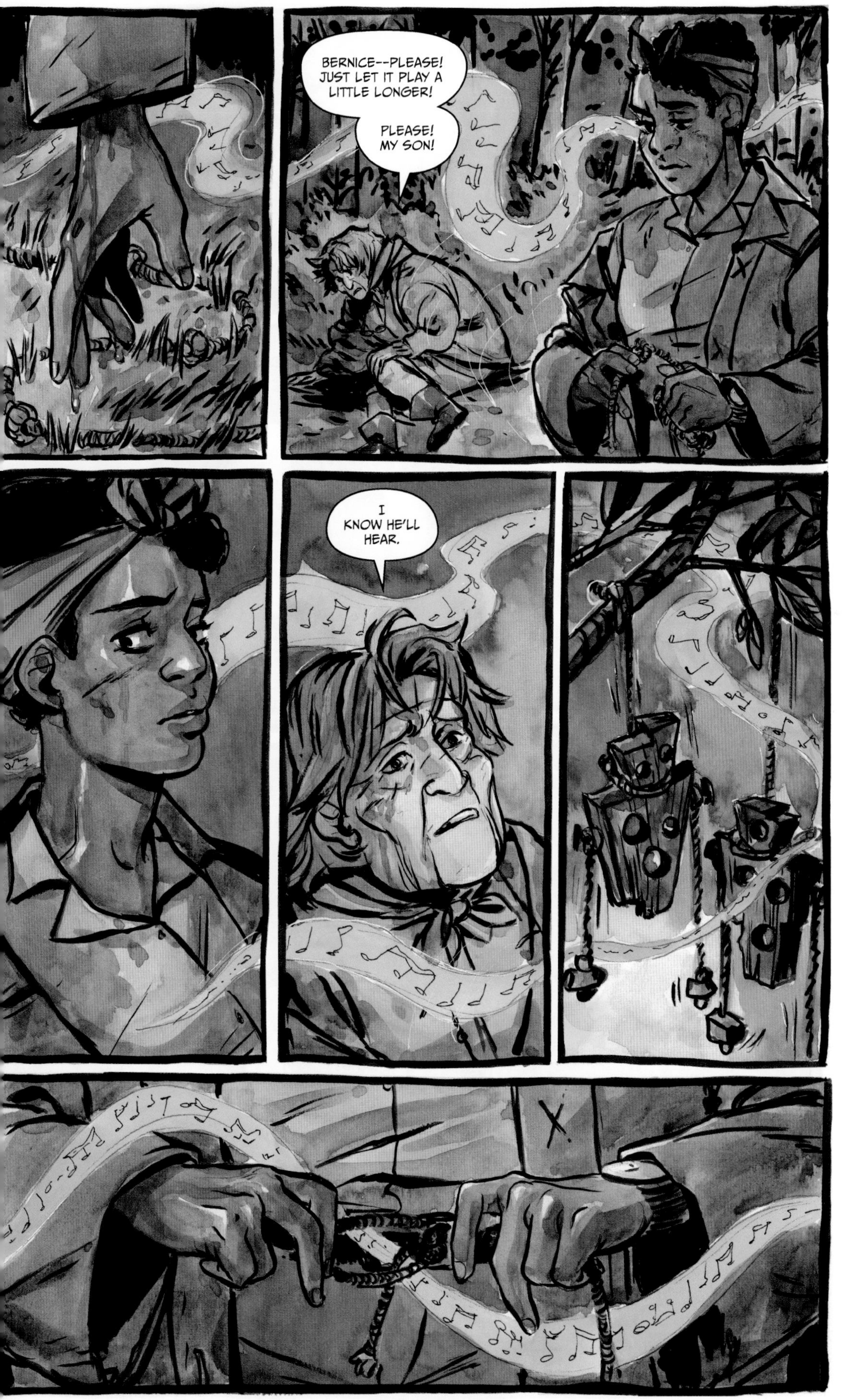
BERNICE--PLEASE! JUST LET IT PLAY A LITTLE LONGER!
PLEASE! MY SON!
I KNOW HE'LL HEAR.

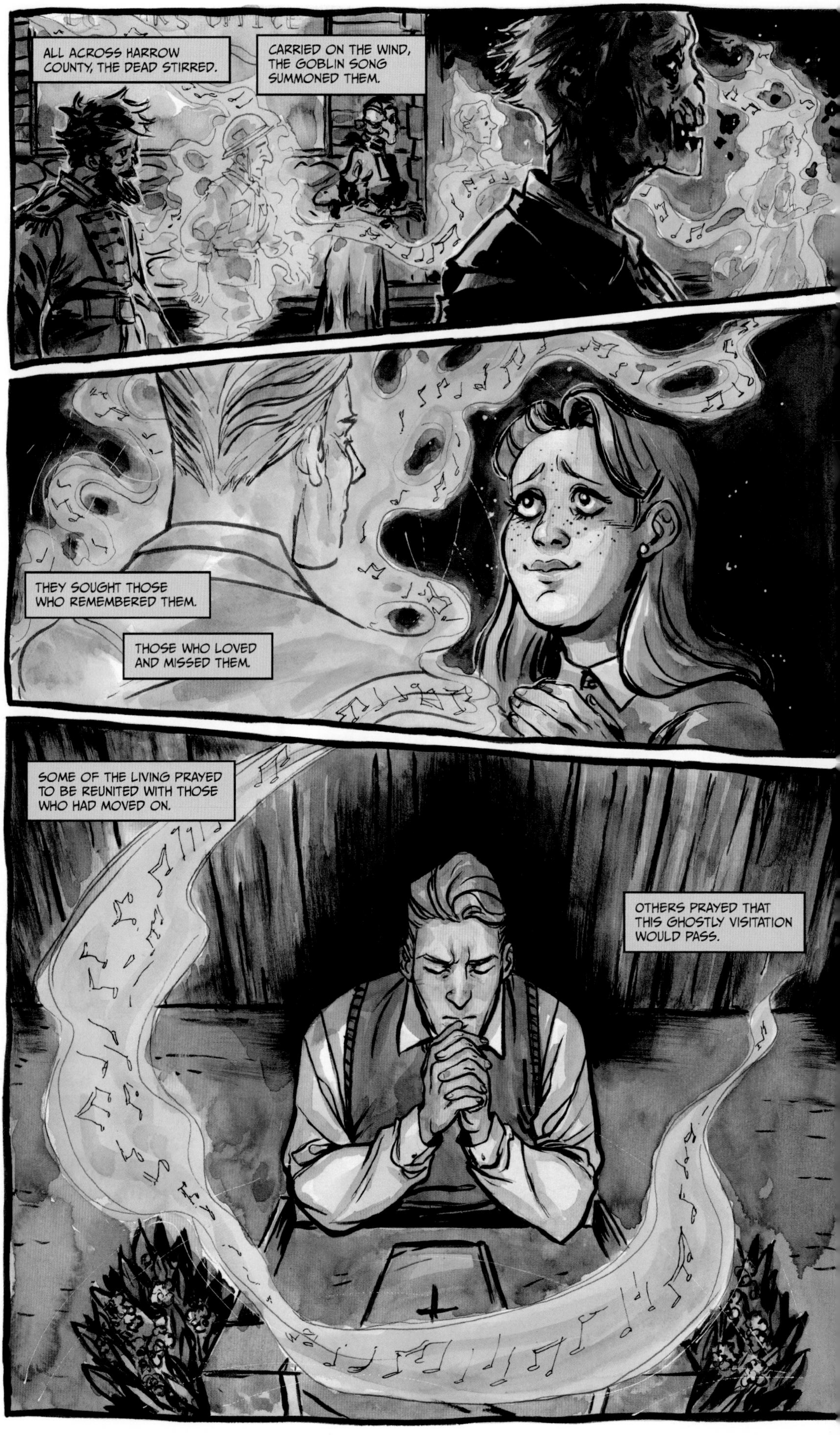
ALL ACROSS HARROW COUNTY, THE DEAD STIRRED.
CARRIED ON THE WIND, THE GOBLIN SONG SUMMONED THEM.
THEY SOUGHT THOSE WHO REMEMBERED THEM.
THOSE WHO LOVED AND MISSED THEM.
SOME OF THE LIVING PRAYED TO BE REUNITED WITH THOSE WHO HAD MOVED ON.
OTHERS PRAYED THAT THIS GHOSTLY VISITATION WOULD PASS.

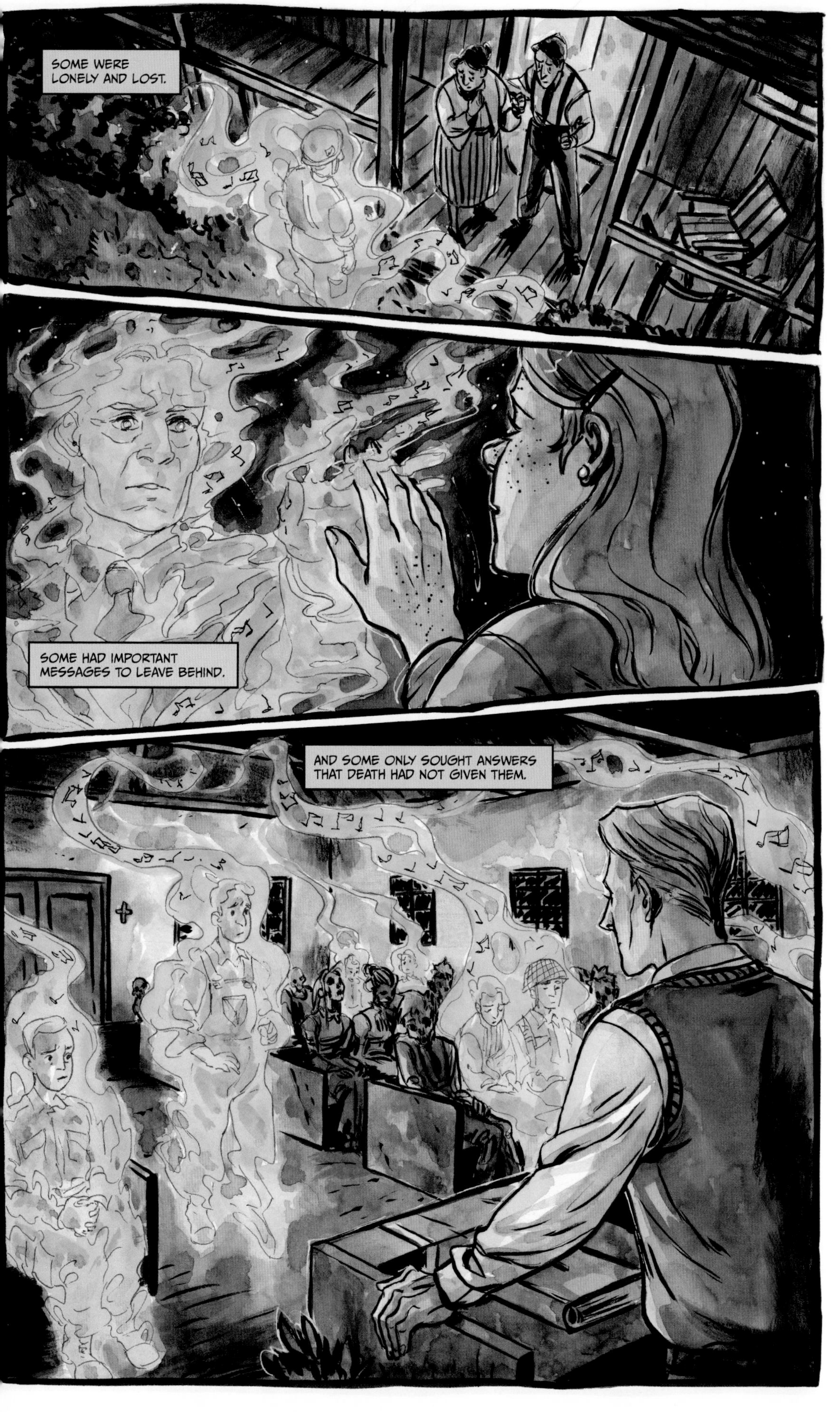
SOME WERE LONELY AND LOST.
SOME HAD IMPORTANT MESSAGES TO LEAVE BEHIND.
AND SOME ONLY SOUGHT ANSWERS THAT DEATH HAD NOT GIVEN THEM.

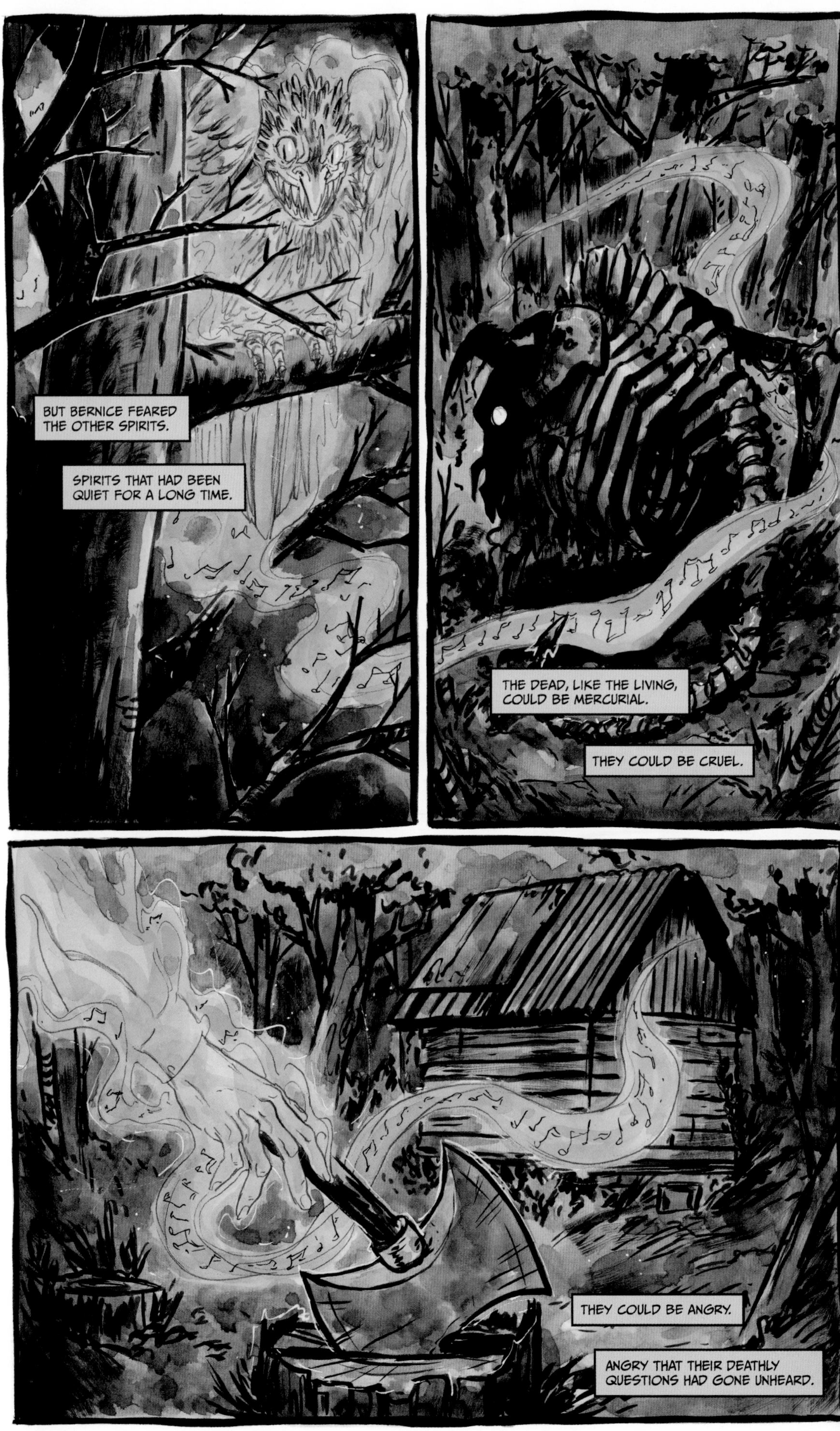
BUT BERNICE FEARED THE OTHER SPIRITS.
SPIRITS THAT HAD BEEN QUIET FOR A LONG TIME.
THE DEAD, LIKE THE LIVING, COULD BE MERCURIAL.
THEY COULD BE CRUEL.
THEY COULD BE ANGRY.
ANGRY THAT THEIR DEATHLY QUESTIONS HAD GONE UNHEARD.

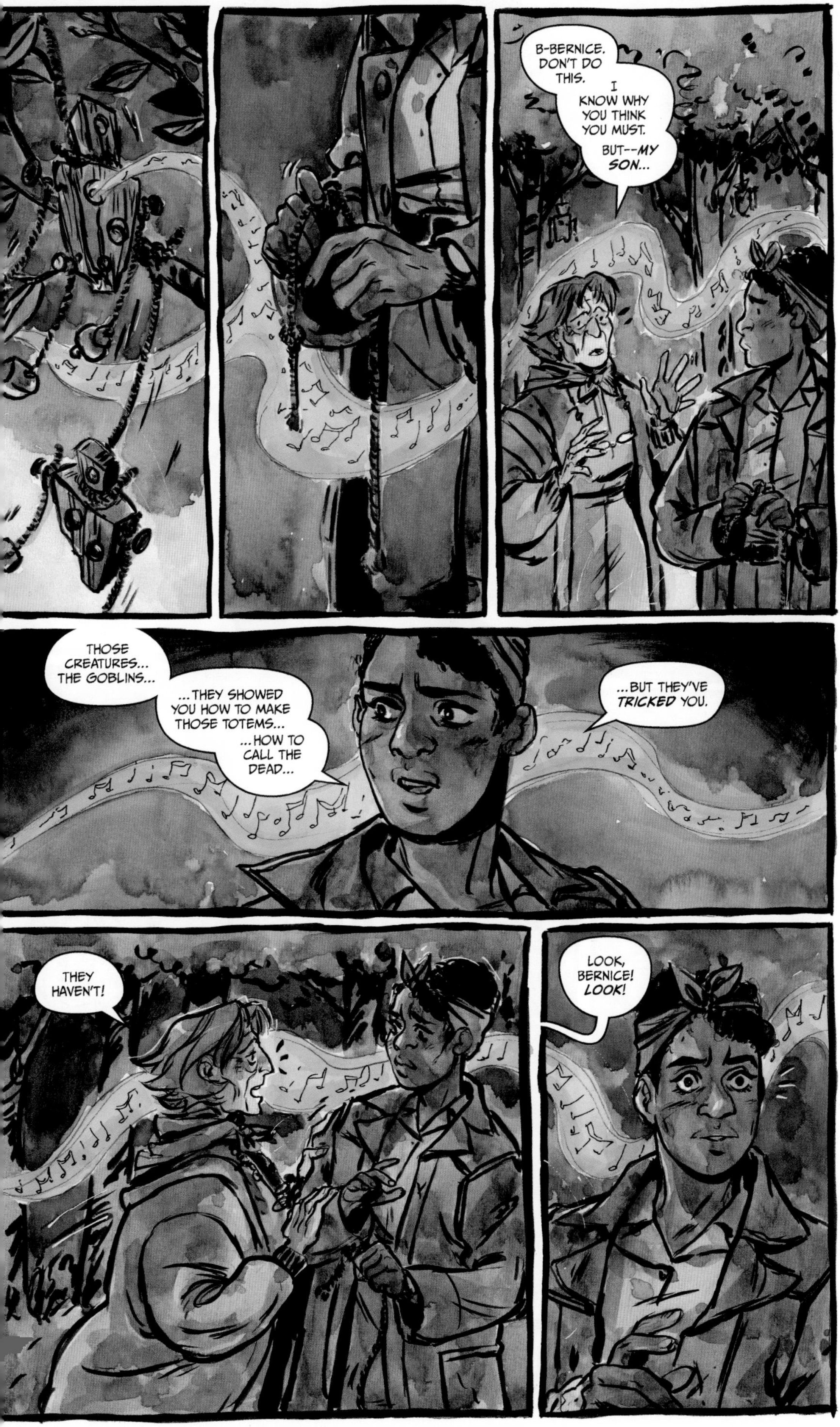
B-BERNICE. DON'T DO THIS.
I KNOW WHY YOU THINK YOU MUST.
BUT--*MY SON*...
THOSE CREATURES... THE GOBLINS...
...THEY SHOWED YOU HOW TO MAKE THOSE TOTEMS...
...HOW TO CALL THE DEAD...
...BUT THEY'VE *TRICKED* YOU.
THEY HAVEN'T!
LOOK, BERNICE! *LOOK!*

THERE ARE SO MANY OF THEM!

THEY'VE HEARD THE SONG!

THEY'RE SEEKING OUT THEIR LOVED ONES!

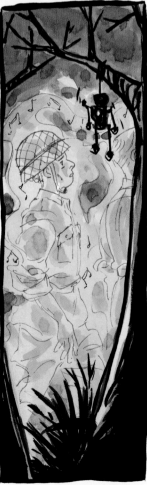

DO YOU THINK--?

COULD GERALD BE AMONG THEM?

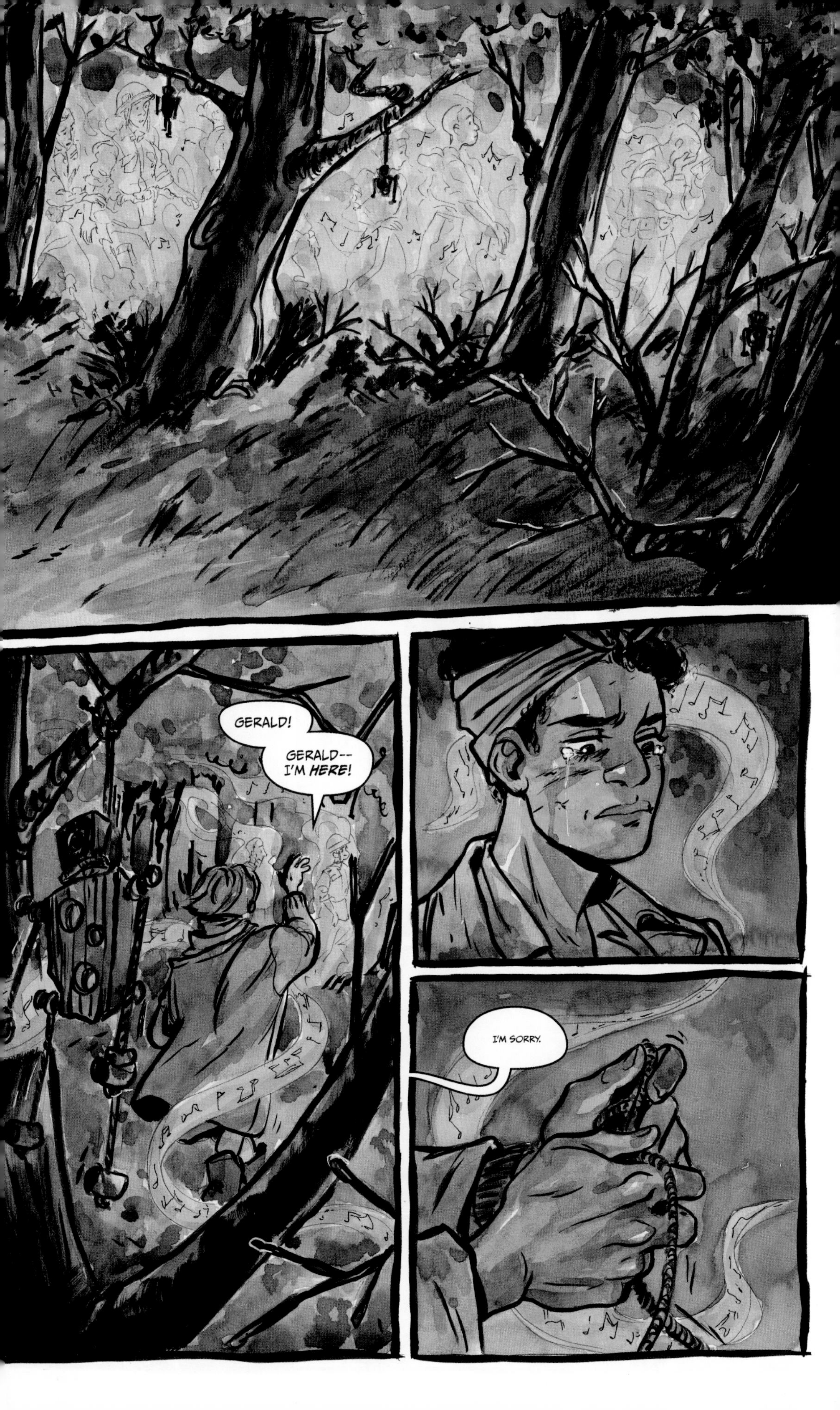
GERALD!
GERALD-- I'M HERE!
I'M SORRY.

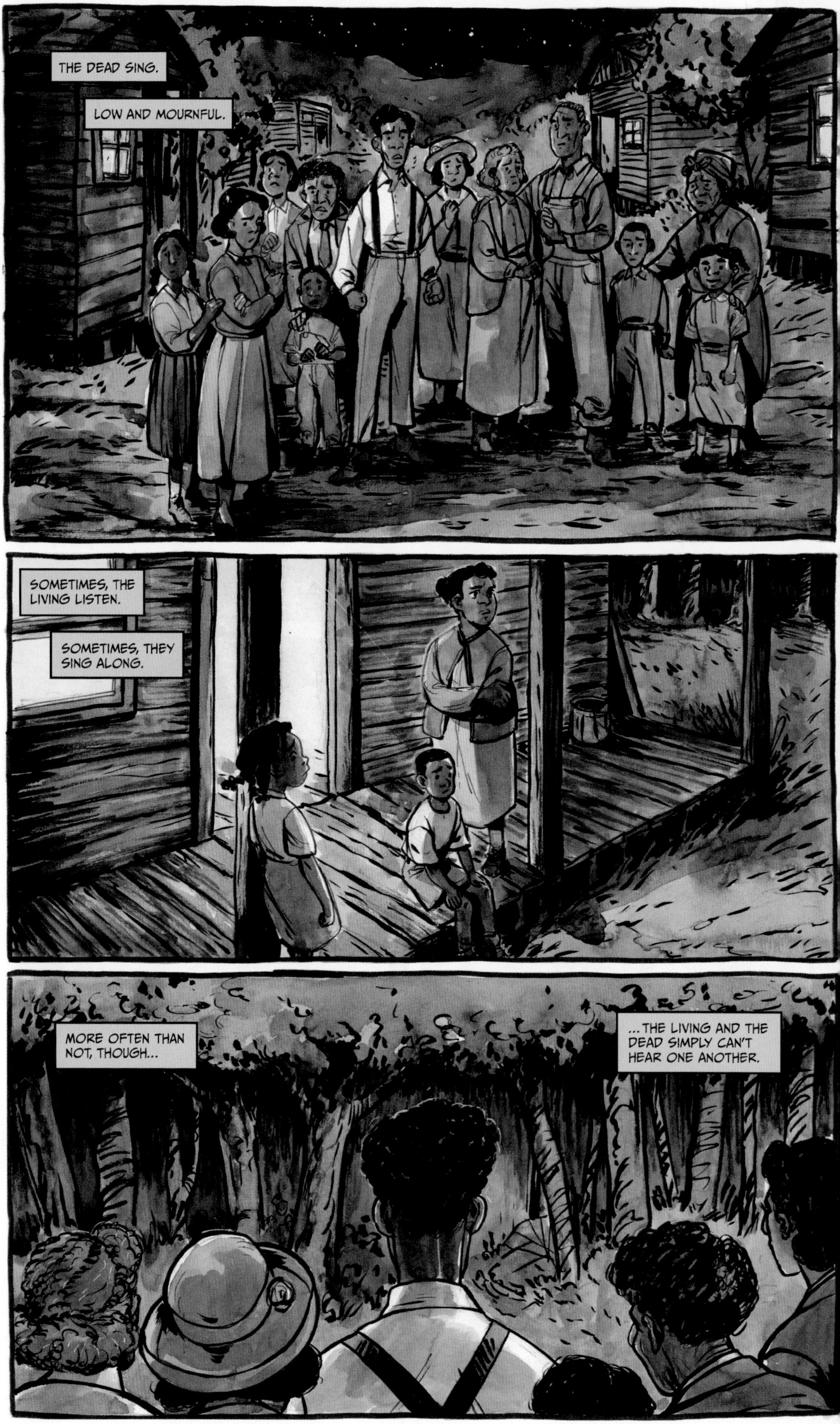
THE DEAD SING.
LOW AND MOURNFUL.
SOMETIMES, THE LIVING LISTEN.
SOMETIMES, THEY SING ALONG.
MORE OFTEN THAN NOT, THOUGH...
...THE LIVING AND THE DEAD SIMPLY CAN'T HEAR ONE ANOTHER.

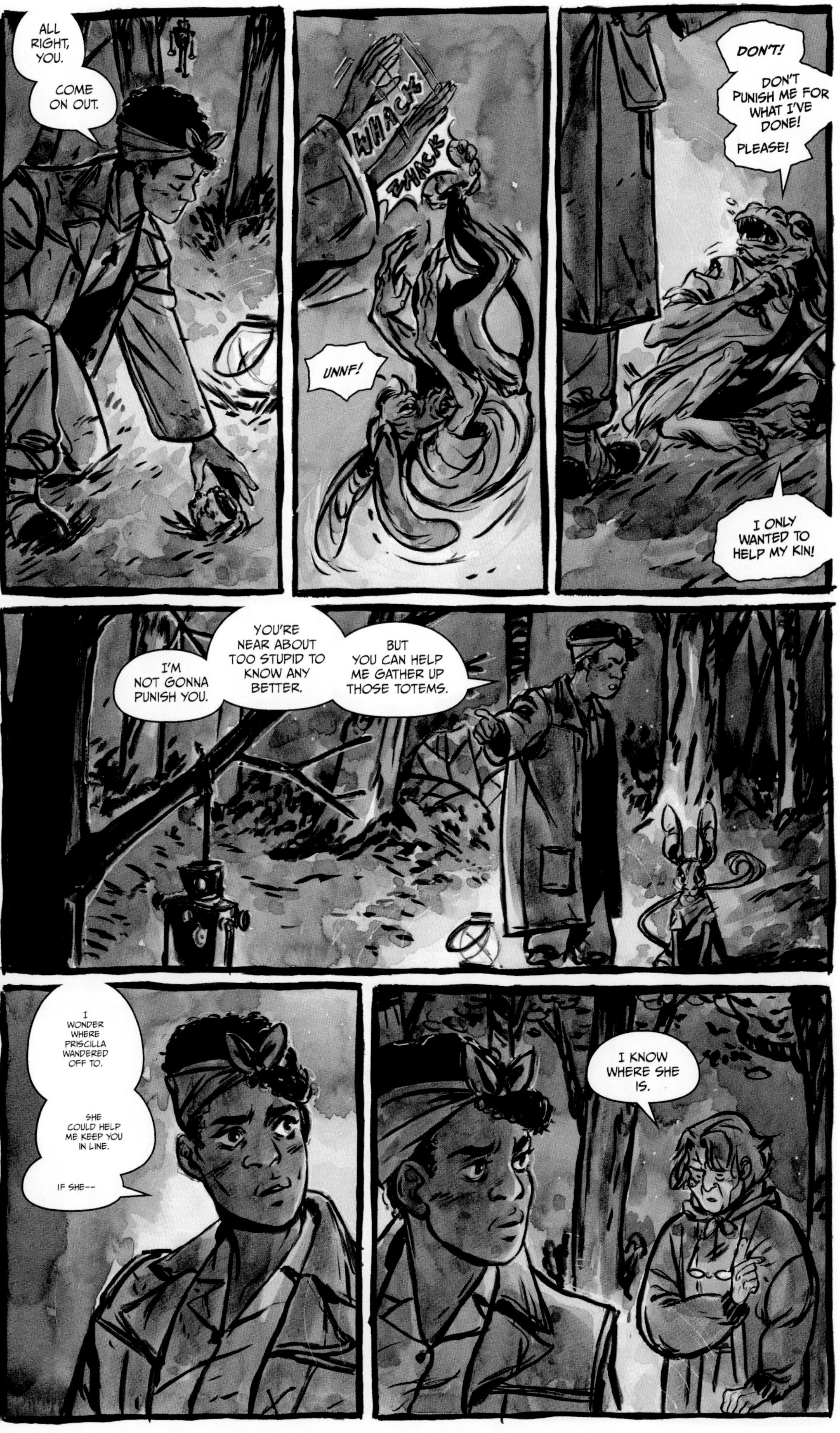
ALL RIGHT, YOU.
COME ON OUT.
WHACK
WHACK
UNNF!
DON'T!
DON'T PUNISH ME FOR WHAT I'VE DONE!
PLEASE!
I ONLY WANTED TO HELP MY KIN!
I'M NOT GONNA PUNISH YOU.
YOU'RE NEAR ABOUT TOO STUPID TO KNOW ANY BETTER.
BUT YOU CAN HELP ME GATHER UP THOSE TOTEMS.
I WONDER WHERE PRISCILLA WANDERED OFF TO.
SHE COULD HELP ME KEEP YOU IN LINE.
IF SHE--
I KNOW WHERE SHE IS.

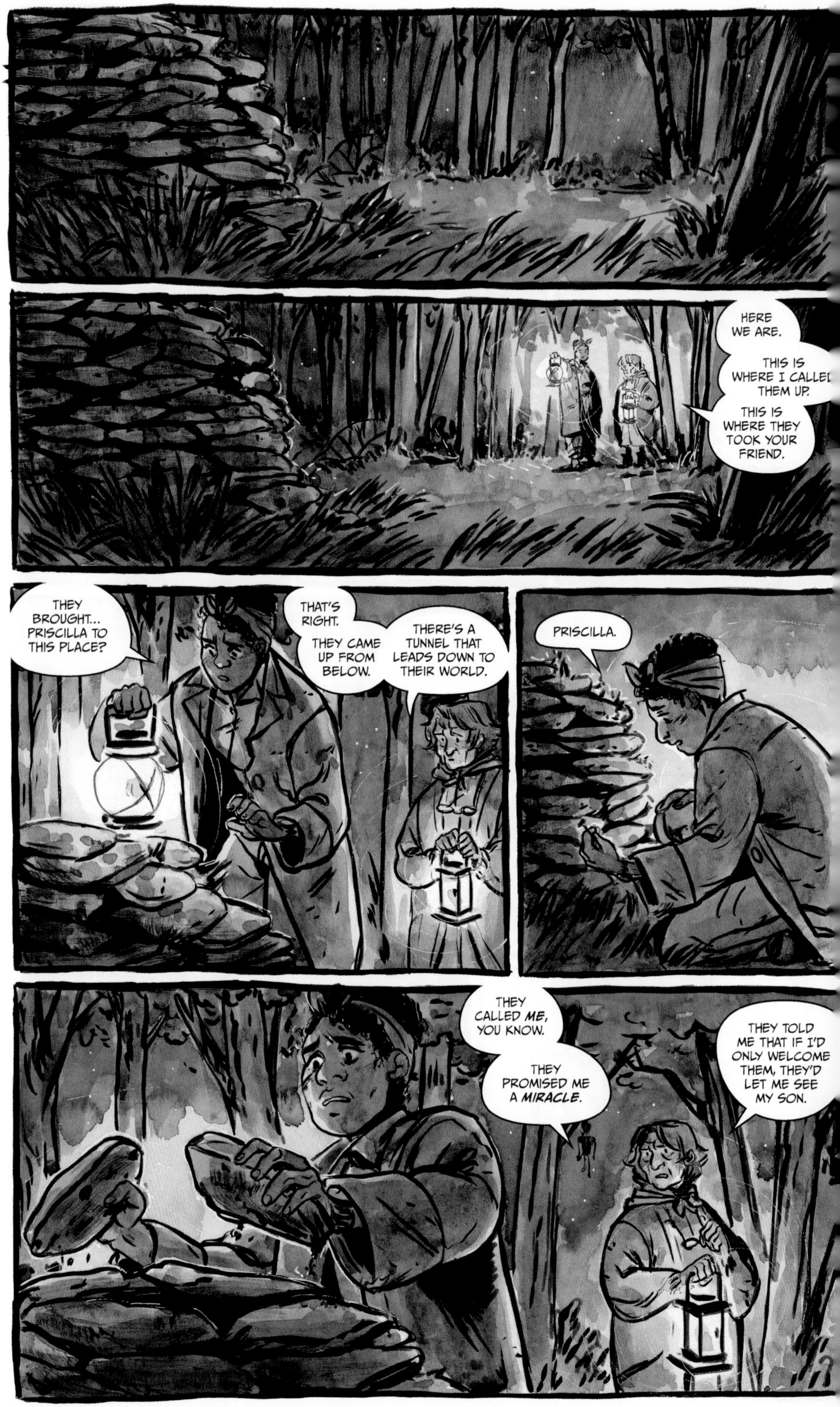
HERE WE ARE.
THIS IS WHERE I CALLED THEM UP.
THIS IS WHERE THEY TOOK YOUR FRIEND.
THEY BROUGHT... PRISCILLA TO THIS PLACE?
THAT'S RIGHT.
THEY CAME UP FROM BELOW.
THERE'S A TUNNEL THAT LEADS DOWN TO THEIR WORLD.
PRISCILLA.
THEY CALLED *ME*, YOU KNOW.
THEY PROMISED ME A *MIRACLE*.
THEY TOLD ME THAT IF I'D ONLY WELCOME THEM, THEY'D LET ME SEE MY SON.

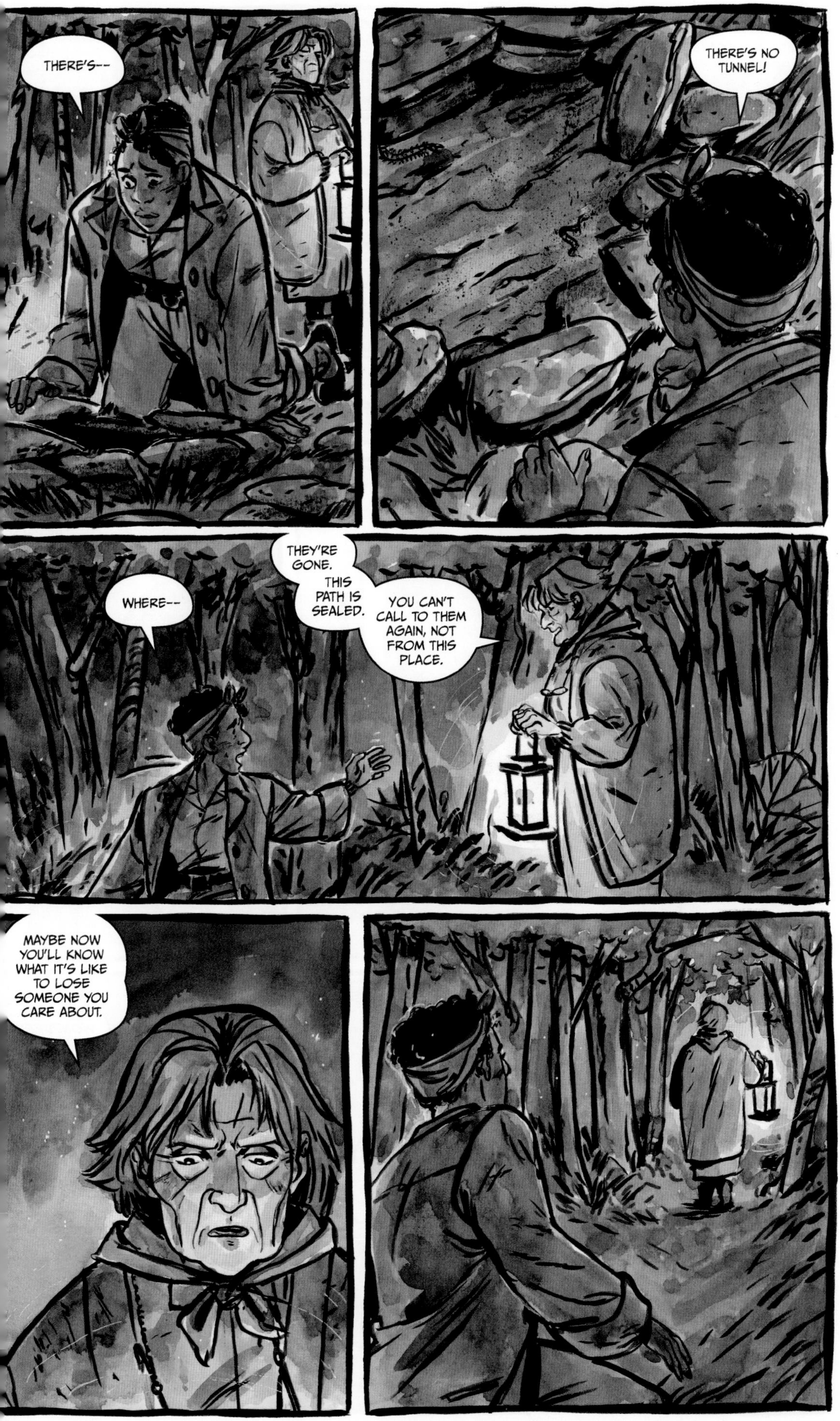
THERE'S--
THERE'S NO TUNNEL!
WHERE--
THEY'RE GONE.
THIS PATH IS SEALED.
YOU CAN'T CALL TO THEM AGAIN, NOT FROM THIS PLACE.
MAYBE NOW YOU'LL KNOW WHAT IT'S LIKE TO LOSE SOMEONE YOU CARE ABOUT.

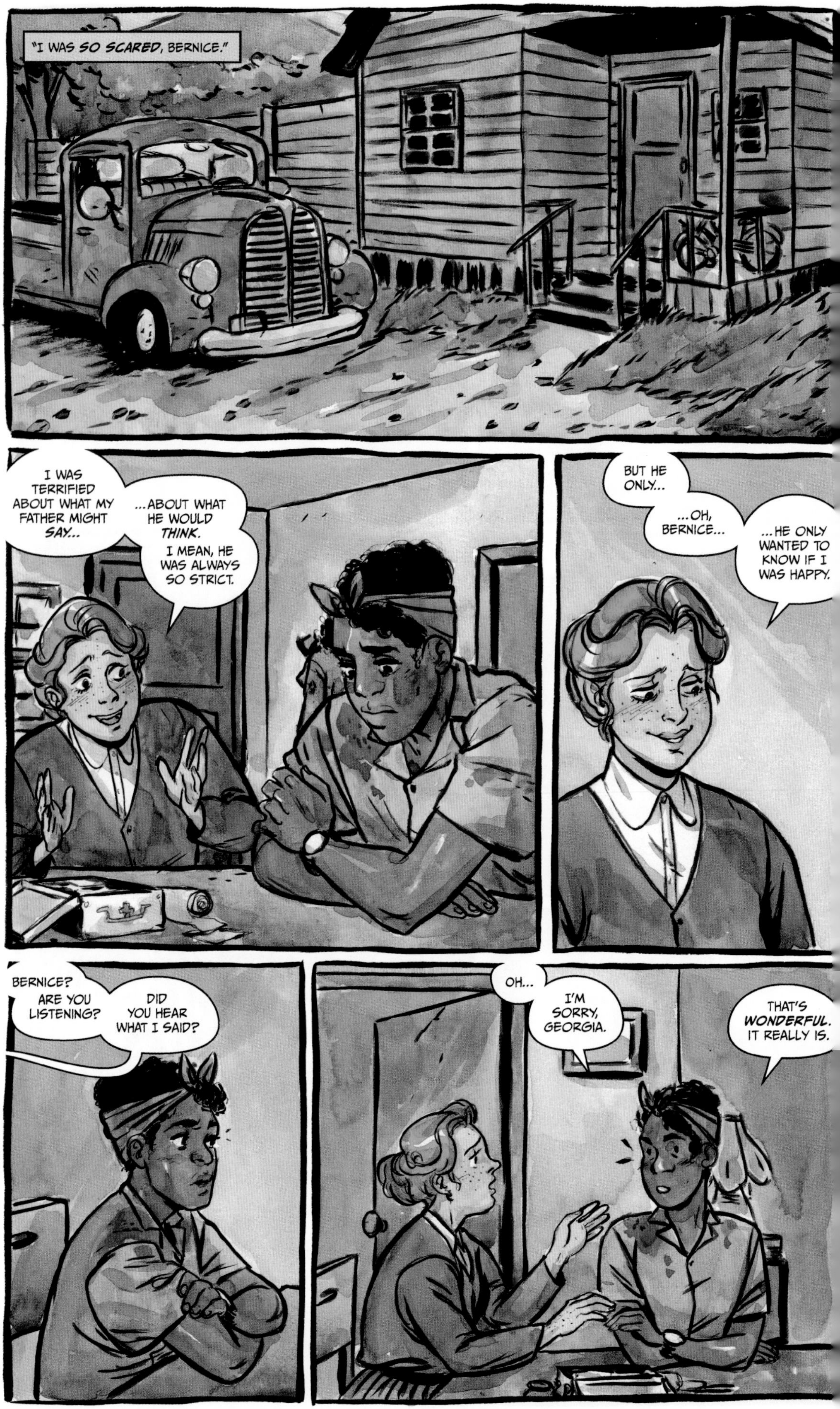
"I WAS SO SCARED, BERNICE."
I WAS TERRIFIED ABOUT WHAT MY FATHER MIGHT SAY...
...ABOUT WHAT HE WOULD THINK.
I MEAN, HE WAS ALWAYS SO STRICT.
BUT HE ONLY...
...OH, BERNICE...
...HE ONLY WANTED TO KNOW IF I WAS HAPPY.
BERNICE? ARE YOU LISTENING?
DID YOU HEAR WHAT I SAID?
OH...
I'M SORRY, GEORGIA.
THAT'S WONDERFUL. IT REALLY IS.

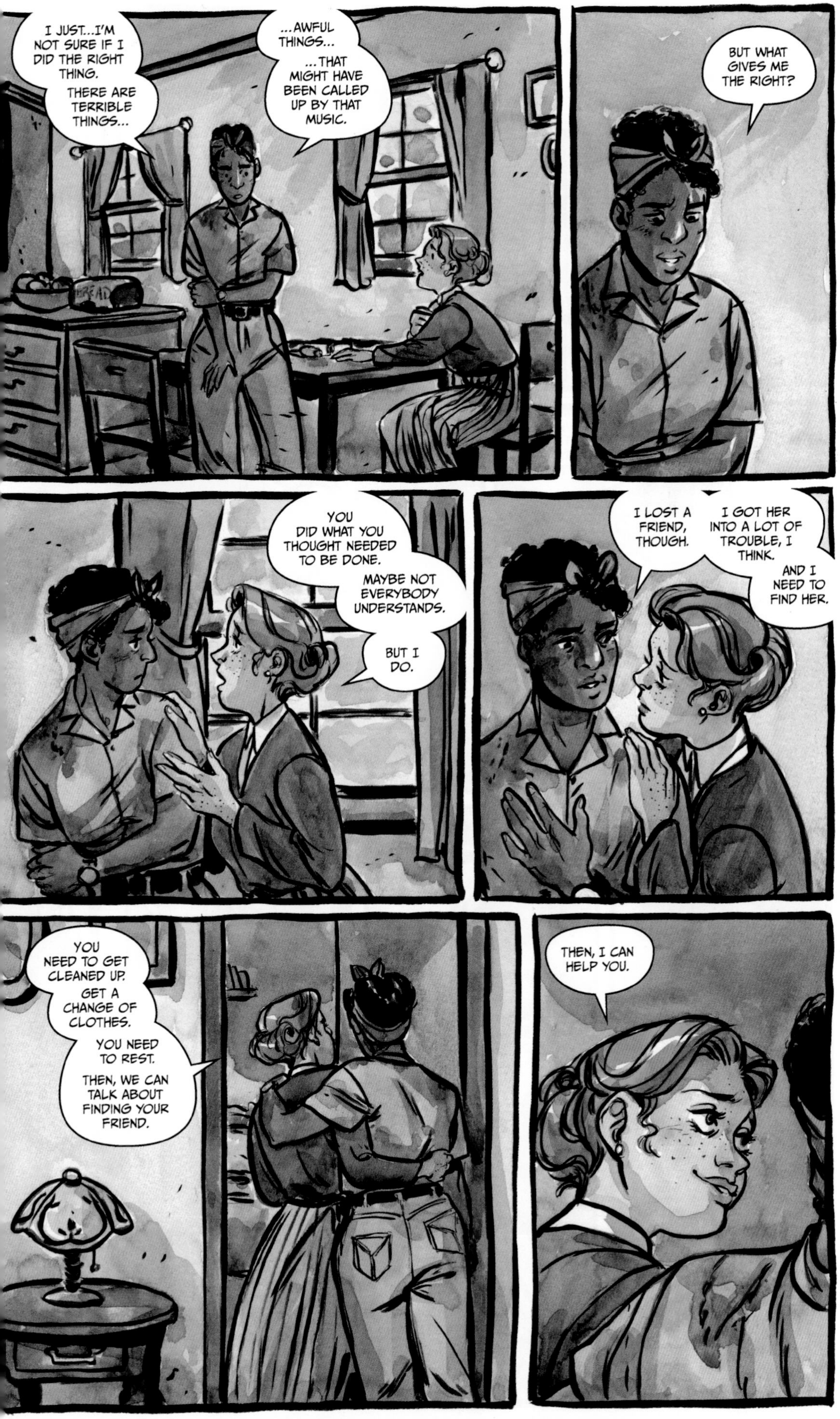
I JUST...I'M NOT SURE IF I DID THE RIGHT THING.
THERE ARE TERRIBLE THINGS...
...AWFUL THINGS...
...THAT MIGHT HAVE BEEN CALLED UP BY THAT MUSIC.
BUT WHAT GIVES ME THE RIGHT?
YOU DID WHAT YOU THOUGHT NEEDED TO BE DONE.
MAYBE NOT EVERYBODY UNDERSTANDS.
BUT I DO.
I LOST A FRIEND, THOUGH.
I GOT HER INTO A LOT OF TROUBLE, I THINK.
AND I NEED TO FIND HER.
YOU NEED TO GET CLEANED UP.
GET A CHANGE OF CLOTHES.
YOU NEED TO REST.
THEN, WE CAN TALK ABOUT FINDING YOUR FRIEND.
THEN, I CAN HELP YOU.

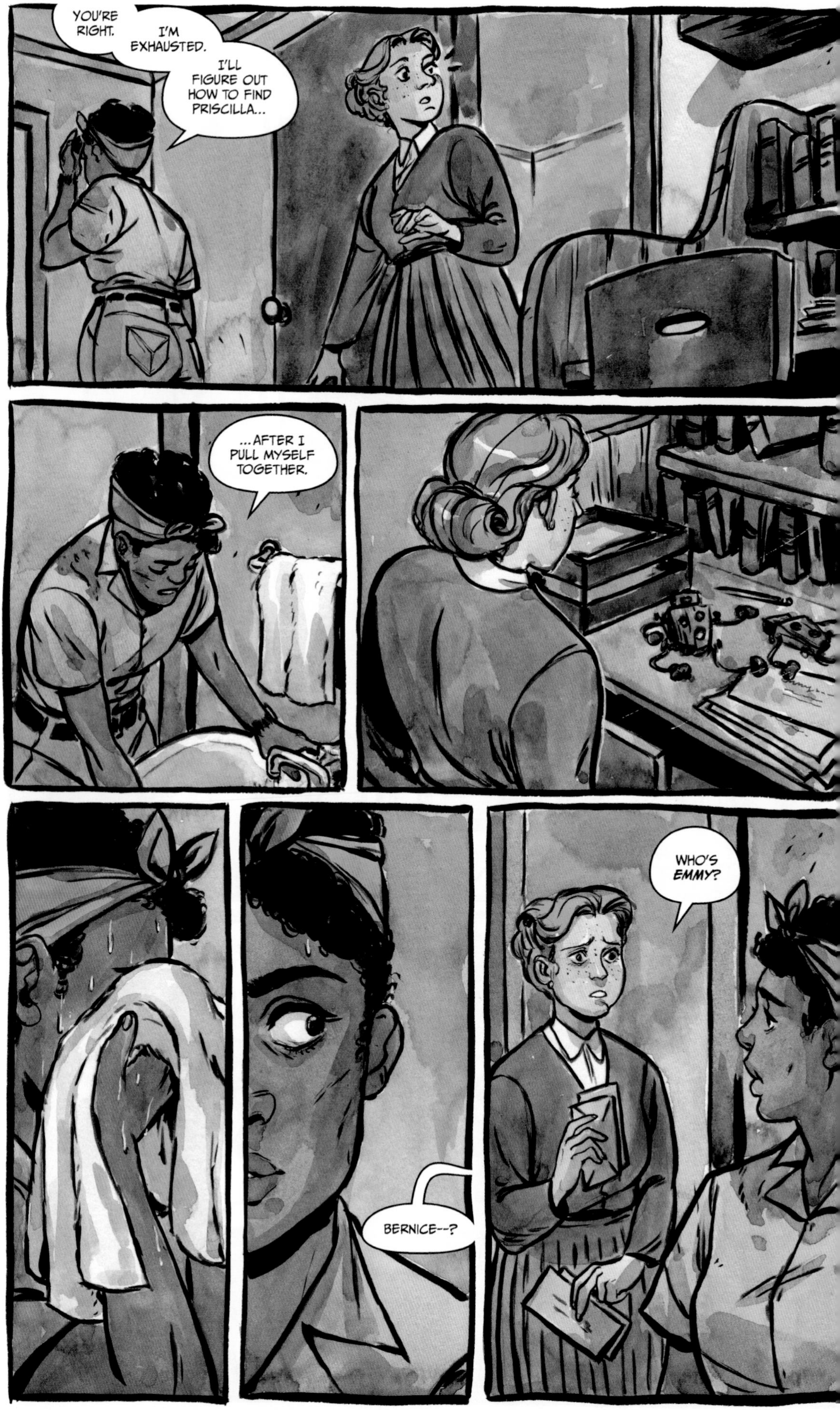
YOU'RE RIGHT.
I'M EXHAUSTED.
I'LL FIGURE OUT HOW TO FIND PRISCILLA...
...AFTER I PULL MYSELF TOGETHER.
BERNICE--?
WHO'S EMMY?

TALES FROM HARROW COUNTY SKETCHBOOK

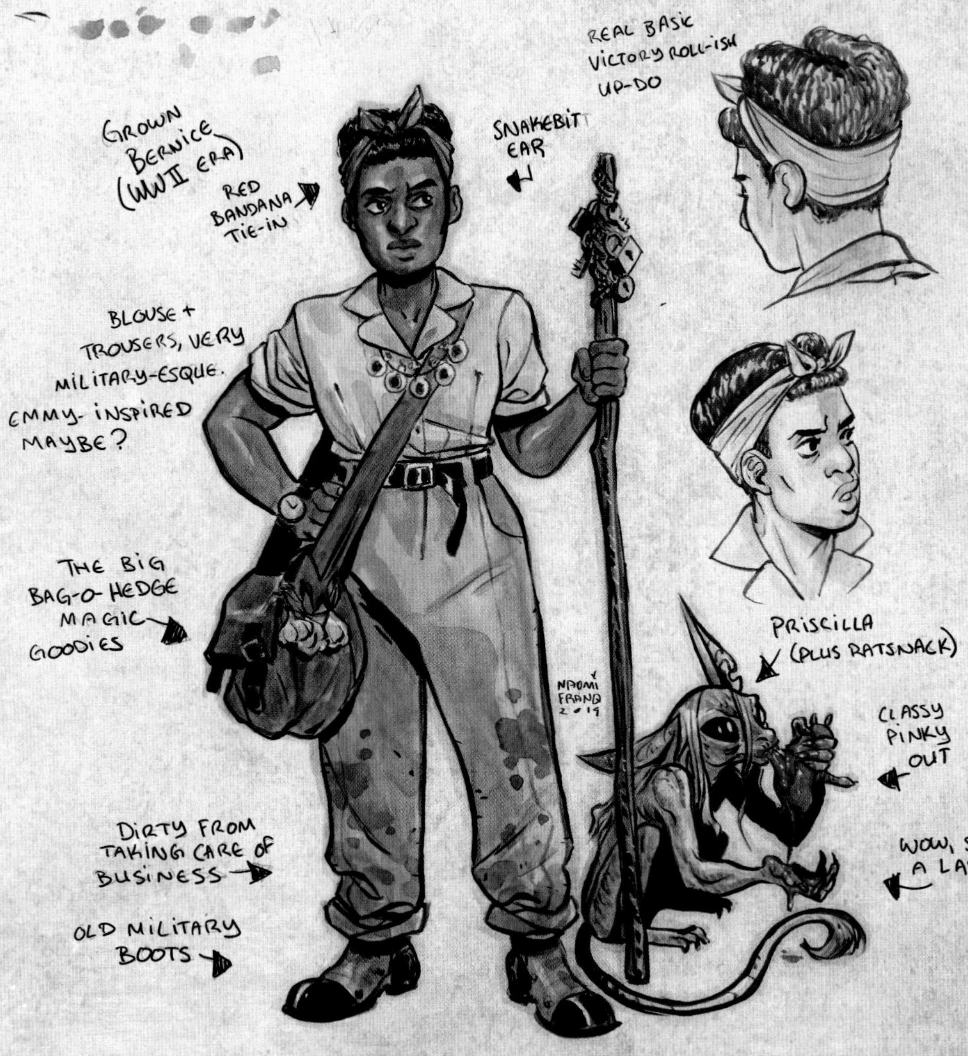

NOTES BY
NAOMI FRANQUIZ

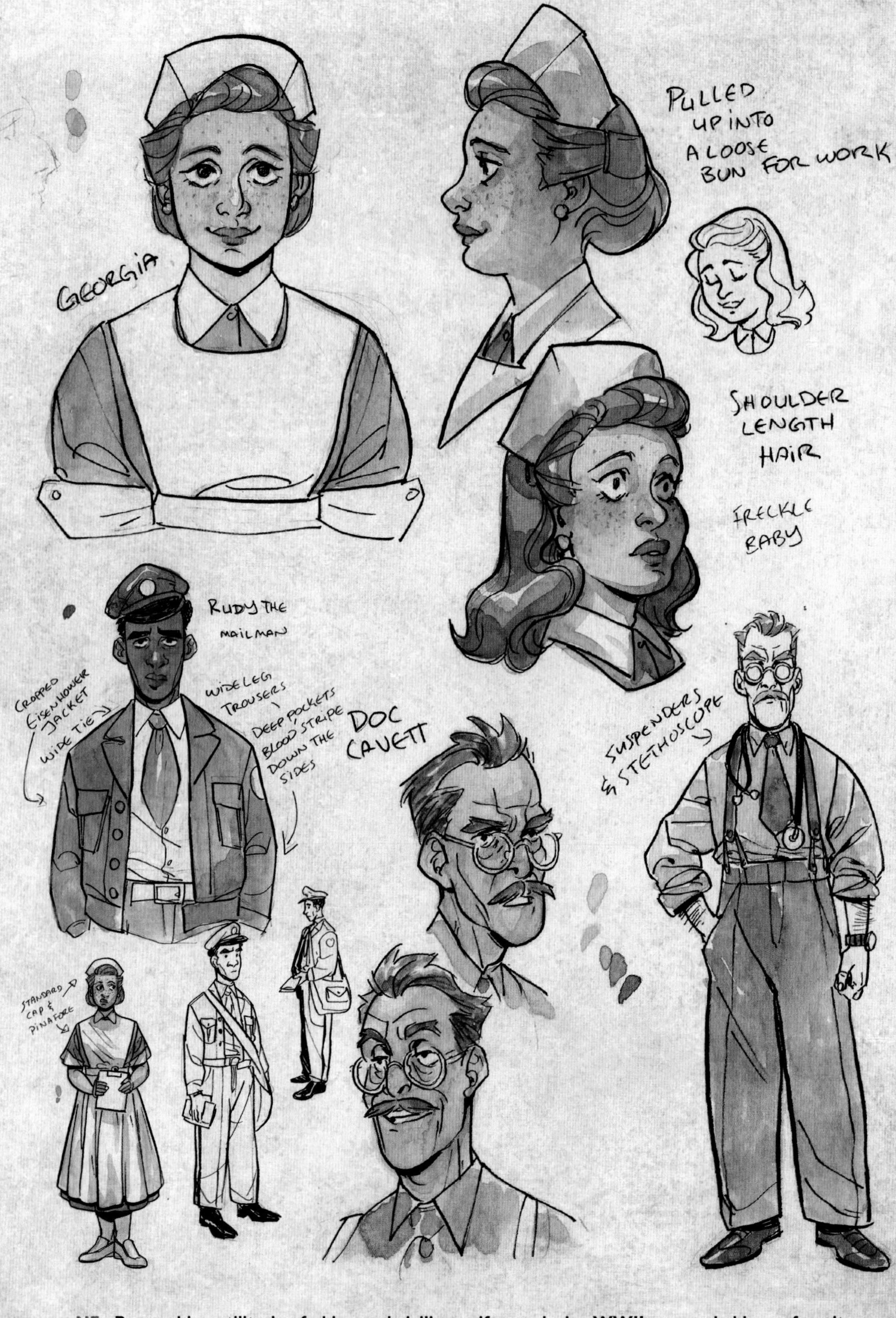
PULLED UP INTO A LOOSE BUN FOR WORK
GEORGIA
SHOULDER LENGTH HAIR
FRECKLE BABY
RUDY THE MAILMAN
CROPPED EISENHOWER JACKET
WIDE TIE
WIDE LEG TROUSERS
DEEP POCKETS BLOOD STRIPE DOWN THE SIDES
DOC CAVETT
SUSPENDERS & STETHOSCOPE
STANDARD CAP & PINAFORE

NF: Researching utilitarian fashion and civilian uniforms during WWII was probably my favorite part of these designs. Bernice wearing functional clothes, used men's coats, and old military boots is something I wanted most. She strikes me as the type to favor what works over what's aesthetic (except for a nice picnic date). Georgia's uniform is civilian but even then, all civilian uniforms were heavily military inspired.

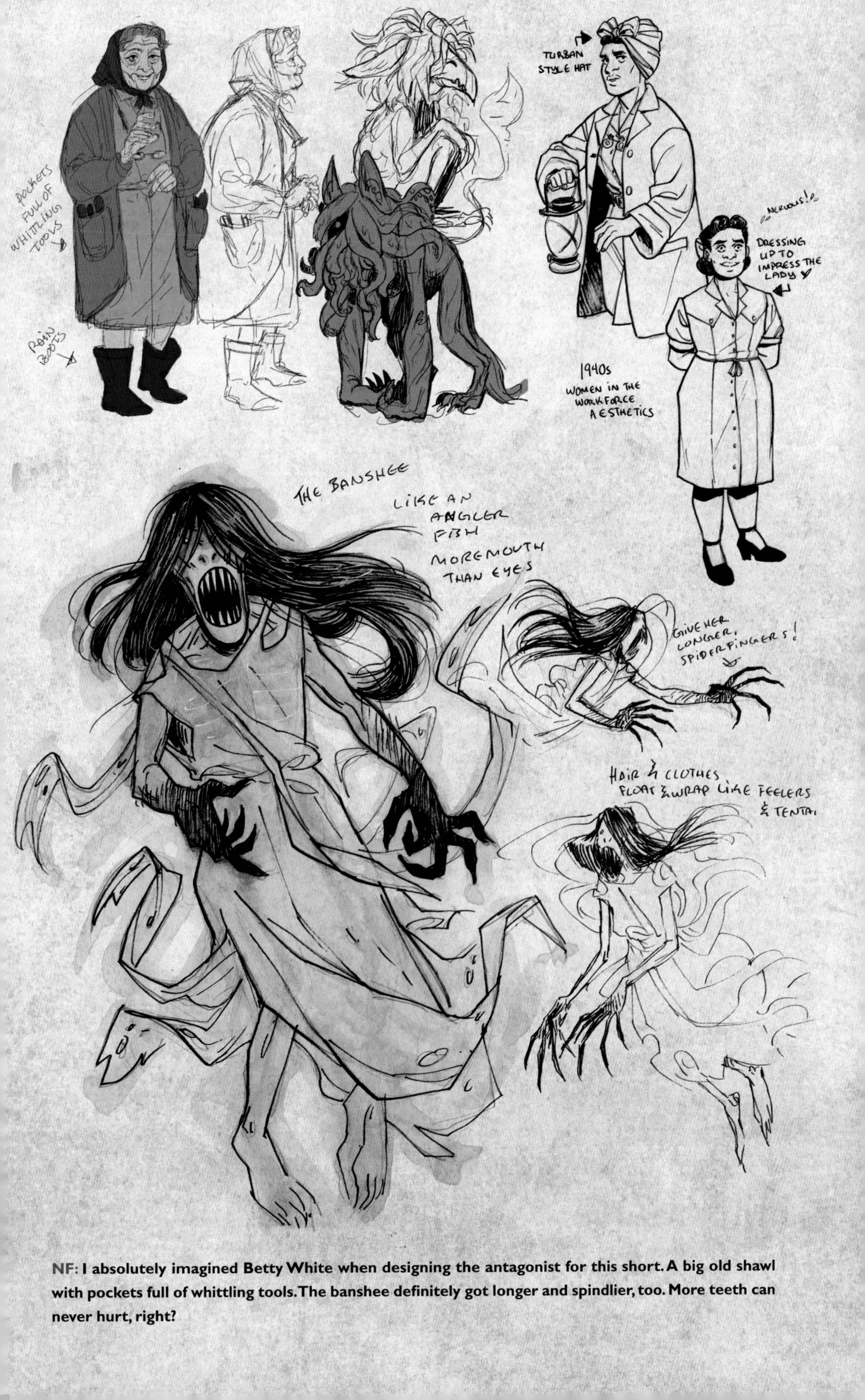
POCKETS FULL OF WHITTLING TOOLS
RAIN BOOTS
TURBAN STYLE HAT
NERVOUS!
DRESSING UP TO IMPRESS THE LADY
1940s WOMEN IN THE WORKFORCE AESTHETICS
THE BANSHEE
LIKE AN ANGLER FISH
MORE MOUTH THAN EYES
GIVE HER LONGER, SPIDERFINGERS!
HAIR & CLOTHES FLOAT & WRAP LIKE FEELERS & TENTA

NF: I absolutely imagined Betty White when designing the antagonist for this short. A big old shawl with pockets full of whittling tools. The banshee definitely got longer and spindlier, too. More teeth can never hurt, right?

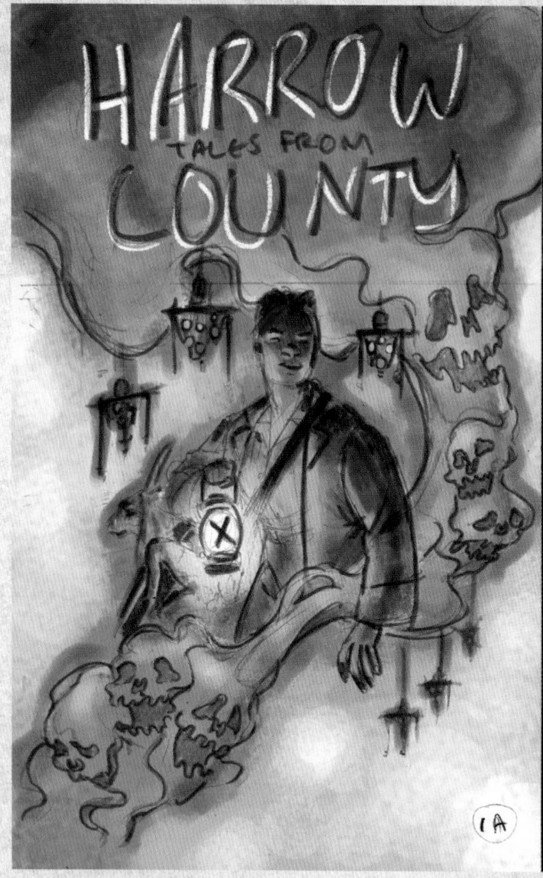
HARROW
TALES FROM
COUNTY
1A

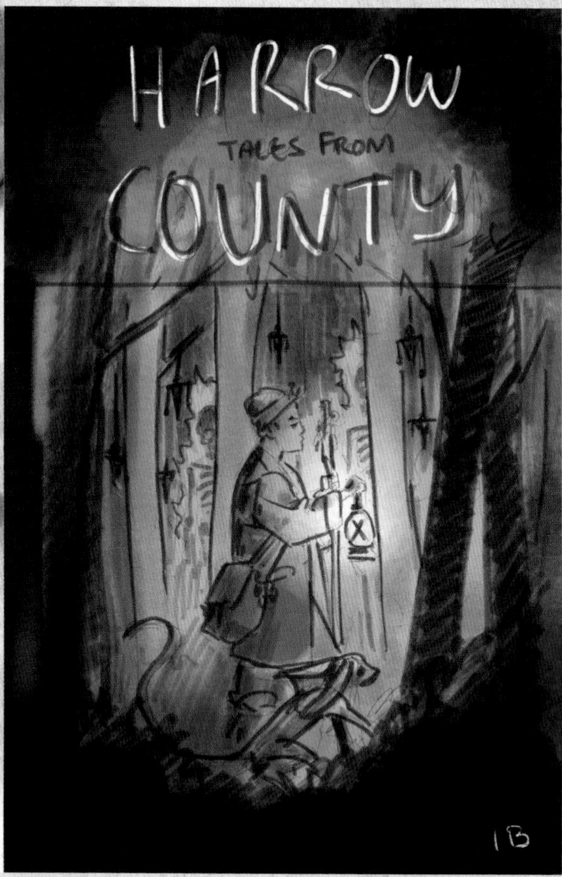
HARROW
TALES FROM
COUNTY
1B

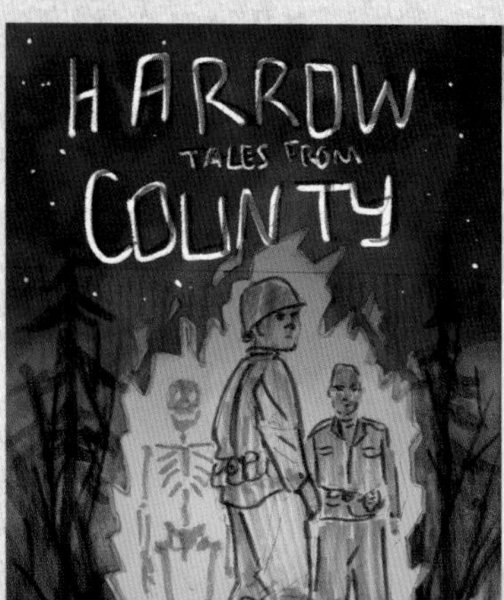
HARROW
TALES FROM
COUNTY

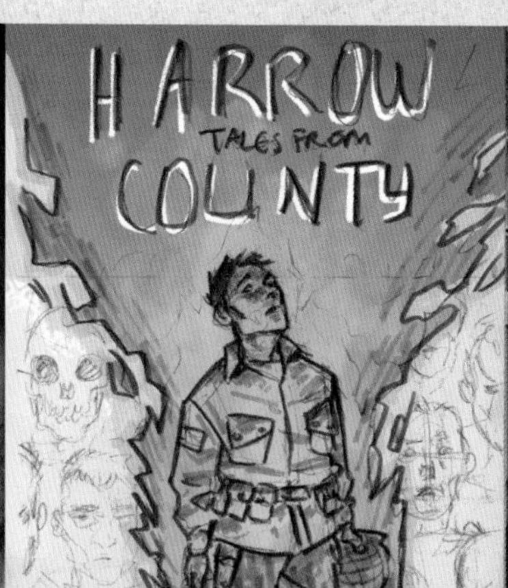
HARROW
TALES FROM
COUNTY
2B

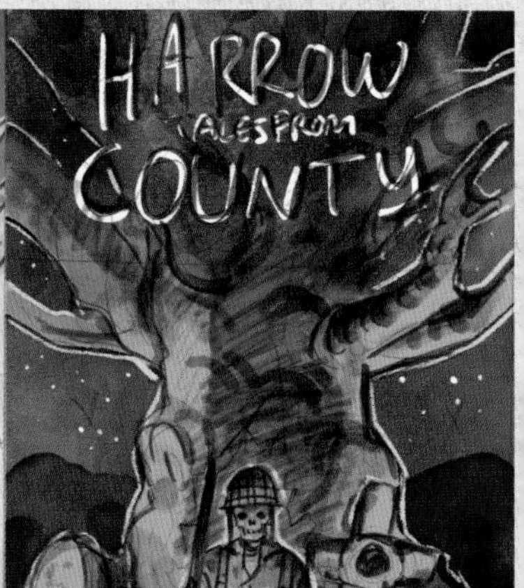
HARROW
TALES FROM
COUNTY

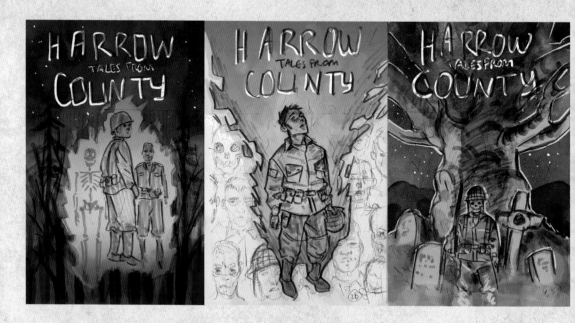

NF: With the first issue, I wanted to highlight Bernice and Priscilla for the start. You knew exactly who this story was gonna be about. I favored covers with light, textured backgrounds because it was reminiscent of *Saturday Evening Post* cover illustrations. It also felt like a good compositional contrast to Tyler's amazing covers, which are frequently really dark and black and ominous. Tonally, it has an eerie, fake veneer of something lighter, which I felt fit well with the home-front efforts during and after WWII.

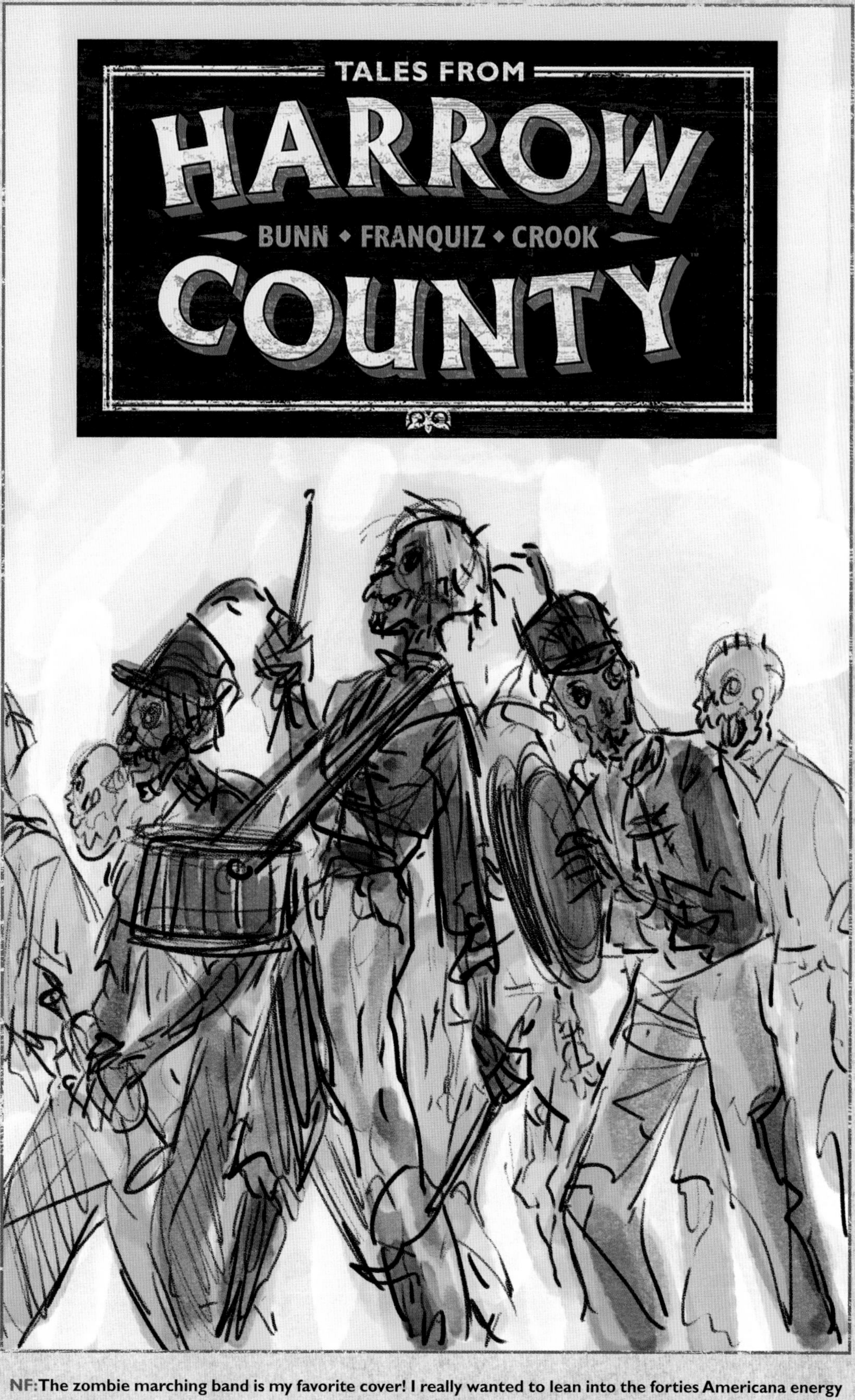
TALES FROM
HARROW
BUNN • FRANQUIZ • CROOK
COUNTY

NF: The zombie marching band is my favorite cover! I really wanted to lean into the forties Americana energy with a red, white, and blue marching band . . . of the undead. I love trumpet zombie. He plays a mean horn.

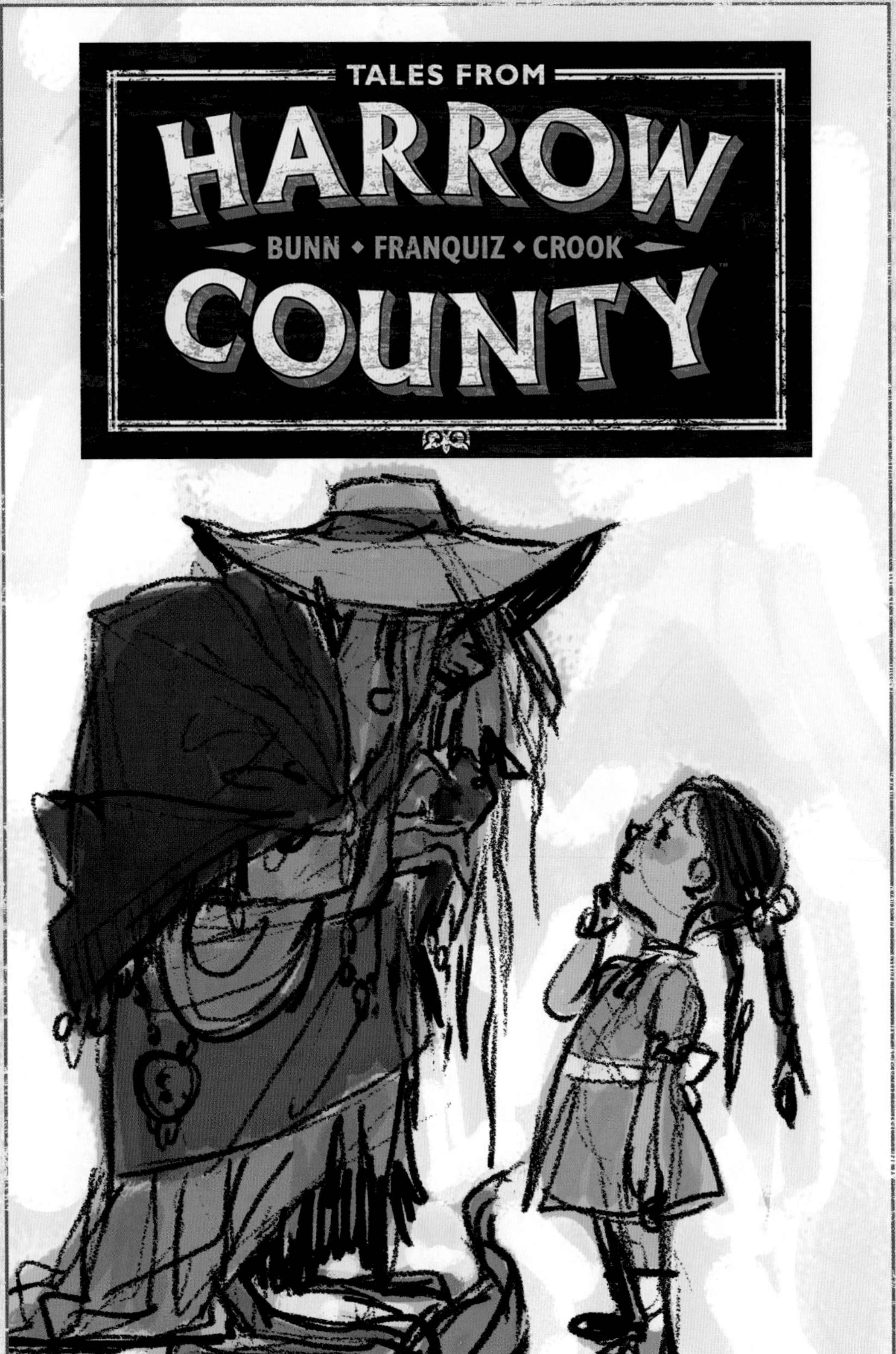

TALES FROM
HARROW
BUNN • FRANQUIZ • CROOK
COUNTY

NF: This wasn't one of my favorites, and I didn't end up choosing it. I didn't know yet who the final villain was, but I had an image of a goblin disguised as an old woman to trick humans. I just really like the goblins, honestly.

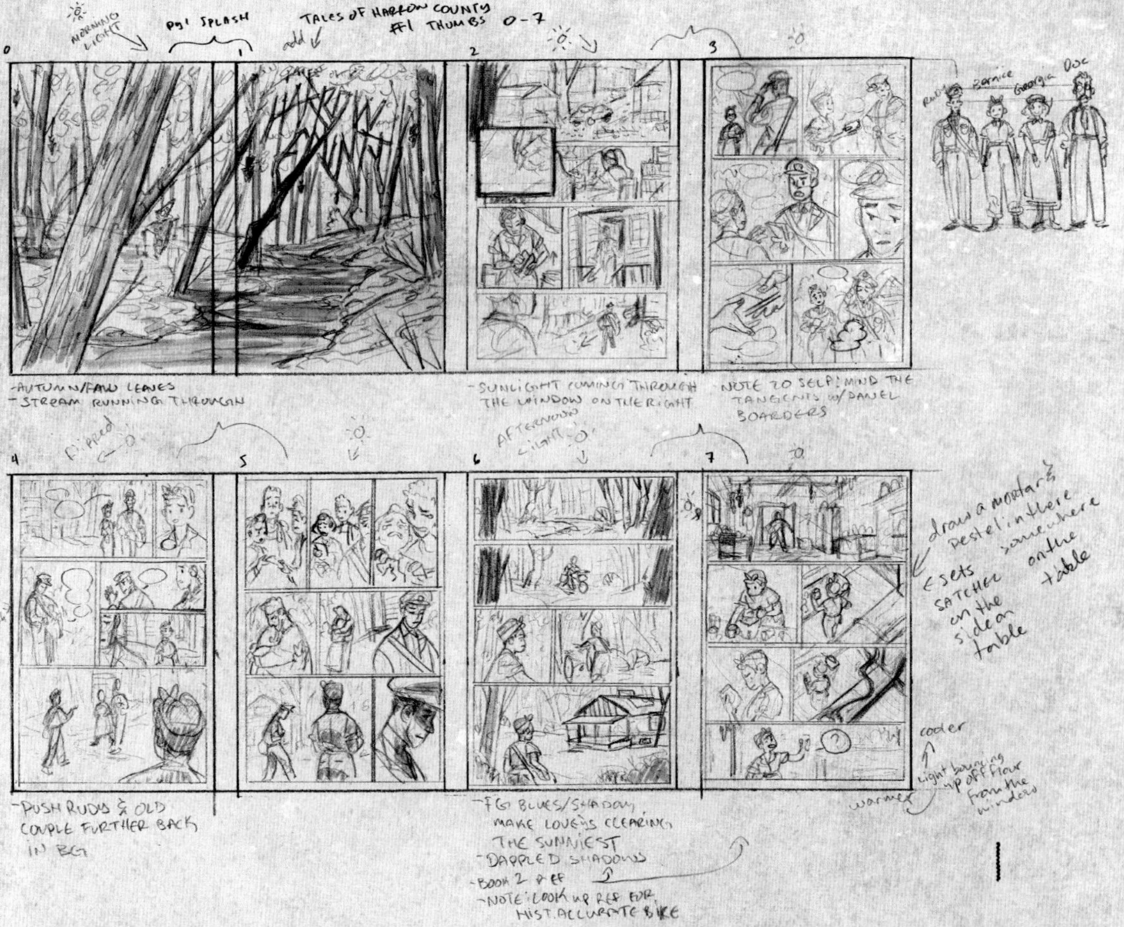
MORNING LIGHT
PG1 SPLASH
TALES OF HARROW COUNTY #1 THUMBS 0-7
add
Rudy Bernice Georgia Doc
-AUTUMN/FALL LEAVES
-STREAM RUNNING THROUGH
-SUNLIGHT COMING THROUGH THE WINDOW ON THE RIGHT
NOTE TO SELF: MIND THE TANGENTS W/ PANEL BOARDERS
flipped
AFTERNOON LIGHT
draw a mortar & pestel in there somewhere on the table
sets satchel on the side on table
cooler
light bouncing up off floor from the windows
warmer
-PUSH RUDY & OLD COUPLE FURTHER BACK IN BG
-FG BLUES/SHADOW MAKE LOVE'S CLEARING THE SUNNIEST
-DAPPLED SHADOWS
-BOOK 2 REF
-NOTE: LOOK UP REF FOR HIST. ACCURATE BIKE

NF: Thumbnailing pages is always the hardest part for me. I spend probably too much time on them, but I really try to work out the hardest parts in this stage. Perspective, exact placements, character actions, and details I need to highlight in the final pages—I'm a heavy planner, apparently.

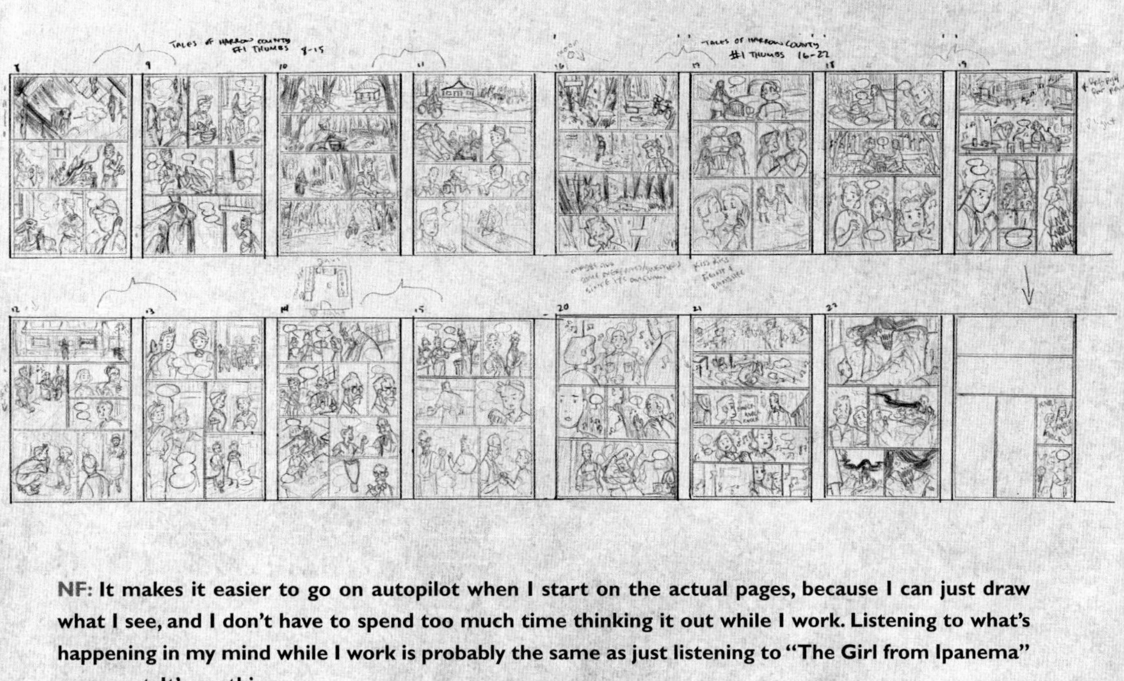
TALES OF HARROW COUNTY #1 THUMBS 8-15
TALES OF HARROW COUNTY #1 THUMBS 16-22

NF: It makes it easier to go on autopilot when I start on the actual pages, because I can just draw what I see, and I don't have to spend too much time thinking it out while I work. Listening to what's happening in my mind while I work is probably the same as just listening to "The Girl from Ipanema" on repeat. It's soothing.

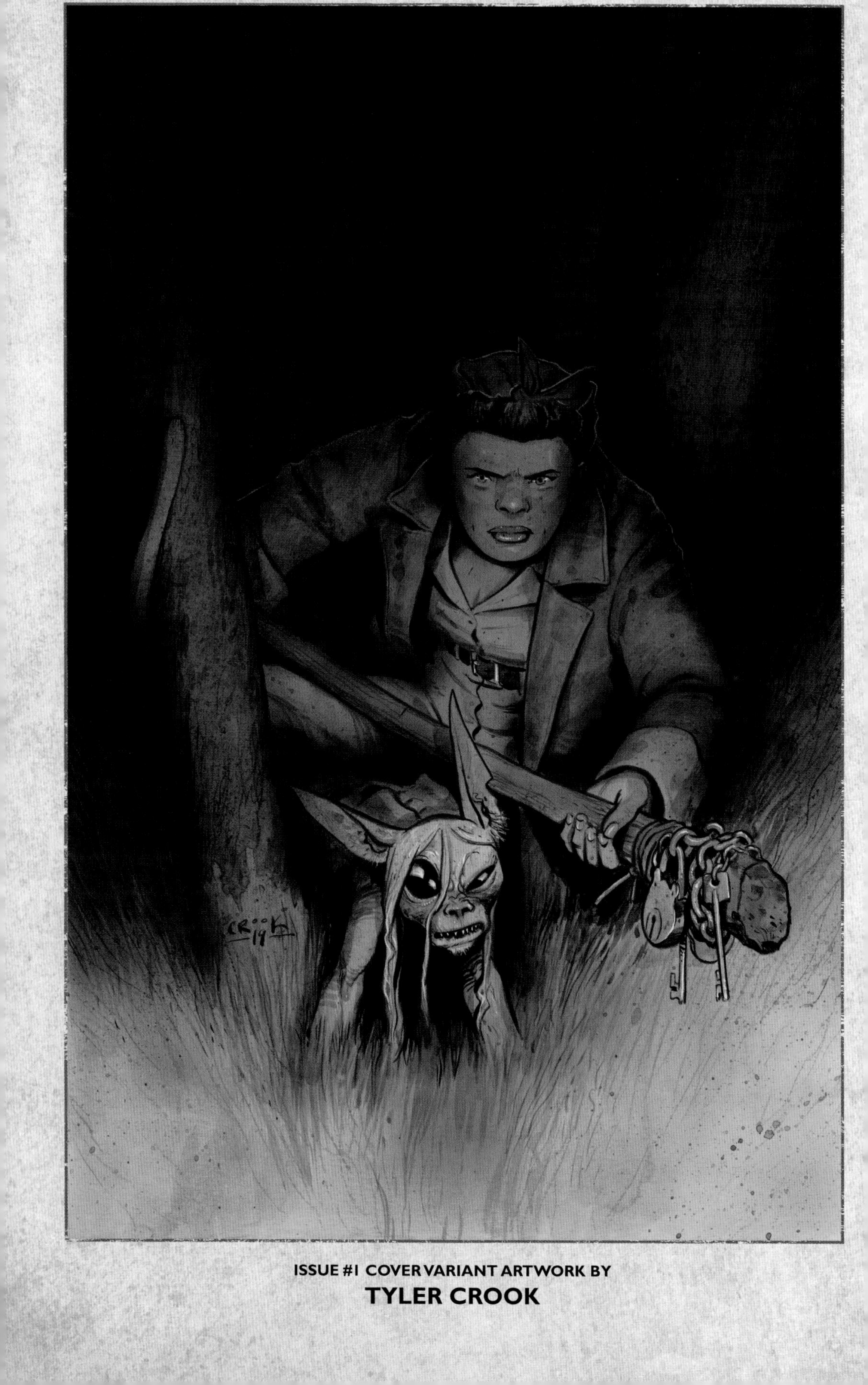
CROOK 19

ISSUE #1 COVER VARIANT ARTWORK BY
TYLER CROOK

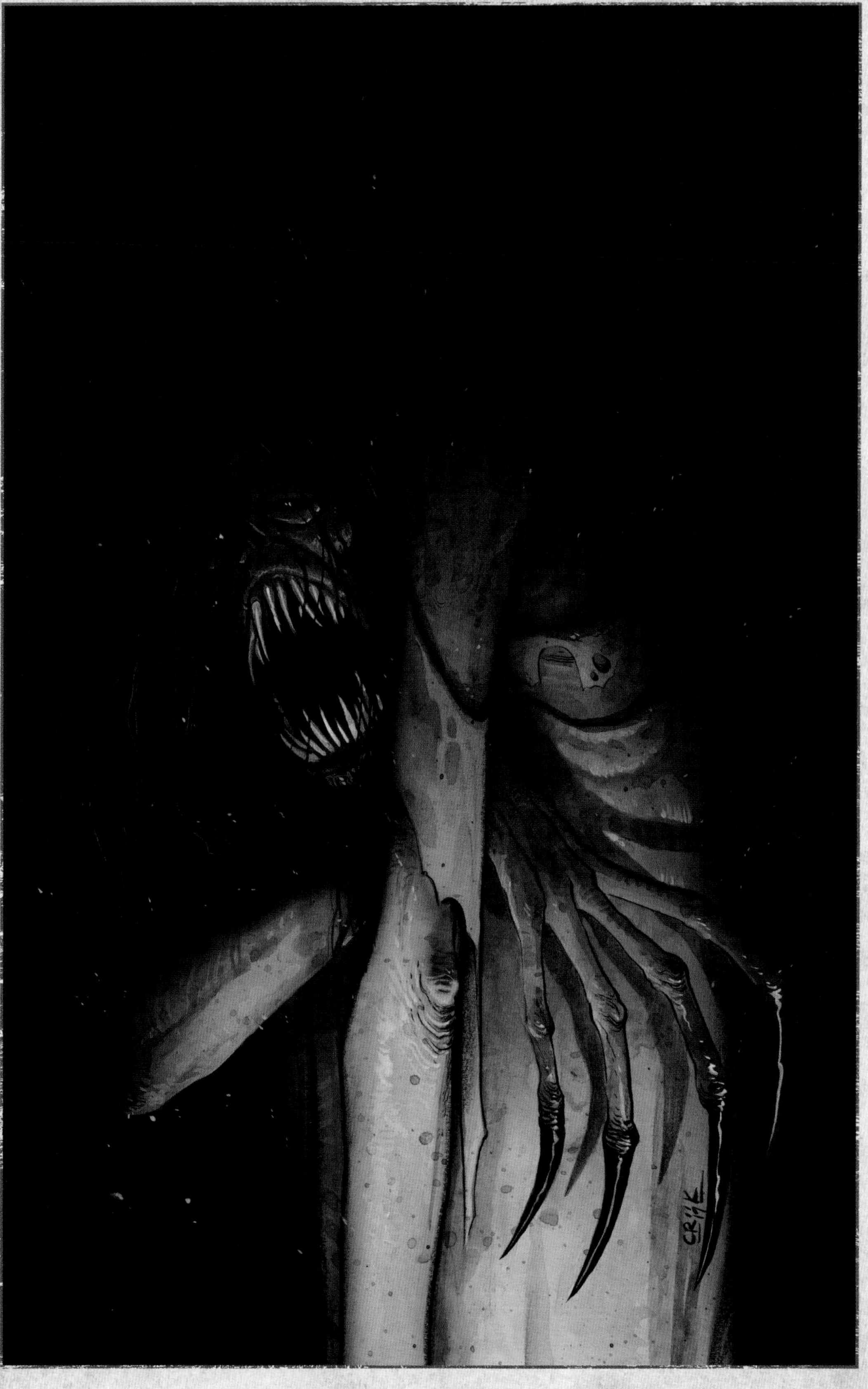

ISSUE #2 COVER VARIANT ARTWORK BY
TYLER CROOK

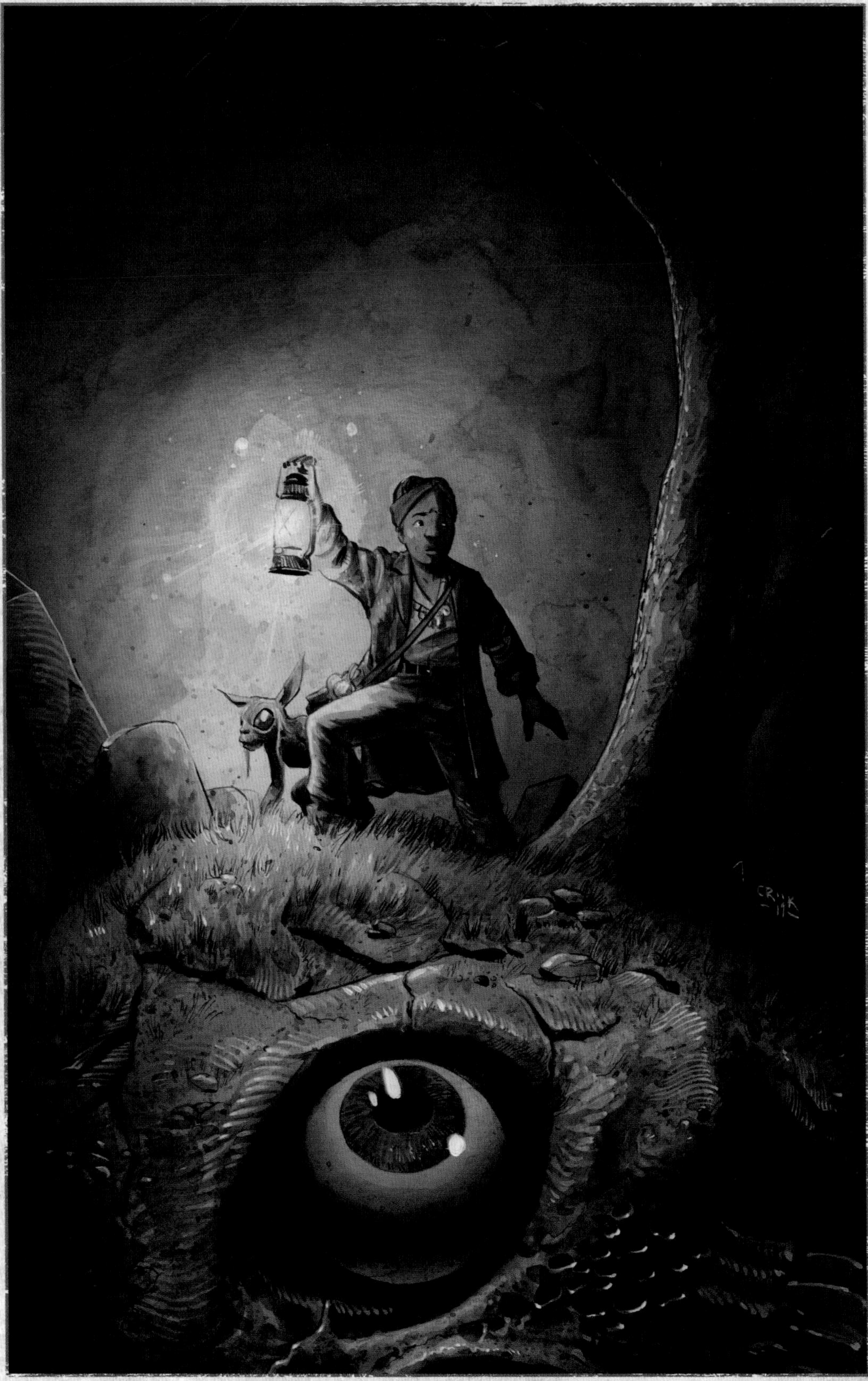

ISSUE #3 COVER VARIANT ARTWORK BY

TYLER CROOK

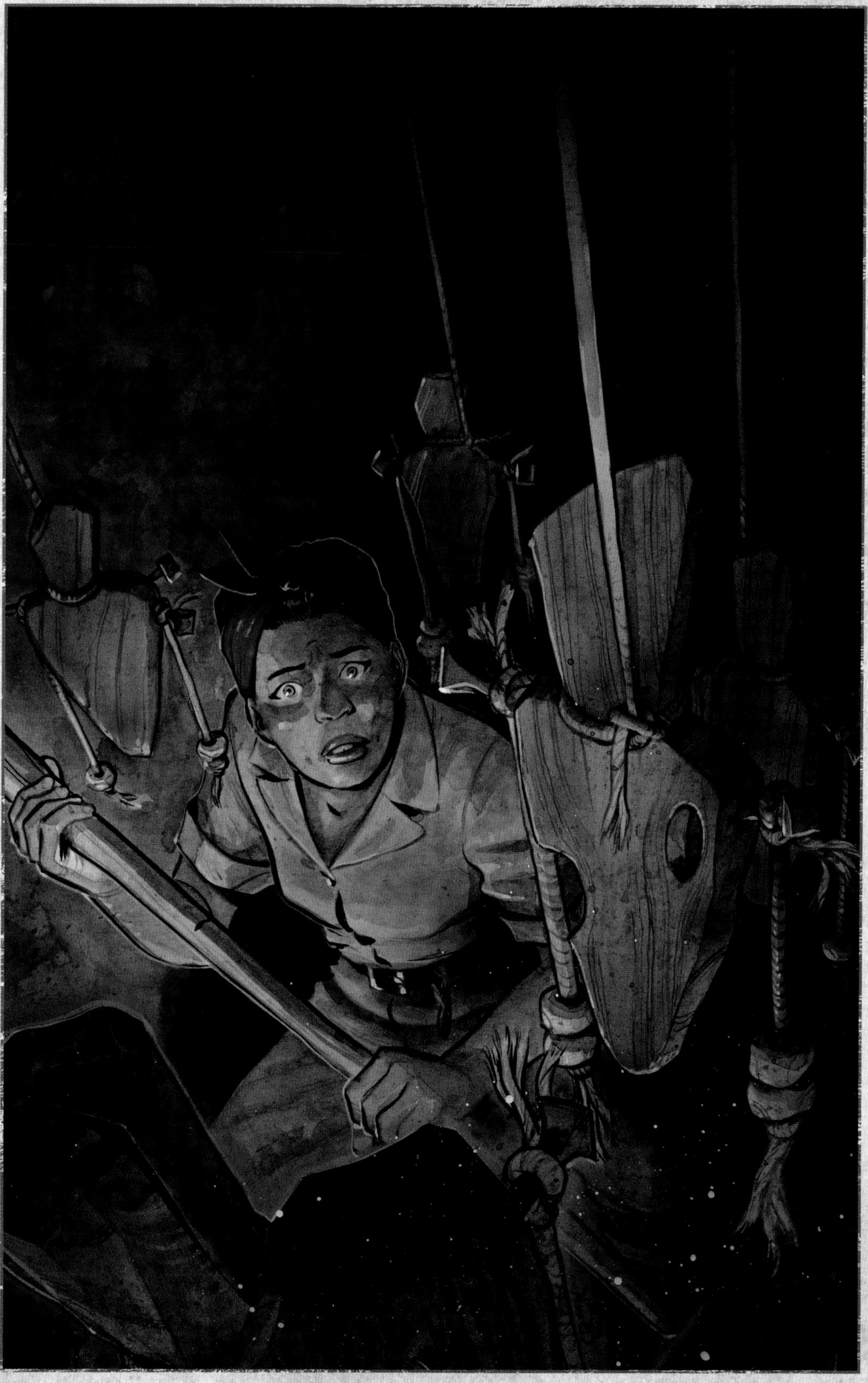

ISSUE #4 COVER VARIANT ARTWORK BY
TYLER CROOK